The Ultimate
Encyclopedia of

Gaelic
Football
& Hurling

Allianz, the world's largest insurer, is delighted to be associated with this exclusive publication, which is a fitting tribute to the deeds and memories of the marvellous players who have graced the GAA fields for well over 100 years.

Through our involvement as sponsors of the Allianz Leagues and the Church & General Cumann na mBunscol Leagues, we are proud to have played our small part in the development of these games which continue to be a unique part of our country's culture and tradition.

John O'Hanlon.

John R. O'Hanlon
Chief Executive, Allianz

Allianz ⑪

Project Editors: Martin Corteel & Vanessa Daubney
Project Art Direction: Mark Lloyd
Design: Neil Wallace
Jacket Design: Gavin Tyler
Picture Research: Debora Fioravanti
Production: Lisa French

The Ultimate Encyclopedia of

Gaelic Football & Hurling

Martin Breheny & Donal Keenan

CARLTON
BOOKS

CONTENTS

FOREWORD

There have been chronicles of the activities of the GAA since the early days of the Association. Indeed, the playing of the national games has prompted recording and analysis by historians and sociologists over five and six centuries.

In the last two decades we have enjoyed a great expansion of our library with publications that reflect the rich history and tradition of the association as a whole and the games of Gaelic Football and Hurling especially.

The celebration of our Centenary Year in 1984 prompted a greater awareness that we should record in detail our achievements, our development, the growth in strength of an Association that had such humble beginnings and is now such a vibrant body.

Now we welcome the latest addition to the library. *The Ultimate Encyclopedia of Gaelic Football and Hurling* is different in concept and design to anything previously. It is a hugely attractive historical and contemporary account of the development of our two national games into the major sports that they are today. The Encyclopedia is a combination of things — a concise history of the origins of the GAA and the games, a record of achievement and a chronicle of the great personalities and games.

It was clearly a major undertaking for the publishers and the authors and the final product is a testament to their painstaking efforts. From the inspiration of Michael Cusack and Maurice Davin to form a national organisation to promote the national pastimes, to the heroic deeds of men like Christy Ring and Mick O'Connell, to the achievements of modern heroes like D J Carey and Maurice Fitzgerald, the Encyclopedia gives us an entertaining, colourful and precise insight into the games and the people of the GAA.

We meet the great families and once again live through the great games through the decades. The Encyclopedia provides us with biographies of the legendary figures of the GAA and details the great managers and coaches. It provides us with a social as well as sporting perspective of the place the GAA and the games have in Irish society.

This publication will be treasured by all of us who love the games of Gaelic Football and Hurling; indeed, sports followers everywhere who wish to get a flavour of what makes our games so special. I congratulate everyone involved and thank you for your efforts.

Sean McCague, President of the GAA

INTRODUCTION

WHEN the Gaelic Athletic Association (GAA) was founded in 1884 by a small group of dedicated visionaries, they could never have envisaged the seismic impact the organisation would have on Ireland's sporting, cultural and social life. Launched with the basic aim of preserving and cultivating national pastimes, the GAA quickly put down strong roots which have continued to deepen.

While the GAA has always placed great emphasis on its role in promoting a national identity, it is as a games organisation that it has achieved the proud position it currently occupies in the hearts and minds of Irish people, both at home and abroad. Despite fierce competition from international sports, Gaelic games continue to prosper and now enjoy unrivalled popularity in terms of the numbers playing and watching the games.

This book is a celebration of two marvellous sports which are ideally suited to the Irish personality. Although vastly different in technical terms, Gaelic football and hurling share a common requirement for high skill levels, unflinching courage and genuine integrity.

Some players have successfully mastered both sports at the highest levels. Their remarkable talents demand special recognition which they are afforded in a chapter on the great dual players. Choosing the leading dual players was relatively easy, certainly by comparison with selecting the twenty players for the chapters on the Legends of Hurling and Gaelic football.

The chosen ten in each code are men of extraordinary talents, who imposed their skills and personalities on the games to such a degree that they are all guaranteed permanent places in history. If choosing the legends was a tough assignment, so too was selecting the 100 hurlers and footballers for the chapters on the all-time greats. The lists could easily have extended to 500, such is the deep well of marvellous players who have graced the playing fields over the past 100 years.

Had this book been written 30 years ago, there would have been no chapter on managers as, up to then, teams were looked after by groups of selectors and coaches, often with no overall boss. However, as part of the ever-evolving process, Gaelic games embraced the team manager concept in the 1970s and, as the relevant chapter shows, managers are now vital components in both codes.

The choices for the chapters on great games were made under a variety of headings, including standard, atmosphere, unpredictability and importance. All share one basic quality – they touched the spirit of the time in a real and meaningful way and left fans with great memories.

While the GAA story has been one of great achievement, it was inevitable that controversies and scandals would weave their way into the fabric of the Association. The main ones are dealt with in detail while the exciting package is wrapped into context by chapters on the origin of Gaelic Games, the history of the rules and the All-Ireland championships, close-ups on the famous stadiums, plus a records section on the major competitions.

Martin Breheny
Donal Keenan

1

THE ORIGIN OF GAELIC GAMES

The earliest references to hurling go back to 1272 BC

I n the modern era the games of the Gael, hurling and Gaelic football, are inextricably linked under the banner of the Gaelic Athletic Association. But the origins of the two games are vastly different, hurling's antiquity making Gaelic football a comparatively new pastime.

A valid claim can be made that hurl-ing is a uniquely Irish game, developing over 1,000 years but maintaining its original form right up to the present period.

Gaelic Football appears to have evolved from a variety of inspirations, other forms of football being imported from Europe and England from the sixteenth century right up to the nineteenth century.

The games as we know them today, with their rules and competitive struc-tures, evolved from the founding of the GAA in Hayes' Hotel, Thurles, on 1 November 1884. But the history of both goes back much further.

HURLING

In historical texts the earliest reference to hurling appears to have been made about 1272 BC at the battle of Moytura, near Cong in County Mayo. The Firbolgs were rulers of Ireland and were protecting their place in a battle against the Tuatha de Danaan. While preparing for battle, the Firbolgs challenged the invaders to a hurling contest in which teams of 27-a-side took part. The Firbolgs won the contest but lost the battle.

Even the legal system of the time, the Brehon Laws, took account of the existence and popularity of hurling. The Laws provided for compensation for injuries arising out of participation in the game of hurling. It was also a punishable crime under the Brehon Laws to deliberately strike another with a hurley. There are many references to the game of hurling in the centuries before the birth of Christ.

There is evidence that hurling was an essential part of life for young men preparing to be warriors. This gives rise to some of the legends of early Irish history which are still being taught to schoolchildren. The most famous warrior of all was Cúchulainn who, as the boy Setanta, engaged in great deeds of hurling. The legend is based around the period of the birth of Christ and is contained in early writings, including what is known as the Book of Leinster.

Tales of his exploits are taught to this day. When he was only eight years old, Setanta left his home in Cooley to join his uncle King Conor MacNessa at his palace in Emhain Macha, where boys were taught the skills of hurling and of war. On the long journey he amused himself by hurling his bronze ball long distances and then throwing his hurley after it so that it struck the ball in mid-air. On arrival in Eamhain Macha he took part in a game of hurling in which he single-handedly defeated 150 boys. He earned the name Cúchulainn when he killed the savage hound owned by the blacksmith Cúlann by hurling his ball into the hound's throat.

So popular was the game that it

Prior to the foundation of the GAA in 1884, hurling resembled hockey

spread to England and Scotland. In Ireland, while the natives continued to play, the invaders too became fascinated by the game. The authorities became concerned about it, considering it a threat to security. The Statute of Kilkenny of 1336 banned the playing of the game. The ban had little effect and 200 years later, in the Statute of Galway of 1537, the playing of hurling was again banned.

In later centuries the rulers and landowners adopted a more accommodating approach. The landowners actually organised games between teams comprising their tenants. Local rivalries grew and large sums of money were wagered on the outcome. Two forms of the game were noted: a summer game, from which today's game evolved, and a winter game which resembled hockey. This style seems to have lost popularity in the seventeenth and eighteenth centuries.

Hurling was commonly played in Dublin, the rest of Leinster and Munster. There is some evidence of

the game in the north of the country, while there also are references to games between parishes in Galway, including areas in the north of the county which would now be regarded traditionally as football strongholds. A number of newspaper reports in the middle of the eighteenth century mentioned games between the provinces of Leinster and Munster, as well as games between counties. At the end of that century, however, a change was taking place which would have a major effect on hurling.

A growing sense of nationalism among the Irish people and the formation of the United Irishmen led to an increase in political tension. The landowners, generally English and Protestant, began to fear large gatherings and withdrew support from the game. The Rising of 1798 deepened divisions and the Act of Union, which made Ireland part of the United Kingdom, also changed the way of life. Barony hurling, which was organised by landlords and comprised teams made up of their tenants, came to an end in the early part of the nineteenth century.

The Great Famine had an even more devastating effect on the people and the ancient game. Yet it survived, and there are accounts of games being played again in various counties by 1850. The first Rules of Hurling were drawn up by Pat Larkin of Killimor in Galway and were printed in 1885, although it is thought that they had been in use for at least a decade before that.

While the gentry and the landlords had abandoned hurling, the game was still played at Trinity College in Dublin. A set of rules, very different to Larkin's, was drawn up by the Dublin University Hurling Club. When modified in the 1860s and 1870s, these rules made such fundamental changes to the game that the form of hurling played resembled hockey.

The native game was struggling to survive. Though some clubs were formed, especially in Dublin, the changes in Irish society had a grave effect on the game. Significantly, it was in the 1870s and 1880s that Michael Cusack began to take an active interest in the game and would soon head the movement that led to the foundation of the Gaelic Athletic Association.

GAELIC FOOTBALL

In the Statutes of Galway of 1527, which banned the game of hurling, there appears to be a reference to Gaelic football, the first mention of the game which can be found. The Statutes actually exempted the game from the ban. Football must have been played widely but there is no historical reference until 1670 in a poem by Seamus Dall MacCuarta, called 'Iomàn na Bionne'. While the use of the word 'Iomàn' might suggest the poet was describing the game of hurling, historian Marcus de Búrca has revealed that in parts of Leinster the word 'Iomàn' was used for football and 'Iomàin le camàin' for hurling.

The poem described a game at Fennor in which wrestling was

Michael Cusack: one of the founding fathers of the GAA

allowed. Another poet, Matt Concannon, described a game played in North Dublin in 1719. There are other texts which suggest that North Dublin, Meath and Louth were football strongholds during the sixteenth and seventeenth centuries. In his biography of Maurice Davin, former GAA president Séamus O'Ríain quotes a poem by Réamonn Ua Murchadha entitled 'Iomàin Leana ba Bhabhdhuin' which describes an eight-a-side football game in Omeath in 1750, lasting from midday until sunset. Davin, from Carrick-on-Suir on the border of Tipperary and Waterford, was a brilliant sportsman. In his late teens he was a boxer and later an oarsman of some distinction. However, it was in field athletics that he would become a nationally-renowned figure. Between 1875 and 1879 he won 10 Irish championships in the hammer and shot. He also won two English championships in 1881 in the 16-lb hammer and 16-lb shot. His brothers, Pat and Tom, were both champions in the high jump and long jump and the three brothers were selected for an Ireland team to compete against England at Lansdowne Road in 1875.

Davin, who had been forced to

end his formal education at the age of 18 in 1859 following the unexpected death of his father, had inherited the nationalist views of his parents and became interested in fostering the Irish language. It was a combination of his interest in athletics (including hurling and football), nationalism and the language which would bring him into contact with people such as Cusack.

Various versions of the game were played in different parts of the country. The games were played between parishes or baronies and sometimes would last for hours. However, there was no organised form of the game and little interaction between the various regions. The rules varied according to region, some games being more disciplined than others. The number of players on each team varied from place to place, although the basic principle of moving the ball from one end of the field to the other was the same. The ball was generally round, but that depended on the materials used. Sometimes the ball would be oval-shaped, by accident rather than design.

In Ireland, in the late 1800s, rugby was beginning to become popular, and quite well-organised in some areas. Michael Cusack taught at two rugby-playing schools, Clongowes and Blackrock, and played the game himself for a time. It was the game of the gentry and Cusack found that his peers did not share his nationalism, so he stopped playing.

In fact, the connection between the playing of football games and meetings of militant Irish nationalists such as the Fenians and later the Irish Republican Brotherhood meant that the authorities became concerned about the games. The link between nationalism and the native games became stronger through the nineteenth century and would have a major bearing on the founding and subsequent development of the GAA.

The first known rules were drawn up by the Commercials club in Limerick but these were not used on a widespread basis.

THE GAA

In the turbulent history of nineteenth-century Ireland, various nationalist groups were gaining in strength and popularity and were becoming more active. There was a growing sense that Ireland was being Anglicised, that the native language and games were being lost. The founding of the Land League by Michael Davitt, the growth of the Gaelic League and the rise of Charles Stewart Parnell and his Parliamentary Party were among the most significant developments of the time, leading to a greater awareness of the danger of losing native pastimes and customs.

The Irish Republican Brotherhood, a more militant body, was still in existence but was less influential. Its members included many nationalists who were prominent in sporting activities, including the brilliant Mayo athlete P W Nally. In the 1870s he formed a close relationship with the schoolteacher Michael Cusack which would ignite the spark leading to the founding of the Gaelic Athletic Association.

The two men regularly discussed the formation of a body to control Irish athletics and to revive the national games. Cusack, a native of Clare who ran his own school in Dublin,

was a nationalist but less revolutionary than Nally. Cusack was a staunch member of the Home Rule movement and had been heavily involved in attempts to organise athletics on a formal basis. He had also been involved in 1882 with the Dublin Hurling Club, one of the first attempts to revive hurling, which did not last very long.

As Cusack himself put it later, there was a need to form a body such as the GAA 'for the preservation and cultivation of the national pastimes of Ireland'. A single-minded and tough-talking individual, Cusack regarded those who were involved in the administration of sports at the time with disdain. His vision of a new organisation was not as a parent body just for hurling and football but athletics as well. In fact, it is clear he himself was a late convert to the game of hurling and it was Maurice Davin, the first president of the GAA, who was the strong advocate of Gaelic football.

Davin would be a hugely-influential figure in the founding of the GAA. While Cusack's almost missionary zeal got the association started, it was Davin's stewardship which ensured that it survived a difficult first decade. In fact, Cusack's volatility meant that he was removed from office as the first secretary of the association after 20 months.

With P W Nally imprisoned in 1883, Cusack worked almost alone in trying to establish a new sports organisation. He attended sports meetings around the country where he spoke of his desire for an Irish governing body for Irish athletics. He also wrote regularly to the newspapers about his ambitions. He organised successful hurling games in Dublin's Phoenix Park and even brought a team to Ballinasloe for a game in 1883.

A number of preliminary meetings were held during 1884, with Maurice Davin attending. From a strong nationionalist and sporting family, Davin was one of Ireland's best-known athletes, having held the world hammer-throwing record. Another influential figure was Michael Davitt, founder of the Land League, who gave his enthusiastic support to Cusack.

Among a number of significant meetings was one held in Loughrea in County Galway in August 1884. William Duffy, a friend of Cusack, had arranged a meeting with the Bishop of Clonfert, Dr Patrick Duggan. The objective was to ask Dr Duggan for his support and to act as a patron of the new body. Dr Duggan supported the ideals but asked that they turn to a younger man, Dr Croke, the Archbishop of Cashel, to act as patron.

In the meantime, Cusack was continuing his crusade through the columns of the newspapers and in October announced that a meeting would take place in Thurles on 1 November. A circular, signed by both Cusack and Davin, was sent to prominent nationalists and to those involved in the organisation of sports around the country. Cusack knew he had backing in Cork, Kerry and Dublin and was anxious to see if he could garner support from other areas.

The billiards room at Hayes' Hotel in Thurles was the setting for the first meeting. It was not an auspicious start. Although there is some

Maurice Davin, the first President of the GAA, 1884–87

Dr Thomas W Croke, Archbishop of Cashel, the GAA's first patron

confusion over the exact details, apparently only seven people turned up. They were Davin, Cusack, John Wyse Power, John McKay, James Bracken, Joseph O'Ryan and Tomas St George McCarthy.

Wyse Power was editor of the *Leinster Leader* newspaper and would play a big role in the fledgling organisation. McKay was also a journalist, while Bracken was a building contractor and a prominent member of the IRB. O'Ryan and St George McCarthy took no active part in the GAA following the first meeting.

Davin, with his high profile and popularity, was appointed president and Cusack, Wyse Power and McKay were appointed joint secretaries. It was significant that Dr Croke, Charles Stewart Parnell and Maurice Davitt were chosen as patrons. These three men were held in awe by Irish nationalists and their support for the new movement was crucial.

That there was a political element to the new organisation could not

be denied. Although Cusack's interest was in promoting the national games, others who became aligned to the GAA were clearly thinking along nationalist lines. Even Dr Croke's letter, which has become the charter of the GAA, outlined the depth of feeling among nationalists. He wrote:

'One of the most painful, let me assure you, and at the same time one of the most frequently recurring reflections that as an Irishman I am compelled to make in connection with the present aspect of things in this country, is derived from the ugly and irritating fact that we are daily importing from England not only her manufactured goods, which we cannot help doing since she has practically strangled our own manufacturing appliances, but together with her fashions, her accents, her vicious literature, her music, her dances and her manifold mannerisms, her games also and her pastimes, to the utter discredit of our own grand national sports, and to the sore humiliation, as I believe, of every genuine son and daughter of the old land.'

The GAA had a stormy beginning. The Irish Amateur Athletic Association was formed in February 1885 in direct opposition to the GAA. A number of athletics meetings had been held quite successfully by the GAA shortly after it had formed but the new body then organised an event in direct conflict with a GAA event in Tralee, County Kerry, in June 1885. Cusack acted as starter at the Tralee event and it was a huge success, while the IAAA event was noted as a disaster.

The dispute between the two bodies led indirectly to Cusack's removal from the post of secretary in July 1886. Both the GAA and IAAA had banned their members from competing in events organised by the opposing body. GAA patron Dr Croke was unhappy with any such ban and urged its removal. Cusack then became involved in a row with the *Freeman's Journal*, edited by a friend of Dr Croke. When Dr Croke wrote in support of the editor, Cusack responded with a letter which he later admitted was offensive to the Archbishop.

At the same time Cusack was

involved in a dispute with the GAA in Cork. His brusque manner did not make him an easy man to deal with. While he was a brilliant organiser and a passionate man, Cusack obviously did not work well with others. A general meeting of the GAA was called for Thurles in July 1886 when Wyse Power made several complaints about Cusack's conduct. Wyse Power was supported by GAA treasurer John Clancy and, when Cusack walked out of the meeting, a proposal to remove him from office was carried.

This was a dramatic end to Cusack's term. In the 20 months since he had inspired the founding of the GAA it had grown dramatically, despite organised and powerful opposition. At the time, most of the events held by the GAA were athletics meetings but there are records showing that hurling and Gaelic football were increasingly being played all over the country. Cusack had steered the GAA through a troubled infancy and it is generally accepted that the association would never have survived were it not for his energy and drive. He tried to regain his position of influence in the following years but became more and more isolated.

What followed was a difficult period for the GAA. Internal bickering was having a serious effect on the development of the association. During this period, however, Davin did complete an outline of the rules of both football and hurling, but he resigned as president in 1886 in a dispute which involved the barring of RIC members from membership of the GAA. Wyse Power also resigned around this time. A rancorous annual convention in Thurles in 1887 caused a serious split. While some had tried to keep the GAA out of politics, militant nationalists had exerted considerable control during 1887. Davin and Dr Croke met to plan a strategy to save the GAA from collapsing and a special convention in 1888 restored some order. At executive level the bitterness remained, but this had little effect on the rank-and-file membership, which continued to grow.

The real strength of the new association could be found on the playing fields. The playing rules adopted in 1885 were now widely-used and the first known game played under the auspices of the GAA was at Feagh, near Tynagh in Galway, when Killimor beat Ballinakill.

In 1887 the first entries for the All-Ireland football and hurling championship were sought. It was agreed that the winner of the local championship in each county would represent the county in the All-Ireland championships. Twelve counties entered, although only five actually contested the hurling championship. The administrative squabbling meant that the finals were delayed until 1888, the hurling final taking place on 1 April in Birr between Meelick (Galway) and Thurles (Tipperary). The official record shows that Thurles won by 1–1 to 0–0: in the early days a 'forfeit' point was awarded when the defending team knocked the ball over their own endline, and Tipperary was awarded one of these.

The football final was played at Clonskeagh in Dublin between Commercials of Limerick and Dundalk Young Irelands of Louth. Commercials won by 1–4 to 0–3. Although there are no attendance figures available, records show gate receipts of £200 which suggests a very large attendance at the final on 29 April 1888.

The championships of 1888 were never completed. The GAA, despite its infancy, agreed to send teams to the United States for a series of exhibition games. This became known as 'The American Invasion' and while it was a great success, the visit left the championship at home in a shambles. In addition, many of the best players remained in America, where work was far more plentiful, and were lost to the game at home.

The problems off the field were not abating. Political tensions were rising and the GAA was tearing itself apart. Ironically, the GAA in America was gaining in strength and in late 1891 the Gaelic Athletic Association of America was formed. At home, teams were reduced to 17-a-side from 21 and a goal was deemed worth five points. No team from Connacht or Ulster contested the football championship from 1893 to 1899, a period during which a goal's value was reduced to three points.

As the twentieth century dawned, the GAA began to find a firmer footing. The conclusions of championships were still delayed – the final of 1900 was not actually played until 1902 – but by this time the first steps towards organising a provincial structure such as exists today had begun, and this led to the rapid development of the GAA during the early part of the century. James Nowlan of Kilkenny would serve as president for 20 years and with the secretary, Luke O'Toole from Wicklow, would guide the GAA into calmer times.

From a promotional point of view it is now generally accepted that the 1903 All-Ireland final between Kerry and Kildare, played in 1905, was the contest which first really gripped the imagination of the general public. Three games were needed to decide the issue, at the end of which even the national newspapers began to realise that there was something worth reporting in Gaelic games. Up to then the newspapers had all but ignored the growing association.

The first game of the 1905 final, played in Tipperary, had to be abandoned when the crowd invaded the field following the disallowing of a Kerry goal. Such was the controversy that a huge crowd attended the rearranged game in Cork, when the teams finished level, Kerry 0–7, Kildare 1–4. The third game, also played in Cork, was a Kerry triumph by 0–8 to 0–2.

The War of Independence and the Civil War had a severe effect on the GAA but the foundations remained secure. When the political situation began to settle by 1925, the National Leagues were introduced and the ensuing period of stability ensured the structures could be strengthened.

One of the most significant events was the appointment of Pádraig Ó Caoimh as general secretary in 1929. Born in Roscommon, he had grown up in Cork and had been active in the GAA from an early age. He also was very involved politically and

was arrested in 1920, at a time when he was secretary of the Cork GAA Board. Although sentenced to 10 years in jail, he was released after one year under a general amnesty.

He served from 1929 to 1964 and has been described by former GAA president Alf Murray as 'the architect of the modern GAA'. Ó Caoimh oversaw the development of Croke Park, put the GAA on a sound financial footing and ensured the policy of providing facilities in every parish and town was implemented.

Another significant event occurred in 1938, when Micheál Ó Hehir carried out his first commentary on Gaelic games, featuring the Galway-Monaghan All-Ireland football semi-final in Mullingar on 14 August.

Ó Hehir's love of the games was apparent in his voice. It would become the most famous voice in Ireland, and when Ó Hehir later transferred to television he became an even bigger star than those who played the game. He did more to make football and hurling glamorous than any amount of promotion.

By the 1960s, the GAA held a position of influence in every sector of Irish society. Hurling and Gaelic football were thriving throughout the country, including the six counties of Northern Ireland. The desire of the founders to preserve and cultivate the national pastimes has been fulfilled.

Men with a mission. Hurling's capacity to unite parishes has always been one of its strong points

2

THE HISTORY OF THE ALL-IRELAND CHAMPIONSHIPS

Declan Meehan is challenged by Noel Kennelly in the 2000 football final

When the first All-Ireland Gaelic Football and Hurling championships began in 1887 (the finals taking place in 1888), the greater part of the Irish population was unaware of what was happening. Many of those who did know were blissfully unconcerned.

The national newspapers of the time paid scant regard to the fact that Meelick of Galway beat Thurles of Tipperary in the first All-Ireland hurling final or that Commercials of Limerick beat Young Irelands of Louth in the football final. When the 1888 championships were not completed because most of the players were visiting the United States (some never came back) it hardly raised a ripple in public attention.

But the seeds were sown then for the competitions that would, just a few decades later, grip the imagination of the Irish public more than any other national sporting event.

THE ALL-IRELAND CHAMPIONSHIPS

The GAA championships are now a multi-million-pound extravaganza, dominating the lives of the players and supporters for most of the year. Heroic deeds, players and games of the past and the present are treasured in the history of Gaelic Games, from the early part of the twentieth century right up to modern times.

WEXFORD'S FAMOUS FOUR-IN-A-ROW

Mention Wexford to casual sports followers and they will immediately think in terms of hurling. Stories abound of epic feats by great Wexford heroes and while the county's All-Ireland haul is modest by comparison with Kilkenny, Cork and Tipperary, the area is still regarded as a major hurling power.

It wasn't always so. Indeed, there was a time when Wexford were setting the football agenda and, in the process, setting impressive records. Wexford appeared in six consecutive All-Ireland football finals in the 1913–18 period, winning the last four. It was the first time that the four-in-a-row had been achieved. Kerry have emulated it twice since then, winning four consecutive titles in the 1929–32 seasons and again in 1978–81. However, no county has won five in a row so Wexford still hold a share in one of the great landmark achievements of Gaelic football.

The first seeds of the glory run were sown in 1911 when Wexford won the Leinster junior football title. The All-Ireland championship

had not yet been introduced at junior level so Wexford didn't get an opportunity to test themselves against the best from the other provinces. However, several of the Wexford junior side progressed quickly to the senior grade, where they carved out a special piece of history.

Keen observers of Wexford football history believe it all started with a stroke of good fortune in the 1913 Leinster semi-final. Laois were leading by two points with two minutes left when Wexford were awarded a close-in free. The kicker stubbed his toe in the ground but with the Laois defenders jumping in the air, anticipating a rising shot, the ball rolled under their legs into the net for a truly amazing goal.

Encouraged by the helpful intervention from the fates, Wexford went on to win the game and captured the Leinster title by beating Louth before easily dismissing Antrim's challenge in the All-Ireland semi-final. Kerry also had qualified for the All-Ireland final, which was played in Croke Park on 14 December. It turned out to be an amazing game. All the scoring was done in the second and third quarters, with Kerry eventually winning by 2–2 to 0–3.

A year later, Kerry and Wexford met again in the All-Ireland final. A crowd of 20,000 turned out in Croke Park, expecting a classic encounter. Wexford had improved dramatically since 1913 and their fans were confident that the All-Ireland title was on its way to the South-East for the first time. Their optimism seemed well founded when goals by Sean O'Kennedy

and Aidan Doyle gave Wexford a 2–0 to 0–1 half-time lead. Kerry were far from finished, however, and with Pat 'Aeroplane' O'Shea in inspired form at midfield, the revival was quick and effective. Paddy Breen got in for a Kerry goal and they added two further points to bring the game level. The replay was played four weeks later and, once again, Wexford were on top in the first half. They were helped enormously by a strong wind and scored six points without reply. But, as in the drawn game, Kerry improved in the second half and goals by Paddy Breen and Johnny Mahony brought them level. They then added three more points to win by 2–3 to 0–6.

In 1915, Wexford and Kerry met for the third consecutive year in the All-Ireland final and this time the balance had very definitely swung Wexford's way. Some of the Kerry team had emigrated while they were also weakened by injury problems. Wexford, who were now desperate to land an All-Ireland crown, were dealing from a full hand.

Wexford took an early lead but Kerry fought back and a goal by Dan Doyle raised their spirits. However, Wexford were playing with poise and purpose and a goal by Aidan Doyle set them on their way to a 1–2 to 1–0 lead at half-time.

It was tight and tense right through the second half but Wexford held their nerve and finished strongly to carve out a famous win, 2–4 to 2–1. Wexford had finally won the All-Ireland title and were about to embark on a magical adventure, winning the next three finals.

Jack Lynch: GAA dual star, politician and statesman

Mayo qualified to meet Wexford in the 1916 All-Ireland final, which was played on a bitterly cold day in December. Croke Park was under a blanket of heavy frost but the match went ahead. Only 3,000 fans attended and the game turned out to be a real lottery as the underfoot conditions made it very difficult for the players to remain on their feet. Wexford's experience proved decisive and they cruised to victory by double scores, 2–4 to 1–2.

Wexford completed the hat-trick of All-Ireland titles against Clare in 1917. In an effort to match their outstanding rivals, Clare went into collective training for two weeks before the final but even that wasn't enough to tip the scales their way as Wexford won by 0–9 to 0–5. That victory brought Wexford alongside Dublin as the only county to

have won three consecutive All-Ireland football titles so the quest for a place in the record books was the over-riding ambition in their minds as they set out on the 1918 championship journey.

Once again, Wexford qualified for the final, where their opponents were a young, emerging Tipperary side. The game wasn't played until February 1919 and turned out to be an outstanding encounter. Team captain Jim Byrne was a hugely influential figure for Wexford but they looked in trouble at half-time when they led by only one point after playing with the wind behind them. It called for calm heads and dogged determination, qualities which abounded in the team, and they edged home by the minimum margin, 0–5 to 0–4. The four-in-a-row had been achieved. It was a

special era for Wexford football and while their fortunes have dipped alarmingly since then, the 1915–18 squad ensured that the county's name will always feature prominently on any list of great achievements.

CORK'S FOUR-IN-A-ROW

The outbreak of World War II and an epidemic of foot and mouth disease caused great difficulties for those pursuing sporting interests from 1939 to the late 1940s. But the determination of people to live life as normal was shown in the successful running of both the football and hurling championships during those years. The Cork hurling team would emerge as one of the greatest ever to play the game,

winning four championships in a row between 1941 and 1944 and adding a fifth title in 1946.

It was in the famous 1939 final that some of the Cork players were seen on the biggest stage for the first time. Jack Lynch, later to be Taoiseach and still the only man to win six All-Ireland championships in succession (including football in 1945), led the team in what become known as the 'thunder and lightning final'.

Cork and Kilkenny had qualified to meet in the final and the fact that it was the first time in eight years that the two great powers had met added further interest. Two days before the game Germany invaded Poland, signalling the start of the Second World War, but in Ireland the interest was focused on Croke Park and less serious matters.

The Cork team which won the first of four consecutive All-Ireland hurling titles in 1941

Torrential rain had fallen on the Saturday night before the game and continued into the morning. It had stopped by the time the game started, but as the *Irish Independent* of the time reported: 'The game had just restarted when the crowd and the players were startled by a clap of thunder. It was a portent of things to come. What followed was a storm of extraordinary proportions. So bad did conditions become that spectators could not make out the identity of some of the players, leading to confusion immediately afterwards over the identity of the Kilkenny player who scored the winning point.

'The spectators who were out in the open had to seek refuge from the elements at stages during the second half. The journalists in the press box situated in the front row of the Cusack Stand tried to find alternative accommodation to allow them to take notes and remain dry.' Confusion over who scored the winning point continued until the following day. The newspapers reported that Terry Leahy scored the point. It was, in fact, Jimmy Kelly who had done so to give Kilkenny a 2–7 to 3–3 victory.

Cork were defeated in the Munster final of 1940 by Limerick but it would be their last championship

defeat until 1945. They won the National League in 1941 but the Munster championship was badly disrupted by the spread of foot and mouth disease. By August the Munster Council decided Cork and Limerick would play to decide who would go through from Munster to the All-Ireland series, despite the fact that Tipperary had already qualified for the Munster final. Kilkenny were not allowed to participate in Leinster and Dublin were nominated to go forward and meet Cork in the final.

Fuel shortages meant that only 26,150 attended but they saw a young Christy Ring score three points as Cork won easily by 5–11 to 0–6. Ring collected the first of eight medals that day. Ironically, in the delayed Munster final Tipperary beat the new All-Ireland champions.

Limerick provided the most stern test of the champions in 1942, in a Munster semi-final regarded as one of the best games of the period. Con Murphy, later to be a GAA president, had joined Lynch and Ring on the team and Cork easily accounted for both Tipperary and Galway on their way to the All-Ireland final. Again Dublin were the opponents but this time they were much sturdier and it was only late in the game that Cork were assured of victory.

Led by Mick Kennefick, Cork went in search of a third title, a feat achieved only once before by a Cork team in the very early years of the championship. The 1943 championship threw up a major surprise when Antrim, the Ulster junior champions, were allowed to play Galway in the All-Ireland senior quarter-final. They won and then caused a sensation by beating Kilkenny in the semi-final, played in Belfast's Corrigan Park.

The occasion proved too much for Antrim and Cork were too strong in the final, winning comfortably by 5–6 to 0–4.

In search of four in a row, Cork again found their toughest opponents in Limerick in the Munster final and replay. The second game was another epic in the long saga between the two counties. Ring produced some magical moments, including the decisive goal in the final minute.

This championship would turn out to be the most difficult of all to win. Galway produced their best display in years and almost snatched victory. Cork were without Jack Lynch and John Quirke because of injury. Sean Condon came to the rescue with eight points and Cork won narrowly by 1–10 to 3–3. Dublin again provided the oppos-

ition in the final. They had a great start but could not sustain the effort and Cork won easily by 2–13 to 1–2.

Nine Cork men played in all four victories – Willie Murphy, Batt Thornhill, Alan Lotty, John Quirke, Jack Lynch, Christy Ring, DJ Buckley, Jim Young and Paddy O'Donovan, who played in 1942 and '44 and went on as a sub in 1941 and '43.

The unbeaten run ended when Tipperary beat Cork in the Munster championship of 1945. Jack Lynch went on to win an All-Ireland football medal that year and in 1946 Cork were back on the hurling title trail again. They met old rivals Kilkenny in the final and an attendance of 64,415 watched, with an estimated 5,000 locked out. The game produced one of Ring's most famous scores when he soloed for almost 70 yards, beat three tackles and flicked the ball to the net. It was one of ten goals scored in the game as Cork won by 7–5 to 3–8

Alan Lotty of Cork

and earned their own special place in history.

THE POLO GROUNDS FINAL 1947

In the long history of the All-Ireland championships there is hardly a more colourful event than the All-Ireland football final of 1947. In a move that was outrageously audacious for the time, the authorities decided that the final should be played in New York, the only time in the history of the championships that a final would be played outside Ireland. Kerry and Cavan, two great rivals of the time, were the participants in a final full of intrigue, drama, excitement, history and adventure.

Irish teams had regularly visited the United States since the foundation of the GAA. One of the first championships in 1888 was unfinished because so many of the leading players had travelled to America for a series of exhibition games and did not return. Contacts were very strong right up to the outbreak of World War II.

It was at the end of that war that the Irish-Americans who ran the GAA in New York began to experience a crisis. Immigration from Ireland had slowed to a trickle. The generation that had played Gaelic games in the 1930s were now getting too old and there were fears that the association in the city was losing momentum. A dramatic gesture was needed.

John O'Donnell, whose nickname 'Kerry' indicated his roots, was a highly successful businessman in New York who had become a central figure in the GAA. On a visit to Ireland in 1946 he attended the drawn All-Ireland final between Kerry and Roscommon. It was there that an idea took root. He thought it would be just the boost New York needed if the replay were staged in the city. Logistically it was not possible, but O'Donnell set events in motion that would lead to the Polo Grounds final of 1947.

With the assistance of Tipperary-based priest Canon Michael Hamilton, who represented New York's interests on the GAA's Central Council, O'Donnell began planning. It was Canon Hamilton who convinced his native county, Clare, to submit a motion to the annual Congress proposing that the final be held in New York. Opposition was fierce and in the build-up to the Congress it was felt that the motion would be rejected. But Canon Hamilton tugged at the heartstrings of delegates with an emotional appeal. Congress agreed that the feasibility of staging the final in New York should be investigated.

The general secretary of the GAA, Pádraig O'Caoímh, and the secretary of the Connacht Council, Tom Kilcoyne, travelled to New York to assess the situation. They travelled by ship from Southampton. They met New York officials, including O'Donnell. They checked possible venues including Yankee Stadium and the Polo Grounds, home of the New York Giants baseball team. The Polo Grounds had staged exhibition games in both hurling and football during the 1930s and was considered the best venue.

When they returned to Ireland the two men had to report to the GAA's Central Council. Opposition to the idea was still strong but on a vote of 20–17 the decision to stage the final in New York was taken. A full-time office was opened in the Woodstock Hotel in New York and the organising committee promised they would ensure that advance sales of the 35,000 tickets would be a priority. The GAA initially sent Paddy McNamee to man the office on their behalf and O'Caoímh followed later after reorganising the championship to ensure the participants would have been decided in good time for the final on 14 September.

To ensure that the teams would have time to secure visas and to receive vaccinations against smallpox, which were compulsory at the time, the four provincial championships were run off much quicker than ever before. The provin-

cial finals in Connacht, Leinster and Ulster were on the same day, 20 July, with Roscommon, Meath and Cavan emerging as champions. The following Sunday Kerry retained their Munster title and would meet Meath in the semi-final.

Roscommon were seeking consolation for the manner in which they lost the 1946 title, having led by six points in the drawn game. Their semi-final with Cavan was a repeat of the 1943 final which Roscommon won after a replay. This time, however, Cavan were superior, while Kerry proved too strong for Meath.

On 2 September the first group of players and officials, a mixture from the two counties, left Ireland on the SS *Mauritania* from Cobh for the six-day trip to New York. The rest of the party travelled a few days later on a TWA flight from Shannon. It was an exhausting trip with stops in the Azores, Gander in Newfoundland, Boston and eventually New York. The teams received a rousing welcome. The Mayor, Bill O'Dwyer, was a native of Mayo and hosted a civic reception. This was followed by a tickertape parade through Broadway, the Irish footballers being the centre of attention.

The intense heat did not make it easy for the players as they prepared for the final. Because of the heat, training was limited so that the players could conserve energy for the final. On the night before the game heavy rain fell and there were fears briefly about the state of the ground. However, circumstances dictated that the game would go ahead one way or the other and almost 35,000 packed into the Polo Grounds for the eagerly-awaited clash.

After 15 minutes of the game, refereed by Martin O'Neill, the fear was that it would not be a contest. Cavan were very slow to start and were soon eight points behind, Batt Garvey and Eddie Dowling scoring goals for Kerry in the first seven minutes as Cavan tried to find their feet. Dowling suffered an injury which forced him out of the game and that contributed to the turning

of the tide. Cavan began to enjoy some dominance and Peter Donohue found the range from frees and play. By half-time Cavan were leading 2–5 to 2–4, the goals coming from Joe Stafford and New York-born Mick Higgins.

The second half turned into a thriller, the teams exchanging scores and playing the game at an exceptional pace given the heat and the hard surface. Cavan lasted the pace better, with free-taker Donohue contributing eight points in all as they won by 2–11 to 2–7.

As an occasion, the final was a major success. The meticulous planning had paid off and the Polo Grounds final took its place in the history of the championship.

FIRST ACROSS THE BORDER

Until 1960 no team from across the border, in the Six Counties of Northern Ireland, had ever won the All-Ireland senior football championship. The great Antrim team of the 1940s, with Kevin Armstrong among their number, were extremely unlucky to come through at a time when there were a big number of contenders for the Sam Maguire Cup.

During the late 1940s there were signs that the Six Counties were becoming even more competitive. Tyrone won the All-Ireland minor championships of 1947 and '48, while Armagh won the title in 1949. Cavan had represented the province of Ulster well but there was a burning desire among those involved in Gaelic football in the Six Counties that one of them would finally break the jinx and carry the trophy back across the border.

Maurice Hayes was one of those dreamers. As secretary of the Down County Board, he worked day and night during the 1950s organising games and players. He not only dreamed, he believed that one day it would happen despite the fact that the county had never won an Ulster senior title. They reached the

Seán O'Neill (far left) and James McCartan (foreground) helped Down to success in the 1960s

final in 1958 but lost to Derry. They returned in 1959 and beat Cavan to take the Anglo-Celt Cup for the first time. Although they lost to Galway in the All-Ireland semi-final, it was the start of a great era.

On 25 September 1960 Down created history and earned a special place for the county in GAA folklore when they became the first All-Ireland champions from north of the border. A record crowd of 87,768 attended the final against Kerry in Croke Park and the scenes that greeted the victory were described as the most incredible ever seen.

Having retained the Ulster title, Down played Offaly in the All-Ireland semi-final. They struggled to a draw, having been seven points down at half-time. A late penalty, controversially awarded for a foul on Jim McCartan, had kept them in the championship. Standing on Hill 16 that day Peter McDermott, the former All-Ireland-winning captain from Meath, was an interested observer. He wrote to a friend in Down the following day suggesting that their tactics were wrong. McDermott was then invited to coach Down for the replay. He agreed on condition that his involvement remained a secret. The move worked, and Down won the replay by 1–7 to 1–5.

Whatever uncertainties had been in the minds of the players before the final were gone by the big day. Down entered the arena with confidence. They led by two points at half-time, 0–7 to 0–5, and repulsed a number of Kerry attacks. Paddy Doherty, Jim McCartan and Sean O'Neill were causing problems for the Kerry defence and goalkeeper Johnny Culloty pulled off a number of good saves.

McCartan and Culloty would be the central figures in the turning-point of the game. The teams were level 12 minutes into the second half when McCartan got possession 40 yards from the Kerry goal. He sent in a speculative lob that Culloty seemed to have covered. At the last moment the goalkeeper took his eye off the ball, and it slipped through his hands and into the net.

Then Doherty was pulled down in the square and referee John Dowling awarded a penalty. Doherty took the kick, scored another goal, and the championship was decided.

Tens of thousands of Down supporters rushed on to the field at full-time. Down captain Kevin Mussen received the Sam Maguire Cup and was unable to get to the dressing-room for almost 30 minutes because of the crowds. The following day, as the team bus crossed the border, the customs men entered to carry out their official duties. The players disembarked and walked across the border with Mussen carrying the trophy.

Ironically, Mussen lost his place on the team in 1961 when Down successfully retained their title. Led this time by Paddy Doherty, they again beat Kerry (by six points) in the All-Ireland semi-final and played Offaly in the final. A record attendance for the final (that still stands) of 90,556 was reached as Down won a dour game by 3–6 to 2–8.

Doherty, Joe Lennon, Dan McCartan and Sean O'Neill were back in the winners' enclosure in 1968 when Down won a third All-Ireland championship, making the 1960s a memorable decade for the county.

Leabharla... 1150524 Contae na Mí...

Above: 1965, Galway vs. Kerry. All-Ireland final. **Opposite**: 1964 All-Ireland final: Galway's Sean Meade (6) and Noel Tierney challenge Kerry

GALWAY'S THREE-IN-A-ROW: 1964, '65 AND '66

As Galway supporters left Pearse Stadium, Salthill, on a March Sunday in 1962, they were accompanied by an air of unrelenting depression. They had turned out in big numbers to assess the rate of development among their young football team, believing that things were coming together quite nicely.

Wins over Laois, Wicklow and Roscommon and a draw against Offaly had hoisted them up the National League table, so the next match against Dublin was a real attraction for Galway fans. Expectations were high but Dublin re-introduced Galway to reality, winning by 6–7 to 1–4. From a Galway viewpoint, it was every bit as depressing as the scoreline suggested. Nobody could have possibly envisaged the transformation which would come over the Galway team in the following seasons, during which they reached four consecutive All-Ireland finals, winning three and guaranteeing themselves

a place in history as one of the greatest teams of all time. Ten of the team which lost the 1962 League game to Dublin by 18 points would go on to figure prominently in the All-Ireland three-in-a-row side of 1964, '65 and '66.

Galway lost the 1962 Connacht final to Roscommon by a point but in the following National League they showed flashes of the brilliance which would come to be their hallmark in future seasons. Among their victims were Dublin, beaten 2–12 to 0–7 at Croke Park. Clearly, much had changed for Galway since the previous year. They reached the League semi-final but lost to Down by a point in a game which produced a rather curious scoreline: Down 2–8, Galway 4–1.

There were mixed emotions in Galway after that defeat. Few teams score four goals in major games but fewer still manage just one point in 60 minutes. Optimistic Galway fans felt that there was still a whole lot more to come, while the pessimists feared that it would a case of flattery followed by deception. It was

still a young team – indeed, several of them had been on the side which won the All-Ireland minor title in 1960 – so there were doubts about whether they would have the necessary maturity to make a real impact on the 1963 championship.

The answers came quickly and emphatically. Mayo were despatched comfortably, followed by Leitrim, who were totally outclassed as Mick Garrett and his Galway side began to touch new and exciting heights. Despite their impressive form in the Connacht championship, sceptics still doubted if Galway could deliver against Kerry in the All-Ireland semi-final. Kerry were the defending All-Ireland champions and went into the 1963 semi-final as hot favourites, a rating they lived up to in the first half when they built up an 0–4 to 0–1 lead. Kerry increased the lead to five points early in the second half before Galway launched a spirited comeback which peaked with a goal by Pat Donnellan. Galway's confidence soared and two points by Seamus Leydon gave them a 1–7 to 0–8 victory. They

lost to Dublin in the All-Ireland final by 1–9 to 0–10 in a game which was watched by 87,706 spectators, the third highest attendance ever. Galway were badly betrayed by their shooting and could have no real complaints although they felt aggrieved at the referee's decision not to award team captain Mick Garrett a penalty late in the game.

It was all very different in 1964. Wins over Sligo and Mayo were followed by a hard All-Ireland semi-final against Meath which Galway negotiated with considerable difficulty, eventually winning by two points to set up an All-Ireland final clash with Kerry, the 1962 All-Ireland champions. Times had moved on, however, and Kerry failed to quicken to the pace of a lively Galway side who won by 0–15 to 0–10. It was Galway's first All-Ireland senior win since 1956.

This was the start of an amazing era for Galway football. Down had set the standard with a double All-Ireland win in 1960–61 but now Galway set about raising the bar to new heights. They won the

Seán Walsh (Kerry) and Brian Mullins (Dublin) in a high duel

to clinch the three-in-a-row, a feat which up to then had been achieved only by Kerry, Dublin and Wexford. Galway won the 1966–67 National League 'home' final but lost the final proper to New York. Galway fans assumed it was a one-off set-back and that the team would resume with a high-octane performance against Mayo in the first round of the Connacht championship. It didn't happen. Galway collapsed completely and were soundly beaten. Their great run had come to an end and they wouldn't win another All-Ireland senior title until 1998.

The Galway three-in-a-row team are assured of a permanent place in the list of all-time greats. Their skill, movement, fielding and passing took the game on to a new level which others could only admire. The defence was built on the defiant solidity of Noel Tierney at full-back and Sean Meade at centre-back. Tierney was one of the game's great fielders while Meade was a tenacious stopper who never conceded ground. Enda Colleran and Bosco McDermott were the epitome of vigilance as corner-backs. Colleran, who captained the side in 1965 and 1966, had an added dimension to his game for, as well as being a smart defender, he could also get huge distance into his kicks. John Donnellan, who captained the side from right half-back in 1964, also played in 1965, but was replaced by Coleen McDonagh for the 1966 All-Ireland final, while Martin Newell was at left half-back in all three All-Ireland successes.

Goalkeeper Johnny Geraghty had the distinction of playing in three consecutive All-Ireland finals without conceding a goal. He was generally recognised as one of the best goalkeepers in the history of Gaelic football, and some of his reflex saves were breathtaking. His brilliance attracted the attention of Manchester United but no deal was done, although it is virtually certain that he would have been a huge success as a soccer goalkeeper.

Mick Garrett, Mick Reynolds, Pat Donnellan and Jimmy Duggan featured at midfield over the

1964–65 National League title and because the final was played in New York, they were given a bye directly into the Connacht final. Sligo were the opposition and, just as they had done a year earlier, they gave Galway a real fright. Sligo led by 2–3 to 1–2 at half-time but Galway's confidence and experience enabled them to restore equilibrium in the second half and they ran out three-point winners, 1–12 to 2–6. Galway struggled past Down (0–10 to 0–7) in the All-Ireland

semi-final and repeated their 1964 victory over Kerry in the final, although this time the winning margin was down to three points, 0–12 to 0–9.

This was the first time that Galway had won consecutive All-Ireland finals but their appetite for success remained as strong as ever. They lost the 1965–66 National League 'home' final to Longford but were back to their brilliant best in the 1966 championship, beating Roscommon, Mayo, Cork and Meath

three-year period. Duggan was promoted to the side as an 18-year-old in 1966 and settled in very quickly, winning an All-Ireland medal in his first season.

Mattie McDonagh anchored the attack from centre half-forward. His strong, bustling style caused all sorts of problems for defenders and he finished his career as the only Connacht man ever to win four All-Ireland senior medals: he had also played in the 1956 win over Cork.

Cyril Dunne was a consistently reliable free-taker while Seamus Leydon's speed and anticipation were prime weapons in Galway's attacking plans. Christy Tyrrell played at right corner-forward in both the 1964 and 1965 All-Ireland finals but was replaced by Liam Sammon in 1966. Sean Cleary and John Keenan, both hugely effective, were the other two full-forwards in each of the three years.

The 1964–66 period was, by a distance, the most exciting era ever in Galway football. The team not only left an indelible imprint on the minds of their own supporters but also on rivals who came to admire and respect the sheer brilliance of a team which carved its own special place in the history of All-Ireland football championships

Pat Spillane lifts the Sam Maguire Cup after Kerry's All-Ireland football triumph in 1975

HEFFO'S ARMY

In early June 1974, Dublin played Wexford in the first round of the Leinster senior football championship. These were two of the game's forgotten teams, languishing in the lower divisions of the national league, and the meeting generated little interest. The game was, in fact, a curtain-raiser to the league final between Kerry and Roscommon at Croke Park.

A new Dublin manager, Kevin Heffernan, watched his team struggle to success and then waited for the 'big' game. What he saw disheartened him. The gulf in standards was considerable. Privately he wondered if he could ever bring Dublin to a stage where they could compete at that level. It took a mere four months to achieve the seemingly impossible.

Gaelic football was unprepared for Dublin's return. They had been out of the limelight since the early 1960s. Organisation of the game was poor and there was little spectator interest in the affairs of the county team. Soccer was gradually becoming the choice of sport for most young boys growing up in the city and county. The fact that Dublin generally played just one match in the championship did nothing to promote the game.

By the end of 1973 Dublin played in Division Two of the League. The future looked bleak. The county chairman, Jimmy Grey, decided it was time to act. He looked at the possibilities before him. Grey, a suc-cessful hurler with the county, knew Kevin Heffernan. He had admired him as a player and knew that Heffernan was a passionate football man who thought deeply about the game. In conversation Grey mentioned the possibility of Heffernan becoming manager. Heffernan had some conditions, especially in relation to the number of selectors. Dublin teams were chosen by a minimum of five people at the time. Heffernan wanted that reduced to three. Grey agreed and appointed Donal Colfer and Lorcan Redmond to assist his new manager.

Heffernan devised a demanding training regime for his players. The haphazard system of the past was replaced with an almost military-style campaign. He believed that even if his team was not as good as

Mick O'Connell, a Kerry legend, takes control as he did so often in an amazing career

jected to a system radically different from anything he had experienced in Dublin before. Players trained to the point where they became physically sick. The emphasis was on speed, fitness and creating space. Keaveney realised that if Heffernan was successful in implementing his ideas, then Gaelic Football would be transformed.

There were other positive signs. A 19-year-old, Brian Mullins, standing at 6 ft 4 in, was showing remarkable maturity at midfield, which meant that his natural football ability was easily expressed.

Dublin's big test would be a game against Offaly, the All-Ireland champions of 1971 and '72 and the big power in Leinster. A one-point victory, with substitute Leslie Deegan making an invaluable contribution, changed the course of history. Suddenly, everyone began taking an interest. The newspapers began to focus on this new glamour team; Hill 16 at Croke Park became the natural home of the Dublin supporters who fashioned themselves as 'Heffo's Army' and brought to GAA grounds for the first time the terrace chants that had become familiar on BBC's *Match Of The Day*, such as 'You'll Never Walk Alone'.

The Dubs made Gaelic Football fashionable in modern society. The championship began to feature more regularly on radio and television; newspapers devoted more coverage, even on the news pages. When Dublin won the Leinster title for the first time in nine years by beating Meath 1–14 to 1–9, it was a major cultural event.

Heffernan was naturally pleased with the progress but was beginning to become concerned by the hyperbole. The celebrations that followed the Leinster success were raucous. Everyone seemed content, except Heffernan. One night in the middle of training he called the players together. In angry tones he informed them that his ambitions had not been realised, that Dublin football demanded more and that the players should want more.

All-Ireland champions Cork were

others, at least they would be fitter and would last the pace much better, thereby gaining some sort of advantage. He did not have a time limit in his plans, but felt that it would take at least a couple of years to create a winning team.

While the change went almost unnoticed outside, there was a big change in atmosphere within the squad. Players who had been around for a few years, such as Paddy Cullen, Tony Hanahoe, Sean Doherty and Robbie Kelleher, noticed a new confidence growing among the team. Training, though difficult, became something of a ritual that the players did not want to miss. (They would feel the wrath of the manager if they did.)

The result of the first-round game against Wexford did not create any ripples. Significantly, the events of the day convinced Heffernan that a certain course of action would have to be taken. Jimmy Keaveney, a former team-mate of Heffernan at the St Vincent's club, had retired from inter-county football in 1972. He had attended the game against Wexford as a supporter and had no intention of returning. Heffernan had always rated Keaveney as the best place-kicker of a ball he had seen. Though Keaveney was out of the game and considerably out of condition, a phone call had to be made.

Keaveney, then 29 years old, returned and found himself sub-

overwhelming favourites to win the semi-final against Dublin (Galway overcame Donegal in the other semi-final). Theirs was a team packed with top-line stars, such as Billy Morgan, Declan Barron, Denis Coughlan and Jimmy Barry-Murphy. But by now the Dublin team was beginning to play the rapid-fire football, with swift movement off the ball, that Heffernan had been coaching. Cork were caught unawares and Dublin won by 2–11 to 1–8.

The quality of football in the final was certainly not of the highest standard but that took nothing away from the occasion. Galway, the beaten finalists in 1973, showed their experience by settling quickly but missed a few good scoring chances. They were a point ahead when awarded a penalty. Dublin goalkeeper Paddy Cullen saved from Liam Sammon and the tide turned.

When Dublin won the game by 0–14 to 1–6 it unleashed a wild celebration. It was not just that Dublin were back at the top but that they had done so unexpectedly. In a short period of time, Heffernan and his selectors had completely altered the state of Dublin football. The names of Cullen, Gay O'Driscoll, Doherty, Kelleher, Paddy Reilly, Alan Larkin, Georgie Wilson, Steve Rooney, Mullins, Bobby Doyle, Hanahoe, David Hickey, John McCarthy, Keaveney and Anton O'Toole became famous all over the country.

A year later when Kerry emerged to beat Dublin in the All-Ireland final, a new edge was added to the Dublin story. The rivalry between the two became a feature of the decade. By 1976 Dublin had re-structured their half-back line. Tommy Drumm, Kevin Moran and Pat O'Neill had emerged, with Fran Ryder a regular replacement as the manager introduced the squad system to good effect. There was a psychological war to be won. It was always felt over the decades that Dublin could not beat Kerry on the major occasions. The events of 1975 had reinforced that belief. Heffernan and his captain Tony

Hanahoe were determined to bring that to an end.

Kevin Moran, soon to join Manchester United, set the tone in the opening minutes with a blistering run through the Kerry defence that should have yielded a score. If

After those highs came the lows. Dublin and Kerry met in the 1978 final. Kevin Moran returned from Old Trafford, but even he could not prevent the extraordinary turn-around in fortunes during the game that began the break-up of the

Eoin 'Bomber' Liston was a huge influence for Kerry

Dublin had managed to combine accuracy with the precision of their build-up they would have won the game more convincingly than the final score of 3–8 to 0–10.

The 1977 semi-final win – with Tony Hanahoe now player-manager – by Dublin over Kerry (see *The Great Matches*) confirmed their superiority and Dublin went on to a comfortable victory over Armagh in the All-Ireland final.

team. Kerry's success prompted changes in the Dublin team. For the 1979 final a new full-back line of Mick Kennedy, Mick Holden and Dave Foran had arrived. Jimmy Keaveney was suspended; Dublin had lost its most accurate player. Defeat signalled the end of a remarkable era when Gaelic Football enjoyed a profile unprecedented in its history. Dublin had brought glamour to the game.

KERRY'S GOLDEN YEARS

Nobody in their wildest dreams could have imagined the impact a young Kerry team would have on the history of Gaelic football when it first emerged in 1975. Known as 'O'Dwyer's Babes' because the team was so young and almost all were bachelors, they would embark on an amazing journey that would become known as The Golden Years.

What followed was a wonderful rivalry with the resurgent Dublin team of the 1970s. Kerry would contest ten of the next 12 All-Ireland finals, winning eight. With their fast, free-flowing football and liberal use of the handpass, along with the sublime skills of so many great players, they would earn the title of 'the greatest team of all time'.

The beginnings were humble. Kerry had suffered a major disappointment when losing the Munster final of 1974 to Cork. Players like Mick O'Connell and Mick O'Dwyer had come to the end of their careers and it seemed as if a period of reconstruction would have to be undertaken. Dublin exploded on to the scene and won the All-Ireland championship, stealing the limelight with their style and the glamour that attached to them.

Kerry trainer Johnny Culloty decided to step down. The county chairman Gerald McKenna wanted to act quickly. He had watched O'Dwyer look after the Kerry Under-21s and was impressed with his methods. McKenna also liked O'Dwyer personally and regarded him as a man of action who would get things done quickly. Once he had established that O'Dwyer would be interested in becoming manager, McKenna ensured that the appointment was ratified without delay.

The early games in the National League taught O'Dwyer a great deal. He had players with wonderful skills, such as Mike Sheehy, Pat Spillane and John Egan. But they needed a great deal of work on the training field. Quickly O'Dwyer established a reputation as a hard task-master. He drove the players

The Kerry team which beat Dublin in the 1979 All-Ireland football final

to the point of exhaustion in training. He encouraged them to develop their skills and realised that he was more fortunate than most managers because of the amount of natural ability the players had.

The first critical test for O'Dwyer and his new team was the Munster final of 1975 against Cork. Nothing else mattered to the supporters and the team would be judged on that result. When they struggled for long periods against Tipperary in the first round the signs were not very positive. But O'Dwyer responded. The team trained for 27 consecutive nights before they met Cork in the Munster final. O'Dwyer instilled in them the need to win and Cork suffered the consequences.

Although hotly favoured to win, Cork were no match for Kerry. The final score of Kerry 1–14, Cork 0–7 told the story. It had been a hot day and the Kerry players clearly survived the conditions better. They were quicker, slicker, more accurate and more committed. The rest of the country slowly began to take notice, although Kerry remained in Dublin's shadow during that midsummer period. They had a com-

fortable passage through the All-Ireland semi-final, beating Sligo by 3–13 to 0–5 and setting up a dream final against Dublin.

In GAA terms it was the classic confrontation: city versus country. Dublin's flashy new style was expected to contrast with Kerry's traditional game – except by now Kerry had changed their game and would be able to match Dublin's speed and precision. Also, O'Dwyer played the psychological game well. Much of the pre-match publicity centred on Dublin, who were installed as strong favourites. O'Dwyer encouraged such talk, except among the tightly-knit group that was the Kerry squad.

There was a tight opening to the final on a very wet September day. The main talking-point of the first half was a heavy tackle on Kerry captain Mickey O'Sullivan which had him hospitalised immediately. Kerry led by 1–6 to 0–4 at half-time and there had been signs that they could become even more dominant. So it happened. Dublin could not respond in the second half and Kerry were comfortable winners by 2–12 to 0–11.

Although Kerry supporters were accustomed to success, this was special. To beat Dublin in such style with the youngest team ever to win an All-Ireland title for Kerry created an excitement that had never been witnessed previously. The team of Paud O'Mahony, Ger O'Keeffe, John O'Keeffe, Jimmy Deenihan, Páidí Ó Sé, Tim Kennelly, Ger Power, Pat McCarthy, Paudie Lynch, Brendan Lynch, Denis 'Ogie' Moran, Mickey O'Sullivan (sub. Ger O'Driscoll), John Egan, Mike Sheehy and Pat Spillane was fêted throughout the county.

Memories are short, however. Before Kerry would win another All-Ireland in 1978 the knives would be out for O'Dwyer. Defeat in the 1976 All-Ireland final against Dublin, followed by another defeat in the 1977 semi-final, also against Dublin (still regarded as the greatest game of the modern era), caused some to question O'Dwyer's position with the team. But with chairman McKenna remaining in office, O'Dwyer had his champion and would get the opportunity to atone for the two years without success.

It was during the autumn of 1977

after the shattering defeat by Dublin that O'Dwyer began to take stock of the players around him. He knew that he would not survive in his job if Kerry did not win the All-Ireland of 1978. He planned meticulously, trained the team harder than ever before and got the response he desired.

Jack O'Shea and Seán Walsh were fulfilling their potential and established themselves as first-teamers. Throughout the winter league campaign O'Dwyer introduced a few more new names. For the game against Dublin, which drew an unusually large attendance of 25,000 to Croke Park, a big full forward was introduced. His name was Eoin Liston, later to acquire the nickname 'The Bomber', and he would become a major figure. He was tall and gangly, and opinions were divided on his ability. But O'Dwyer and the Kerry players were convinced that he was a star in the making.

Despite the pressure on the team and the manager, Kerry cruised back to the All-Ireland final of 1978. Again Dublin were the opponents. But on this occasion it became clear that the tide was turning and Kerry were now the dominant force, as they showed on a day that would go down in history.

For the first 20 minutes of the game Kerry struggled to contain a rampant Dublin team. Jimmy Keaveney scored five points for Dublin and panic was beginning to spread through Kerry. John Egan scored a goal to help steady nerves but Dublin remained in front and were playing with such confidence that full-backs were joining in the attacks.

Three minutes before half-time referee Seamus Aldridge set in motion one of the most famous incidents in the history of football. Dublin goalkeeper Paddy Cullen and Kerry's Ger Power were involved in a slight collision. Aldridge judged that Cullen was the aggressor. He continued to argue while Dublin's Robbie Kelleher handed the ball to Mike Sheehy.

Sheehy looked up and spotted Cullen away from his goal. He quickly placed the ball and lobbed it into the empty net while Cullen desperately tried to get back to his line. Some Dublin players insisted the free was taken too quickly but the

referee allowed it. At half-time Kerry led by 2–3 to 0–7 and nobody could quite believe what had happened.

The second half was a rout. Dublin scored only two more points and did not score in the final quarter of the game. Mick Spillane, the younger brother of Pat, had an outstanding game at corner-back. Liston was majestic. He scored three goals in the second half to destroy Dublin. Kerry won by 5–11 to 0–9. The first step on an extraordinary journey had been taken.

The team began to take on a familiar shape. Charlie Nelligan was established as first-choice goalkeeper; Tommy Doyle was emerging as a candidate for a place in the starting line-up. The manager always allowed his players time for relaxation towards the end of the year but at the start of January a level of discipline was imposed that had never before been seen in Gaelic games. That the players responded was testament to their own commitment as well as their respect for O'Dwyer. Even when organised training was not taking place, the players trained on their own.

The intentions for 1979 were clear from the first round of the Munster championship. In what became known as 'The Milltown Massacre' Kerry beat Clare by 9–21 to 1–9. Indeed, Kerry faced some criticism for the manner in which they continued to pile on the agony for Clare. But as the players explained later, there was no room for sentiment in this regime and everyone was playing for his place on the team.

Part of the success was because different players starred on different occasions. In the Munster final Ger Power scored 2–3 as Kerry beat Cork by 2–14 to 2–4. Kerry beat Monaghan in the All-Ireland semi-final and prepared for yet another meeting with Dublin in the All-Ireland final. Despite the fact that Páidí Ó Sé was dismissed during the second half, Kerry were comfortable winners by 3–13 to 1–8. The Dublin team was reaching the end of its natural lifespan.

Inevitably talk of a third title in a row began. With Dublin in decline, nobody was quite sure where the greatest challenge would come from.

Cork remained in the doldrums and mounted a tame challenge in the Munster final of 1980, Kerry winning by 3–13 to 0–12. Offaly became the new power in Leinster and the All-Ireland semi-final provided a portent of some of the great occasions to come when these two teams met. Kerry won the game by 4–15 to 4–10 but they were acutely aware afterwards that a challenger had emerged from the pack.

Four days before the All-Ireland final against Roscommon, Eoin Liston was hospitalised with appendicitis. He had become the chief target man for the team and his loss would unsettle them in the final. Roscommon began in whirlwind fashion and were 1–2 to nil ahead after only 11 minutes. Kerry slowly got back into the game, Pat Spillane scoring an important goal. In difficult conditions, the teams were level at half-time, 1–3 each. Controversy would erupt later about the second half. Kerry were very unhappy about what they described as the negative tactics of Roscommon, who seemed to lose the air of confidence that had marked

Offaly celebrate after staging a remarkable finish to beat Kerry in the 1982 All-Ireland football final

the opening of the game. Personal battles erupted around the field. Roscommon had chances to win but a great save by Nelligan and a block by Ó Sé denied them. Kerry maintained their composure and held out for a 1–9 to 1–6 victory.

Only two teams had ever managed four consecutive All-Ireland senior football titles, Wexford from 1915 to 1918 and Kerry from 1929 to 1932. That became the next target for Kerry. By now there was a certain inevitability about the Munster championship. Neither Clare nor Cork was able to mount anything like a real challenge as Kerry romped into another All-Ireland series. In the semi-final Mayo were the opposition. Despite a spirited start, they crumbled in the second half and Kerry won very comfortably by 2–19 to 1–6.

Offaly, who had been so impressive in the semi-final of 1980, were the opponents in the All-Ireland final. For the first time since the emergence of Kerry in 1975, they lined out in a major championship game without Pat Spillane. The knee injury – damage to the cruciate ligament – that would lead to major surgery had struck for the first time. In fact, several other players were beginning to struggle with muscular or joint ailments, including Mike Sheehy. Later the number and extent of the injuries was attributed to the intensity of the training these players did.

The final was not regarded as a classic but Kerry emerged with the desired victory by 1–12 to 0–8. It was not as comfortable as the scoreline suggests as Jack O'Shea, now the most consistent and influential player in the team, scored the only goal just minutes from the end.

Kerry enjoyed the fruits of that success with a world tour that took them through the United States, Hawaii and Australia in October and November. It was a celebration and a reward for what had been achieved. And still the extraordinary story was not complete.

No team had ever won five All-Ireland championships consecutively: Kerry set about completing their fifth in 1982. But the championship got off to a bad start when Jimmy Deenihan broke a leg in a training accident. It ended his career and deprived Kerry of one of the best corner-backs in football.

Pat Spillane played in the first round against Clare, which Kerry won comfortably, but by now the damage to his injured knee was so bad that it was obvious surgery would be required. Spillane went on as a substitute in the All-Ireland final, but made little contribution to the Kerry cause that year. Preparations for the Munster final against Cork were disrupted, with Jack O'Shea also nursing an injury and then being involved in a traffic accident two nights before the game. Internally, a row over sponsorship of the team's kit was causing dissension in the camp. Kerry almost paid the price, being held to a draw, 0–9 each, by Cork.

It was the fright Kerry needed. O'Dwyer was able to re-focus. Young Tom Spillane, the third of the brothers from Templenoe, was gaining experience and played one of his greatest games for Kerry in the replay. Denis 'Ogie' Moran and Mike Sheehy produced some great football and Kerry won by 2–18 to 0–12, re-establishing their dominance and sending out a clear message that they were back on track.

Armagh were the opposition in the semi-final and provided stubborn resistance before eventually succumbing to the Kerry power. By the final whistle the composers were already busy at work, preparing to celebrate 'Five in a row'. Offaly should not have been underestimated. They had shown over the previous two years that they were improving and had some very talented players, none more so than Matt Connor.

The final is now part of football folklore. Kerry had struggled to contain the Offaly forwards in the early stages but managed to gain some control as the game wore on. Conditions were difficult. Sheehy had a penalty saved by Offaly goalkeeper Martin Furlong. Despite that, Kerry built up a four-point lead

with six minutes left and the record seemed in their grasp.

Matt Connor reduced the lead to two points with pointed frees. Then, with 90 seconds remaining, Offaly took a quick free inside their own half. Liam Connor got possession and drove the ball high towards the Kerry goal. Kerry's Tommy Doyle

Ambrose O'Donovan led Kerry to success in the GAA's centenary football final in 1984

which had taken a toll. Questions were asked about the future. Some of the players were clearly coming to the end of their careers, while others wondered if they could maintain the effort. They did so heroically, aided by some new faces and the return of Pat Spillane after a painful period of recovery from major surgery to a knee.

By July of 1984 the engine was running smoothly again. A new face, Ambrose O'Donovan, was proving to be an inspiring captain. John Kennedy had emerged as a player of stature. Liston, Ger Power, Sheehy and Spillane were providing leadership and Páidí Ó Sé was finding some of his best form. They beat Cork in the Munster final and set off again on a path that would lead to three more All-Ireland championships.

Dublin were the victims in the finals of 1984 and '85, though the latter title was not won without a battle. Cork produced one of their best displays in the Munster final, while Monaghan forced a draw in the All-Ireland semi-final and proved they were worthy opponents. The final itself was a severe test when Dublin rallied after a slow start to go within one point of Kerry with only a few minutes left. Kerry eventually won by 2–12 to 2–8.

In 1986 Cork again provided stubborn resistance before eventually losing to a Kerry team for whom Tom Spillane was outstanding. Meath were the next test but their inexperience at this level told and Kerry had a comfortable win. Another new opponent, Tyrone, awaited in the final and they had plenty of surprises in store for Kerry. It took the combined brilliance of Jack O'Shea and Pat Spillane to overcome the challenge. Tyrone led by 1–8 to 0–4 just after half-time having played some inspired football. Although their captain, Eugene McKenna, was clearly hampered by injury, Tyrone were in control. But when McKenna was forced to leave the field the game began to change. Spillane and Sheehy scored two goals and Kerry found the resolve to pull away and win with some

and Offaly substitute Seamus Darby jumped for it. Darby got possession – though it was claimed that he gave Doyle a nudge in the back – turned and sent a fierce shot to the net. Offaly led by 1–15 to 0–17. Kerry tried vainly to get the levelling point but the final whistle came too early. The dream had died.

The recovery was difficult but there were other targets. In 1983 Kerry were going for their ninth Munster title, another record. They met Cork in the final, again on a day when torrential rain fell. Nobody could have foretold how the game would be decided. Kerry held a two-point lead as the game went

into injury time. Tadhg O'Reilly took a free for Cork and dropped it near the Kerry goal. It fell perfectly for Tadhg Murphy, who drove the ball low and hard to the net. The final whistle went. Another last-minute goal had denied Kerry.

Emotions ran high in the aftermath. It had been a long journey

Down and Offaly struggle for superiority in the 1961 All-Ireland football final

comfort, 2–15 to 1–10.

Completing the three-in-a-row was a stunning achievement for Kerry. They had won seven out of the previous nine championships and eight in 12. Páidí Ó Sé, Ger Power, 'Ogie' Moran, Mike Sheehy and Pat Spillane had played in all the winning teams. Charlie Nelligan, Mick Spillane, Jack O'Shea, Seán Walsh and Eoin Liston had won seven medals. Kerry had dominated football like no other team in history.

In 1987 they took Cork to a replay in the Munster final but now the team was clearly in decline. Players began to drift away. O'Dwyer stayed on as manager until 1989, always fiercely competitive but slowly realising the end was nigh. He eventually quit after losing to Cork in the '89 Munster final. It was the final act in the most remarkable tale in the history of football.

FAMOUS FIRSTS ~ OFFALY 1971–81

Offaly is the little county with the big heart. For an area with a small population its achievements in Gaelic Games have been remarkable. In the 30 years from 1970, three All-Ireland senior football titles and four All-Ireland senior hurling titles have been won, a collection that puts Offaly at the very top of the honours list.

The first signs that the midland county would make a mark on Gaelic Games were seen in 1960 and '61 when a very talented football team won successive Leinster championships and was regarded as very unlucky not to win an All-Ireland title. Offaly lost to Down after a replay in the 1960 All-Ireland semifinal and were narrowly beaten in the 1961 final by the same opposition.

In 1969 they reached another final but lost again, this time to Kerry. So when they reached the final of 1971 against Galway the sense of anticipation was enormous. Father Tom Gilhooly, who had master-minded the arrival of Offaly as a football power, was meticulous in his preparations of the team. This time, he vowed, they could not return home without the title.

With players of the stature of Martin Furlong, Paddy McCormack, Nick Clavin, Eugene Mulligan, Willie Bryan and Tony McTague, the Offaly supporters were confident. But the team took time to settle in the final and after a torrid first half – in which heavy tackles were plentiful – Galway led by 1–6 to 0–4, Seamus Leydon scoring the first of two goals. Goalkeeper Furlong had also made a number of excellent saves and Mulligan was producing a display that would earn him the Footballer of the Year award.

Galway missed two more goal opportunities in the second half, including a shot from Liam Sammon that came back off the bar. Offaly levelled the game and then took the advantage when Murt Connor scored a goal. But Leydon replied with his second for Galway and the title was still up for grabs. In the end a late point from Kevin Kilmurray sealed the issue. Offaly won by 1–14 to 2–8. They retained the title in 1972 when beating Kerry by 1–19 to 0–13 in a replay.

In 1969, while the footballers were preparing for their success, the county's hurlers were making a small impression. They reached the Leinster final where they lost to Kilkenny by a very respectable two points. Hopes that it might spark an immediate upsurge in the game faded during the 1970s, however, and it was obvious that a new approach was needed to take the county to the next level.

In the late 1970s a renowned coach from Kilkenny, Dermot Healy, was approached to take over the Offaly hurling team. The transformation from hopefuls to champions began almost immediately. Healy unified the small hurling population in the south of the county, banished club rivalries from the environs of the county dressing-room and coached a more expansive, first-time-striking style of play.

People took some time to notice. When Offaly reached the Leinster final of 1980 just over 9,000 spectators bothered to attend. By 5.00 that evening the whole country was still in shock at the result. The All-Ireland champions, Kilkenny, had been beaten by little Offaly, 3–17 to 5–10.

Offaly lost by two points to Galway in the All-Ireland semifinal, but a year later the two teams met again, this time in a final that would produce as dramatic a finish as was ever seen in the concluding game of the championship.

Galway, winners in 1980, seemed to be on their way to victory as the game entered the closing minutes and they led by two points. Then Pat Delaney got possession for Offaly and bounded up the field. He passed to Brendan Bermingham, who quickly sent the ball to Johnny Flaherty. Surrounded by the goalkeeper and two defenders, Flaherty handpassed

32

the ball to the net. Galway protested that he threw the ball but the goal was allowed. The Galway players were stunned. Danny Owens and captain Padraig Horan added two points and Offaly had snatched the title by 2–12 to 0–15.

MEATH 1949

At the end of the 1940s, a decade that been dominated by Kerry, Cavan and Roscommon, a new name was added to the honours list. Meath had been on the periphery of the big time at various stages during the decade but did not capture a first All-Ireland senior title until the Brian Smyth-led team of 1949 came along to end Cavan's bid for three successive championships.

This Meath team went on to contest the finals of 1951 and '52, which they lost, and the final of 1954, which they won. There are many who still regard the team as one of the most complete footballing

outfits of all time, mixing great strength with football dexterity. The line-up included full-back Paddy O'Brien, Frankie Byrne, Mattie McDonnell and Peter McDermott.

In championship and league in 1949 and 1950 they won 21 consecutive games, losing to Cavan in the league 'home' final of 1950 (at various stages in history New York were permitted to play the 'home' league champions to decide the outright winners).

Meath were a respected outfit when they began the 1949 championship by beating Kildare and Wexford. Then it took three great tussles before they saw off the challenge of Louth in the Leinster semi-final. That saga, more than any other, prepared the team for the tests ahead. They comfortably beat Westmeath in the Leinster final to once again enter the All-Ireland arena. The incentive to beat Mayo in the national semi-final was enormous because it would set up a final against Cavan, the great team of the late '40s and

Meath's great rivals.

Only after they had successfully disposed of the Mayo obstacle did the players became aware of the intensity of the rivalry among supporters. The build-up to the final was extraordinary and caught many of the players unawares. On the weekend of the game the normally quiet roads leading to Dublin were busier than anyone had ever seen them. The entire population of Meath seemed to be going to the final. When the team arrived at the ground on the day of the game it was mobbed and was delayed getting into the dressing-room.

The excitement of the Meath supporters was not tempered by the fact that Cavan were raging-hot favourites to win the title. Even the Cavan players had been unimpressed with the performance of Meath against Mayo and may have been over-confident. By half-time they knew they had a fight on their hands: Meath led by 0–7 to 0–3. Meath's Bill Halpenny and Cavan's

A proud day for Meath as they beat Cavan to win their first All-Ireland football final in 1949

Donegal and Dublin parade before the 1992 All-Ireland football final

Mick Higgins traded goals in the second half, but Meath finished strongest and the last two points, scored by Byrne and Paddy Connell, gave them a 1–10 to 1–6 victory.

During the next few years Meath had many great battles with Louth in Leinster and there is a feeling that they should have won more championships. It was 1954 when they won their second title, led by Peter McDermott who was known as 'the man in the cap' because he wore one while playing to keep his hair in order. They beat Kerry in the final by 1–13 to 1–7.

DONEGAL 1992

After undergoing surgery on a knee in 1991, Donegal midfielder Anthony Molloy decided it was time to give his body a rest and retire from inter-county football. He was not easily persuaded to change his mind. Reluctantly, at the beginning of 1992 he returned, and it turned out to be the most important decision of his life.

The big man from Ardara was the captain and the inspiration as the Donegal class of 1992 brought the Sam Maguire Cup back to the county for the first time. It was a period of high emotion and great drama as a county came ablaze with colour.

At the start of the campaign nobody would have predicted the drama which lay ahead. Donegal almost lost the first-round game to Cavan and depended on the impressive Martin McHugh to gain them a draw. It was a wake-up call of sorts. They won the replay, then beat Fermanagh comfortably by 16 points and the season suddenly changed. The players were getting into their stride, the manager Brian McEniff was pushing them hard in training and everything was falling into place.

They beat old rivals Derry in the Ulster final and were then unconvincing as they beat Mayo in the All-Ireland semi-final by 0–13 to

0–9. It was a significant display because the watching Dublin squad, who had also qualified for the final, were lulled into a false sense of security, while the pundits dismissed Donegal's chances of causing an upset.

Dublin started strongly as the Donegal players were slow to settle into their surroundings. But slowly Molloy, Brian Murray and Barry Cunningham began to get involved at midfield and provide the supply of ball that the talented forward line needed. McHugh, Declan Bonner, Tony Boyle and Manus Boyle began to dominate their opponents. Dublin began to panic and lost shape. Manus Boyle kicked nine points as Donegal won by 0–18 to 0–14.

DERRY 1993

The early 1990s produced a new phenomenon in Gaelic football – Ulster's domination of the All-Ireland senior championship. From a period in the 1980s when the poor standards of the game in the province were decried everywhere, Ulster counties won four All-Ireland titles in a row from 1991 to 1994. Down, previous winners in the 1960s, won in '91 and '94 and Donegal took the title of '92. The Derry team, led by Henry Downey, were newcomers to the steps of the Hogan Stand.

Derry had produced a number of very good under-age teams during the 1980s, winning the All-Ireland minor championship in 1983 and '89. Many of those players graduated to the senior team and they won the National League in the 1991–92 season.

Manager Eamonn Coleman always believed that Derry football was as good as any other. He had one of the game's most respected coaches, Mickey Moran, on the management team with him and they plotted a path that they were convinced would bring them success. The victories of Down and

Donegal also inspired them. Also, they felt that their loss to Donegal in the 1992 Ulster final was the result of poor preparation.

They beat Down in the first round and then overcame Monaghan in the semi-final to qualify for another meeting with Donegal in the Ulster final. That occasion was memorable for all the wrong reasons. The weather was appalling, torrential rain turning the ground at Clones to mud. Most observers agreed the game should not have been played, but with 30,000 supporters converging on the town it was decided to go ahead. Donegal were under-strength through injuries and Derry won a narrow victory, 0–8 to 0–6.

The All-Ireland semi-final against Dublin was a tense affair for Derry. They did not play well in the opening half and were five points down at half-time. But after a verbal lashing by the management team, the players responded and Derry took control and qualified for the final, where they played Cork.

Cork led by 1–2 to 0–0 after five minutes but the game changed when Cork's Tony Davis was harshly sent off. While Cork rallied bravely, Derry slowly got on top. Enda Gormley and Joe Brolly scored some excellent points and in the end Derry won by 1–14 to 2–8.

BACK AT THE WINNER'S TABLE

So many of the greatest occasions in Gaelic football and hurling over the past 120 years have involved counties returning to the victory podium after a long period without success. Size and tradition dictate that many counties can only dream of glory but that does not dull their passion.

The bigger counties, of course, measure success by All-Ireland championships won. In hurling Cork have always enjoyed their share of glory, but the county is also a football stronghold so a wait of 28 years between 1945 and 1973 for an All-Ireland senior football success was

Henry Downey of Derry after the 1993 All-Ireland football final

Billy Morgan: All-Ireland football medallist with Cork in 1973 and manager for their win in 1989–90

regarded as quite unusual. In fact, Cork had contested only three finals in the period between 1945 and 1973.

By 1973, with Billy Morgan as goalkeeper and captain, a talented team had been assembled. The first sign that they would be serious contenders came when they smashed five goals past Kerry in the first half of the Munster final, winning in the end by 5–12 to 1–15. The team contained some great dual players such as Brian Murphy, Denis Coughlan, Jimmy Barry-Murphy and Ray Cummins, who would later go on to win three successive senior hurling championships.

Cork scored five goals in the 1973 All-Ireland semi-final against Tyrone and then ended the long wait for the return of the Sam Maguire Cup by beating Galway in the final by 3–17 to 2–13.

Limerick's hurlers had endured an even longer wait. The last senior All-Ireland had been won in 1940, before almost every member of the 1973 squad was born. Players had been raised on tales of the deeds of Mick Mackey but had never seen a Limerick team win an All-Ireland. But they would create their own legend in the 1973 championship, one of the most eventful of all.

The Munster final against

Tipperary was full of incident and ended in some controversy. The teams were level when Limerick were awarded a '70'. The referee, Mick Slattery, told Limerick's Richie Bennis that this would be the last puck of the game and he would have to score direct. Despite the pressure, Bennis sent the ball sailing towards goal. It veered as it neared the post but the umpire signalled a point. Tipperary protested that the ball was wide but the referee let it stand. Limerick beat London in the All-Ireland semi-final and played Kilkenny in the final.

The switch of Eamonn Cregan

from the attack to centre half-back for the final was regarded as one of the main reasons why Limerick won the final by 1–21 to 1–14.

Sligo's footballers did not often aspire to such lofty heights. They were regarded as one of the weaker football counties, and had captured the Connacht title only once, in 1928. So when a team of contenders emerged in the mid-1970s it was greeted with considerable excitement in the county. The removal of 'the Ban', the rule which barred GAA players from playing soccer or rugby, had been approved in 1971 and Sligo benefitted when David Pugh, a soccer player of considerable quality, joined the Gaelic football squad.

The big star was Mickey Kearins, still regarded as one of the most talented players ever to play the game. He had won a Railway Cup medal in 1969 with Connacht and despite Sligo's lowly status had convinced the selectors of the very first All-Stars team in 1971 of his merits. His greatest year would be 1975 when he was the major influence as Sligo won the Connacht title, by a single point in a replay against Mayo in the final. So wild were the celebrations in Sligo that preparations for the All-Ireland semi-final were badly hampered and the team were no match for Kerry.

In that same year the Galway hurlers were making great strides. They captured the National League title but the search for a first All-Ireland senior hurling title since 1923 went on. They reached the final in 1979 but lost to Kilkenny. A year later, however, the search ended amid some of the most remarkable scenes ever witnessed at Croke Park.

A team which included the incomparable John Connolly and captained by his brother Joe had narrowly beaten the new Leinster champions, Offaly, by two points in the All-Ireland semi-final and set up a final meeting with Limerick. Bernie Forde and P J Molloy scored two early goals for Galway to allow them to settle. It was never comfortable but Galway held their nerve and an explosion of relief at the end engulfed the stadium. Joe Connolly's acceptance speech in Irish is regarded as the greatest ever given on All-Ireland day while Joe McDonagh, later to be GAA president, created a new trend by singing 'The West's Awake' on the steps of the Hogan Stand.

Armagh football followers had waited 24 years for an Ulster championship when the Jimmy Smyth-led team emerged triumphantly in 1977. With players of the calibre of goalkeeper Brian McAlinden, Tom McCreesh, Paddy Moriarty, Colm McKinstry and Joe Kernan

Noel Roche gave outstanding service to Clare football

in the team they marched confidently out of Ulster, beating Derry in the final by 3–10 to 1–5.

They drew with Roscommon in the All-Ireland semi-final and then won the replay by one point. But they found Dublin too strong in the All-Ireland final.

Even when Clare's footballers qualified for the Munster final of 1992 nobody gave them a chance of beating Kerry. Clare, trained by Army officer John Maughan, whose playing career with his native Mayo had ended prematurely because of injury, had received some good reviews for their performances early in the year and the new format 'open-draw' championship introduced in Munster a year earlier allowed traditional powers Kerry and Cork to meet in the semi-final.

What happened when Clare met Kerry at the Gaelic Grounds in Limerick will never be forgotten in either county. It became a tight battle in which Kerry could never get the sort of control they expected. And when, midway through the second half, Colm Clancy and Martin Daly scored two goals, Clare grew in confidence and Kerry began to struggle. Clare held on for a 2–10 to 0–12 victory. It was their first Munster senior championship since 1917 and a reward for players like Noel Roche, who had played for the county in three decades without any reward.

Although they lost to Dublin in the All-Ireland semi-final, they performed with distinction and Clare's status as a football county has remained high ever since.

Little Leitrim has a tiny population and many of the players live and work outside its borders, but this always was a proud football county. Though success was alien, efforts were constantly made to improve its standing. Bringing coaches into the county was a major assistance in improving standards and when Mayo man John O'Mahony was brought on board

in 1993 it was a major step. O'Mahony had taken Mayo to an All-Ireland final in 1989 and would later lead Galway to All-Ireland glory.

Leitrim's path had been blocked by Roscommon on a few occasions in the early 1990s but they got over that hurdle in 1994 and qualified to meet Mayo in the Connacht final. Just reaching that stage created a frenzy of excitement in the county. For players like Mickey Quinn it was the realisation of a dream. He had played for a decade with the county and earned a reputation throughout the country as a player of outstanding ability.

Team captain Declan Darcy, who lived in Dublin but chose to play for the county with which his father Frank had starred, produced an outstanding display in the final. So too did full-back Seamus Quinn, who was decorated as the All-Star full-back later that year. Despite conceding two goals, Leitrim held on for a two-point victory, 0–12 to 2–4. They were beaten in the All-Ireland semi-final by Dublin.

Back in Clare that autumn former star hurler Ger Loughnane was appointed senior hurling manager. Clare had contested the Munster finals of 1993 and '94 and suffered heavy and debilitating defeats. Loughnane brought confidence and authority with him. With his selectors, Mike McNamara and Tony Considine, he devised a training regime the players would later describe as 'cruel'. It made them the fittest team in the country. Loughnane also instilled in the players the self-belief that they could compete at the highest level.

The county had won its only Munster and All-Ireland senior hurling titles in 1914. In the summer of 1995 they went on an adventure that would culminate in provincial and All-Ireland success. It all began when they lost the league final to Kilkenny. Clare had played well despite defeat and felt confident

going into the championship. They played Cork in the Munster semi-final and were two points down with one minute left. Ollie Baker got a late goal to give Clare a one-point win and a place in the Munster final against Limerick.

Limerick, the reigning champions, were favoured to win but this time Clare would make no mistake. They won by 1–17 to 0–11. Galway fell by the wayside in the All-Ireland semi-final and Clare qualified to meet Offaly in the final. It would be one of the most memorable and colourful days in the history of the championship. The game itself was of high quality and the outcome was decided only when substitute Eamon Taaffe scored a late goal to give Clare a 1–13 to 2–8 win.

The new Wexford hurling manager Liam Griffin was inspired during this period to describe hurling as 'the Riverdance of sport' in reference to the hugely successful stage show. Griffin would mastermind Wexford's return to the All-Ireland podium in 1996 after a wait of 28 years. They had endured some agonising defeats in Leinster during the early part of the 1990s but Griffin's charisma and infectious enthusiasm brought a change in approach and attitude.

He blended old with new, encouraging a fast, open style of hurling which endeared them to supporters everywhere. They had a difficult game to open the championship when they played their great rivals Kilkenny in the quarter-final in Leinster. It was a real challenge, but the new Wexford emerged victorious. They beat Dublin comfortably in the semi-final and faced Offaly in the final. Wexford proved that day just how confident they were as they won by 2–23 to 2–15 in impressive style.

Galway tested Wexford fully in the semi-final but could not stop the momentum. Wexford played Limerick in the final and it would prove to be a tough assignment. Wexford corner-forward Eamon Scallan was sent off towards the end of the first half and they had to defend a one-point lead, 1–8 to

0–10, with only 14 men. But with Ger Cushe and Liam Dunne outstanding in defence and veteran George O'Connor providing inspiration at midfield, they held on to win by 1–13 to 0–14.

For a county with such a wonderful football tradition, Cavan had suffered many years of failure until 1997. The county had not won an Ulster title since 1969 and only rarely made an impact within the province. In the mid-1990s they looked outside for assistance. Martin McHugh was a young man with little coaching experience but he had been an outstanding player with Donegal and was eager for the challenge. He transformed an ordinary Cavan team into Ulster champions.

It began in less impressive fashion in early June of '97 when only a point, five minutes into injury time, from Anthony Forde snatched a draw with Fermanagh in the opening game. The replay was just a little more comfortable and Cavan marched on with a three-point win. The Ulster semi-final pitted the manager against his native Donegal but sentiment was set aside and Cavan won by six points.

The final against Derry was a heart-stopping affair for the Cavan supporters. It was tight and tense throughout. The team led by two points with only a few minutes remaining when Cavan goalkeeper Paul O'Dowd made an excellent save to deprive Derry of a goal. Derry's Joe Brolly reduced the margin to a point but that ended the scoring. The long-serving Cavan midfielder Stephen King realised a dream when lifting the Ulster trophy.

The oldest Kildare supporters will have understood how the people of Cavan felt. The county had not won a Leinster championship since 1956 and during the '90s had seen the team go so close on a few occasions. The arrival of Mick O'Dwyer from Kerry as coach had created mass hysteria in the county and by '98 the time for the team to deliver had arrived.

They drew with Dublin in the

first round and won the replay by a single point. The manager had brought a few new faces to the team, including his son Karl and former Tipperary player Brian Lacey. Willie McCreery was developing into a player of quality and young Dermot Earley was maturing well. They comfortably beat Laois in the Leinster semi-final and then faced Meath in the provincial final. Kildare were the dominant team but had seen a three-point lead wiped out as the game entered the final minutes. This time it was Kildare who responded best. Substitute Brian Murphy scored a goal and the dream of a Leinster title was realised.

Kildare reached the All-Ireland final where they faced Galway. No Connacht team had won the title since Galway completed three-in-a-row in 1966. This time John O'Mahony was in charge and his magic touch would be felt. Building a team around Kevin Walsh in midfield and the brilliant Jarlath Fallon at centre-forward, O'Mahony also benefitted from having Michael Donnellan's pace and vision available to him.

Galway had survived a scare in Connacht when they needed a point from a late and controversial free to draw with Roscommon in the final. The replay went to extra time before Galway won through a fortuitous goal. They beat Derry in the semi-final, and the final was regarded as one of the best of the modern era, full of flowing football from which Galway emerged as 1–14 to 1–10 winners.

WATERFORD 1948

When Christy Moylan returned from England at the beginning of the summer of 1948 to visit his sick mother, he could never have believed that his dream of winning an All-Ireland senior hurling championship would be realised. But it was, and the dreams of an entire county came true, when Waterford won its first All-Ireland senior title.

Moylan had been a member of the team which had reached the 1938 final and lost to Dublin. He continued playing for the county until he emigrated in 1945, convinced that the chance of ultimate glory had passed him by.

But when he was home in 1948, Waterford had beaten Clare in the Munster semi-final and Moylan was drafted into the squad for the Munster final against Cork. Despite a nervous start, Waterford managed to win their first Munster title in ten years, with John Keane the star of the show at centre-forward. Though renowned as one of the greatest centre-backs in the history of the game, Keane moved into the attack for 1948 to provide strength and sublety.

Having beaten Galway in the All-Ireland semi-final, a Waterford team that included great players such as Jim Ware, Vin Baston, Andy Fleming and Mick Hayes played Dublin in the All-Ireland final. The fierce hunger for a first All-Ireland success was quickly sated. Waterford led by 2–5 to 0–2 at the interval and were convincing winners in the end, 6–7 to 4–2. A crowd of 25,000 greeted the team in Waterford city the following day.

CHANGING CHAMPIONSHIP FORMATS

Although the inaugural hurling and football championships in 1887 were played on an open-draw basis, the GAA moved quickly towards the concept of using provincial championships as a qualification route to the All-Ireland series. Limerick, represented by the Commercials club, beat Louth (Dundalk Young Irelands) by 1–4 to 0–3 in the first All-Ireland football final while Tipperary (Thurles) beat Galway (Meelick) by 1–1 to nil. Between 1887 and 1891, teams had 21 players and a goal outweighed any number of points. Teams were reduced to 17 players

in 1892, while the value of the goal was set at five points. Four years later, the goal was re-set at three points, a value it has retained ever since. Teams were reduced to 15 players in 1913.

As the GAA grew in organisational strength and efficiency, the provincial system worked particularly well in football as the standards were fairly even across the country. However, hurling was a different matter. Leinster and Munster were way ahead of Connacht, where Galway was the sole power base, and Ulster, where Antrim generally reigned supreme. The Leinster and Munster hurling championships were launched in 1888 and grew in quality and stature

Waterford, winners of the county's first All-Ireland Senior hurling title in 1948

each year. The first Ulster hurling championship was played in 1901 and, with a few exceptions, continued until 1946. No Ulster senior championship was played between 1947 and 1989, when it was revived. The first Connacht hurling final was played in 1900 but with Galway vastly superior to the rest, the championship was scrapped in 1923 and wasn't revived until 1995, when Roscommon returned to provide opposition for Galway in the final. However, after a series of heavy defeats, Roscommon withdrew in 2000, leaving Galway to qualify automatically as Connacht champions. Between 1959 and 1969 Galway played in the Munster championship, but after winning only one of 12 games they opted out and decided to take their chance as Connacht champions in the All-Ireland semi-final.

An important change was introduced to both the All-Ireland football and hurling championships in 1970 when games were extended from 60 to 80 minutes. With fitness levels rising and preparation

methods becoming more sophisticated, it was felt that an hour was not long enough to decide an important championship clash. The 80-minute experiment lasted for five seasons; then 70-minute games were introduced in 1975 and have remained ever since.

In the mid-1990s, a groundswell of opinion grew up in favour of introducing change to the All-Ireland hurling championships. Many people felt that the game would benefit from the addition of more high-profile matches in the July–August period. Also, there was disquiet over the All-Ireland semi-finals. The Ulster champions were no longer providing competitive games for their Leinster and Munster counterparts, which meant that one All-Ireland semi-final was virtually a foregone conclusion.

A new system was introduced in 1997, and the beaten Leinster and Munster finalists re-entered the All-Ireland championships at the quarter-finals stage to meet Galway and the Ulster champions respectively.

Supporters of the plan, which became known as 'the back door', justified it on the basis that it would provide additional high-quality games and better semi-final pairings, while critics argued that the real beneficiaries would be the stronger Leinster and Munster counties and that it would do nothing for the weaker counties.

Kilkenny and Tipperary were the first teams to get a second chance as provincial final losers in 1997. Kilkenny beat Galway and Tipperary beat Down in the All-Ireland quarter-finals and Tipperary went on to reach the All-Ireland final by beating Wexford in the semi-final. Thus Tipperary became the first team to reach an All-Ireland final having earlier lost a provincial final. However, they lost to Clare, just as they had done in the Munster final.

A year later, Offaly created history by becoming the first county to lose a provincial final before going on to win the All-Ireland title. Offaly lost the 1998 Leinster final to Kilkenny but beat Antrim and Clare in the All-Ireland series to qualify for the final, where they avenged the earlier defeat by Kilkenny.

They also reached the 2000 All-Ireland final via the 'back door' but this time were well-beaten by Kilkenny.

In October 2000, experimental change was introduced to the All-Ireland football championship format. For the 2001–2002 seasons, it was decided to run a special open-draw competition, running parallel to the provincial championships.

The four provincial winners now qualify for the All-Ireland quarter-finals, where they are joined by the four survivors from an open-draw competition, which is played off between all losers, up to and including provincial final level. In effect, it means that every county is guaranteed a minimum of two championship games. The impact of the new format will be examined at the end of the 2002 season.

Opposite: Liam McGrath of Tipperary battles Down in 1997. **Above**: Offaly fans protest after the 1998 All-Ireland hurling semi-final first replay

3

THE LEGENDS OF FOOTBALL

Legends in opposition: Kerry's Mick O'Connell out-jumps Down's Seán O'Neill (left) in the 1968 All-Ireland final

Gaelic football has a broader parish than hurling and, while that in no way gives it precedence in terms of affection in the public mind, it has resulted in a more even spread of heroes throughout the country. With the exception of Antrim, Down and Derry, the main hurling action is confined to the south of a line drawn between Galway and Dublin, whereas football is fairly evenly spread throughout the country. Each county has its own heroes and legends, although men like Seán Purcell (Galway), Mick O'Connell and Mike Sheehy (Kerry) and Seán O'Neill (Down) transcend every boundary when it comes to assessing the true masters of Gaelic football.

Offaly legend Matt Connor (left) in classic shooting pose against Dublin in 1980

MATT CONNOR

Club: Walsh Island

County: Offaly

Honours: 1 All-Ireland senior title (1982); 3 Leinster senior titles (1980, '81, '82); 3 All-Star Awards (1980, '82, '83).

A remarkable talent who contributed so much to Offaly's exciting times in the early 1980s, Connor was at his prime when his career was tragically ended in a car accident on Christmas Day 1984. Unfortunately, he sustained a serious back injury which has left him confined to a wheelchair ever since. He was only 25 years old at the time of the accident.

The injury robbed Gaelic football of a special talent; one which was apparent from his early days with his club, Walsh Island. Connor was a beautifully-balanced player, equally comfortable off left or right,

and was also a consistently-accurate place-kicker.

He was born into a famous football family. His father, Jim, was an accomplished club player, winning six county championship medals in the 1930s and 1940s, while his older brother, Murt, was a member of the Offaly squad which won consecutive All-Ireland titles in 1971 and 1972. Another brother, Richie, played alongside Matt on the Offaly team for several seasons.

Matt made his senior debut with Offaly at the age of 17 in 1977, at a time when the side was beginning to re-emerge after a lean spell. He played on the minor (Under-18), Under-21 and Offaly senior teams that year, and in a short space of time made it abundantly clear that he possessed a rare and wonderful talent. Offaly reached the 1979 Leinster senior final where they lost to Dublin, but made amends a year later when they took the provincial title for the first time since 1973. They were beaten by

Kerry (4–15 to 4–10) in the 1980 All-Ireland semi-final but Connor emerged as a real star, scoring 2–9, 2–3 from play.

His scoring exploits were again influential in 1981 as Offaly retained the Leinster title and reached the All-Ireland final, where they lost to Kerry by 1–12 to 0–8. A year later, Offaly resumed their rivalry with Kerry in the All-Ireland final and emerged one-point winners in a remarkable game. Kerry were bidding to become the first county to win five consecutive All-Ireland titles but, after leading for most of the way, were caught by a late goal from Seamus Darby which gave Offaly a one-point win, 1–15 to 0–17.

Connor's consistent scoring rate played a major part in Offaly's great run in 1982. He scored 0–7 in the All-Ireland final and set up several chances for his attacking colleagues. The victory was made all the sweeter for the Connor family by the fact that Matt's brother Richie captained the team while first cousins Liam and Tomás Connor also featured prominently, at full-back and midfield respectively.

Matt was the country's top marksman for five successive years (1979–83) and scored a total of 82 goals and 606 points in 161 games for Offaly. As well as anchoring the Offaly attack for several seasons, he also had a massive influence on Walsh Island, helping them to win six consecutive county titles between 1978 and 1983.

He had so much natural talent that consistent excellence came very easily to him, but behind the laid-back approach lay a calculating mind and a willingness to work extremely hard at honing his vast array of skills. One of his favourite training-ground drills was to take the ball to the corner flag and attempt to kick points from apparently impossible angles. He did this repeatedly, so that on match days he never lacked the confidence to shoot from awkward positions. It may have looked quite simple from the terraces but in fact it had been perfected on the training-ground over many nights.

Connor's attention to detail typified the approach of a modest, unassuming man who left an indelible mark on Offaly football.

KEVIN HEFFERNAN

Club: St Vincent's

County: Dublin

Honours: 1 All-Ireland Senior title (1958); 1 All-Ireland Junior title (1948); 3 National League titles (1953, '55, '58); 7 Railway Cups (1952, '53, '54, '55, '59, '61, '62).

To generations of sports fans the name of Kevin Heffernan will be forever linked with his role as coach to the Dublin teams that bewitched the country in the mid-1970s. But as a player, Heffernan had been one of the outstanding exponents of forward invention, and was one of the most respected figures on the field of play during the height of

Hero: Dublin's Kevin Heffernan

his powers in the 1950s.

One of the game's great thinkers, Heffernan is credited with perfecting the role of the roving full forward, which he put to great use during the latter part of the decade.

Unlike many of his contemporaries, Heffernan was not born into a football background. Indeed, his father's sporting interests were far removed from Gaelic games and it was by chance that Kevin would be introduced to the games and become such a proficient player in both Gaelic football and hurling. The family moved to Marino in Dublin when Kevin was very young, and the switch would prove to be very influential on his sporting choices. The local schools treated the games very seriously, and when he attended secondary school he made great progress as a hurler. In 1945 he was a member of the St Joseph's team which won the Leinster Colleges hurling title.

He was still at school when he first played football for Dublin towards the end of the 1940s. Dublin had won the All-Ireland championship in 1942 but had gone into something of a decline. In the search for a new winning formula, they turned to young players like Heffernan. By 1952 he had become an established corner-forward and earned selection on the Leinster team at left half-forward, winning the first of seven Railway Cup medals.

Also in 1952, Dublin showed the first signs of a major revival when they reached the National League 'Home' final, which they lost to Cork. The following year Dublin won their first national title in 11 seasons by capturing the league, but it was not until two years later that the whole country really began to take notice. Playing a fluent, open style of football, Dublin again won the National League and went on to capture the Leinster championship of '55, beating Meath.

However, when they reached the All-Ireland final against Kerry, disappointment followed. Indeed, after that defeat some wondered whether Dublin would ever fulfil their potential. In 1956 they were beaten in the early stages of the Leinster campaign and then in 1957 they lost to eventual All-Ireland champions Louth in the Leinster final.

At this time Heffernan was enjoying spectacular success with a famous St Vincent's team in the Dublin championship. In 1949 they embarked on a 13-year unbeaten run in the Dublin senior championship, winning every title between 1949 and 1962. He was named Dublin's captain in 1958 and, with a team dominated by his clubmates, Heffernan played the roving full-forward role to perfection.

Heffernan had been bitterly disappointed when Dublin lost to Louth the previous year, believing that they had played way below their potential. He was determined that the same would not happen in 1958. The teams met again in the Leinster final and Dublin won by five points, 1–11 to 1–6. Heffernan's ability on the ball, allied to speed of thought, was causing trouble for all defenders and in the All-Ireland semi-final Galway had no answer. In the final against Derry the Dublin team struggled for periods but were comfortable winners in the end by 2–12 to 1–9.

Dublin retained the Leinster title in 1959 but Heffernan's further successes as a player came with Leinster and St Vincent's. He later went on to enjoy great success as a manager (see *The Great Managers*).

He was selected at left full-forward on the Team of the Century in 1984 and the Team of the Millennium in 1999.

JIMMY MURRAY

Club: Knockcroghery

County: Roscommon

Honours: 2 All-Ireland Senior titles (1943, '44); 1 All-Ireland Junior title (1940).

Among the many stories that make up the legend of Jimmy Murray is one of an incident that occurred decades after his illustrious playing career ended. His famous public house in the village of Knockcroghery was on fire and the emergency services were trying to clear the area. To their astonishment, the firemen spotted a figure emerging from the billowing smoke. It was the proprietor, holding a valuable object – the ball from the 1943 All-Ireland football final.

The ball has pride of place in the rebuilt pub, a Mecca for passing sports fans. It is decorated with memorabilia of a great football career which made Jimmy Murray one of the most famous names in the history of the game, and one of the few men to have lifted the Sam Maguire Cup twice.

Jimmy (also known as Jamesie) Murray was born in 1917 in Knockcroghery. His passion for Gaelic games was evident from an early age and he was constantly encouraged by his parents. With his brother Phelim just as passionate about the game, they played football with the local club, St Patrick's, and often cycled six miles to Roscommon town to play hurling.

Roscommon was not a fashionable football county at the time, although inter-club rivalry was fierce and produced some outstanding encounters. Jimmy Murray was as passionate as most and stood out on the field with his shock of red hair. He was as tenacious as he looked, both physically and mentally very strong.

When he first played for Roscommon at adult level they were not even graded as a senior team. In fact, the first taste of success at adult level came in 1940 when they won the All-Ireland Junior title with Murray playing at midfield alongside Eamon Boland. Phelim was a sub in the final.

Two All-Ireland-winning minor teams in 1939 and 1940 ensured that a good supply of players was coming through. When Murray became captain at the beginning of 1943 a new mood of optimism was sweeping the county. Collective training for the players was introduced before the championship, and continued as Roscommon made progress.

His peers reckoned Murray's influence off the field was as important as on it. He was fiercely competitive and drove the other players hard in training. His criticism could be as stinging as his encouragement was comforting. On the field he was getting some crucial scores, too. They had lost two previous Connacht finals to Galway, so revenge in 1943 was particularly sweet. It was also Roscommon's first Connacht senior title in 29 years. Louth were their next victims, as Roscommon qualified for the All-Ireland final for the first time.

Roscommon played poorly but Murray scored a magical goal in the second half to help them to a draw. The replay was a tough encounter, with Cavan's Joe Stafford becoming the first man to be sent off in an All-Ireland final. Roscommon won by five points.

Murray always felt that to prove they were true champions they would have to beat Kerry in a final. The opportunity came in 1944, when they won by two points, 1–9 to 2–4, and gave Murray the greatest satisfaction of his career. Two years later came the biggest disappointment, when the teams met again in the All-Ireland final. Roscommon were six points ahead when Murray had to go to the sideline for treatment on a head injury. It is said that because of the amount of blood on his face a medical assistant told him: 'We'd better clean you up for the presentation.' In his absence Kerry scored two goals and earned a draw – then won the replay, regarded as a football classic.

MICK O'CONNELL

Club: Waterville

County: Kerry

Honours: 4 All-Ireland Senior titles (1959, '62, '69, '70), 6 National Leagues (1959, '61, '63, '69, '71 and '72), 1 Railway Cup (1972), 1 All-Star (1972). Footballer of the Year 1962.

He was the perfect hero – aloof, almost distant; disdainful of fame but having no difficulty in coping with it; a perfectionist whose search for peak physical condition was the catalyst for song and poetry throughout the land; the Islander who enchanted his audience when performing on the big stage but who always yearned to be back in his home place.

Mick O'Connell was Gaelic football's first superstar. Even now, almost three decades after his retirement, his name is still spoken of with reverence wherever football followers gather. His career spanned the 1950s, '60s and '70s when television was beginning to invade not just the living-rooms but the lives of Irish people. Life became centred on personalities and none came any bigger than the man from Valentia Island.

He was the classic catch-and-kick footballer, a brilliant exponent of the traditional game. But he was more than that. His pursuit of physical fitness allowed him to adapt easily to the faster game that developed during the 1960s. He was blessed with great balance, could kick equally well and accurately with both feet and was one of the toughest competitors the game has ever known.

That he was an islander lent O'Connell an air of legend. Some of the mystique was the result of poetic licence by his journalist friends, but there was no doubt that island life had hardened him. It was a tough life where hard work was the norm rather than the exception.

He first wore a Kerry jersey at minor level aged 18 in 1955. Valentia Island did not have its own team, so O'Connell travelled to the mainland for his football, regularly rowing over to play for Waterville or the divisional team, South Kerry. He graduated to the Kerry senior team in 1956 but Kerry lost the Munster final and O'Connell's rise was temporarily halted.

By 1958 the legend was growing and O'Connell won his first Munster championship. Then a year later, as captain of Kerry, he played in his first All-Ireland final. Although Kerry beat Galway in the '59 final O'Connell's memories were not good. He had been sick in the days leading up to the game and then suffered a knee injury, forcing him to leave the field during the final.

He collected the Sam Maguire Cup on behalf of the team but there followed an extraordinary episode that simply added to the growing legend.

O'Connell changed swiftly after the game and travelled home to Kerry by train. He was back on the island that night but had forgotten the cup. Someone came to the rescue and the unconcerned captain

Kerry legend Mick O'Connell lifts the Sam Maguire Cup after winning the 1959 All-Ireland final

Mick O'Dwyer: a great player who became a legend as a manager

Kerry lost to Offaly. Even in defeat, however, the giant shadow of the Islander dominated the football scene. He was chosen at midfield on both the Team of the Century in 1984 and the Team of the Millennium in 1999.

MICK O'DWYER

Club: Waterville

County: Kerry

Honours: 4 All-Ireland senior titles (1959, '62, '69', '70); 8 National League medals (1959, '61, '63, '69, '71, '72, '73, '74); 12 Munster senior titles (1958, '59, '60, '61, '62, '63, '64, '65, '68, '69, '70, '72); 1 Railway Cup title (1972); Footballer of the Year (1969).

Mick O'Dwyer's name is written large across every backdrop to Gaelic football. He played senior inter-county football with Kerry for 18 years and, after a few brief months in retirement, re-invented himself as a manager and went on to become the best the game has known.

When Michael John O'Dwyer was born in Waterville, Co. Kerry on 9 June 1936, nobody could have had any idea of the impact he would have on the country's most popular sport. Famous footballers in Kerry are as common as American tourists in summer but nobody ever made the same enduring impression on the game as O'Dwyer.

He first played for Kerry seniors in October 1956 and by the time he retired in the summer of 1974 he had won four All-Ireland, eight National League and 12 Munster championship medals. He had also won a Railway Cup title and had been chosen as Footballer of the Year in 1969. He started out as a defender but it was as a forward that he made the biggest impact. He was the country's top scorer in 1969 and 1970 and remained a prolific marksman right up to his retirement at the age of 37.

While O'Dwyer's football career

remains as a monument to his greatness, he went on to surpass his playing achievements as a manager. He was appointed Kerry manager after they had been beaten by Cork in the 1974 Munster final. It was a traumatic time in Kerry football: while they had won an All-Ireland final only four years earlier, there was a feeling that they were being left behind in terms of training and preparation. Kevin Heffernan had set the benchmark with his Dublin team, which in 1974 brought fitness levels to a new height.

O'Dwyer responded in style, and by September 1975 the All-Ireland crown was back in Kerry. Dublin regained control in 1976 and 1977 but Kerry took charge again in 1978 and went on to complete their four-in-a-row in 1981. A last-minute goal by Offaly's Seamus Darby in the 1982 All-Ireland final robbed Kerry and O'Dwyer of a place in the record books as the first county to win five consecutive All-Ireland finals, but it didn't quench their spirit and they went on to win three more All-Ireland titles in 1984, '85 and '86.

O'Dwyer stayed in charge for three more years before stepping down at the end of 1989. However, a year later he began the second phase of his managerial career, taking charge of Kildare, whom he coached until 1994.

They failed to make the Leinster championship breakthrough but O'Dwyer returned to deal with unfinished business in 1996, and two years later he masterminded Kildare's great victory over Meath in the Leinster final. It was Kildare's first Leinster final win since 1956, and while they lost the All-Ireland final to Galway it was still a special year for the Lilywhites. They won a second Leinster title under O'Dwyer in 2000.

His hugely-successful playing and managerial careers make him one of the most remarkable men in GAA history. His passion, energy and devotion to Gaelic football are matched by a brilliant tactical mind, which never ceases to come up with new ideas.

and the cup were reunited some days later.

Quite quickly, O'Connell's reputation reached awesome proportions. It led to very high expectations, sometimes unreasonable, which meant O'Connell found himself under close scrutiny at all times. When he added a second All-Ireland medal in 1962, with Kerry easily accounting for Roscommon in the All-Ireland final, he was being talked about as one of the great players of all time. Seven years would elapse before he won his third medal. Kerry lost three finals in between, to Galway in 1964 and '65 and to Down in 1968. But when they faced Offaly in 1969, O'Connell was determined that the losing sequence would end. Kerry won by 0–10 to 0–7. A year later they retained the title by beating Meath in the final. O'Connell played in his last final in 1972 at the age of 35, when

SEÁN O'NEILL

Club: Newry Mitchell's

County: Down

Honours: 3 All-Ireland Senior titles (1960, '61, '68); 7 Ulster Senior titles (1960, '61, '63, '65, '66, '68, '71); 3 National Leagues (1960, '62, '68); 8 Railway Cups (1960, '63, '64, '65, '66, '68, '70, '71); 2 All-Star Awards (1971, '72); Footballer of the Year 1968).

Six minutes into the 1968 All-Ireland senior football final, Down right corner-forward Peter Rooney gained possession deep in Kerry territory and shot for a point. As the ball looped towards the posts, Down full-forward Seán O'Neill raced in towards goal. He was expecting the ball to sail over the bar but he decided to chase it down, just in case.

The Kerry defence saw no danger as O'Neill prowled in on goal, but suddenly the ball thudded off the upright. O'Neill was galloping through in full stride and while the bounce was very awkward, he managed to adjust his body and, in a reflex action, booted the ball to the net for an amazing goal. Kerry fans argued that it was down to pure luck, but that was less than generous to the instinctive finishing skills of one of Gaelic football's finest forwards. Indeed, many shrewd judges believe O'Neill was the only forward of that era who was capable of scoring such a brilliant goal.

Down went on to beat Kerry by two points, 2–12 to 1–13, and brought O'Neill's All-Ireland haul to three. The first two had come in 1960 and 1961, when Down beat Kerry and Offaly respectively.

Prior to 1960, Down had never won the All-Ireland senior title but it all changed that season, as they marched through Ulster before beating Offaly in the All-Ireland semi-final and Kerry in the final. Seán O'Neill played a prominent role in Down's historic adventure and would go on to become one of the most consistently-efficient attackers Gaelic

Seán O'Neill shows his aerial skills in a Railway Cup clash with Connacht

football has ever produced.

His talents first hit the public consciousness in 1958 when he helped Down minors to win the Ulster title. His promotion to the senior side followed pretty quickly as Down set about building a side which would go on to achieve true greatness. That Down team went into history as one of the most innovative ever seen.

O'Neill, whose vision, positioning and general smartness were complemented by dazzling skill and speed, started out as a right half-forward but later switched to full-

forward. While points remain the staple diet for most forwards, O'Neill possessed a more adventurous streak and saw goal chances which others would have missed.

He scored 12–65 in 23 games in 1968, an average of 4.3 points per game, and maintained his high strike rate right up to his retirement. He was a permanent presence on the Ulster team between 1960 and 1974 and became the first Down man to captain the provincial side to Railway Cup glory, in 1960. He won seven more Railway Cup medals in 1963,

'64, '65, '66 , '68, '70 and '71, and three National League medals in 1960, '62 and '68.

O'Neill's excellence in 1968 earned him the Footballer of the Year Award and he was chosen at full-forward on the inaugural All-Stars team in 1971. He won a second All-Star award a year later. He was selected at right half-forward for the Football Team of the Century in 1984, picked to mark the GAA's centenary celebrations, and was also at right half-forward on the Football Team of the Millennium, chosen in 1999.

CIARRAÍ 1-6
MUINEACHAN 2-5

Fielding expertise was one of the many attributes which enabled Kerry's Jack O'Shea to win four Footballer of the Year awards, in 1980, '81, '84 and '85

JOHN JOE O'REILLY

Club: Cornafean

County: Cavan

Honours: 2 All-Ireland Senior titles (1947, '48); 2 National League titles (1948, '50); 4 Railway Cups (1942, '43, '47, '50).

What greater tribute could be paid to a sportsman than to be immortalised in song? 'The Gallant John Joe', written in tribute to Cavan's two-times All-Ireland-winning captain in the 1940s, John Joe O'Reilly, hit the Irish charts in two decades and is still heard around the pubs and community halls of Cavan and places beyond.

It celebrates the career of the young Army officer who died after a short illness at the age of 34 in 1952. By then his name had been indelibly etched on the history of Gaelic football as one of the great leaders of teams and a centre half-back of outstanding quality.

Leadership obviously ran in the O'Reilly family, for John Joe took over the captaincy of the Cavan team in the mid-1940s from his brother Big Tom. It was an easy succession because John Joe had already proved in his schooldays that he had the necessary qualities for leadership, when he was captain of the St Patrick's College team in Cavan town which won two Ulster Senior Colleges titles.

John Joe, born in 1918 near Killeshandra, loved life on the farm. From his earliest days he was an enthusiastic helper, even when some of the tasks were beyond the strength of a young boy, and in the evenings he loved to play football. He was a keen student, too, attended national school in Corliss and received a scholarship to St Patrick's College.

In 1937 he began attending the Army Cadet School in the Curragh where he was able to pursue other sporting interests while at the same time improving his physical condition, which he believed was cen-tral to being a successful footballer. He showed great prowess as a sprinter and as a basketball player, attributes which would help him in his future career as a leading footballer.

O'Reilly was just 19 when he first played for Cavan in 1937. He played at wing-back in those early years with the senior team, with his brother Tom in the centre. They were beaten in the All-Ireland final that year by Kerry, but it was the first of six finals in which John Joe would compete. They also lost in 1943 to Roscommon in a replay and in 1945 to Cork. By then John Joe had moved to the centre half back position he loved, and success was just around the corner.

Cavan's reward for consistency and domination in Ulster came in 1947. John Joe had taken over the captaincy and produced some memorable performances as Cavan reached yet another final and faced old foes Kerry again. This time, however, they would fulfil their ambitions when winning the county's third All-Ireland championship.

At the beginning of 1947 the Central Council of the GAA agreed that the All-Ireland final for that year would be played at the New York Polo Grounds. It provided special lustre for the championship and the 'perfect' pairing emerged when Cavan and Kerry qualified for the trip Stateside.

John Joe was renowned as a pure footballer, a player who did not like to stray from his central role and always commanded his area. He was also an outstanding tackler, dispossessing his opponent with the minimum of physical contact. This was seen to full effect at the Polo Grounds. Cavan got off to a slow start and were behind 2–2 to 0–0 after just 15 minutes. But with P J Duke switched to O'Reilly's right and Simon Deignan playing on his left, Cavan began to gain control. Conditions were difficult but they played flowing football to win by 2–11 to 2–7. A year later they added a second title by beating Mayo in the final. However, they were denied a third title in 1949 when they lost to Meath. Sadly, John Joe never got the chance to play in another final and died at the Curragh Hospital in 1952.

In 1984 he was named as centre half-back on the Team of the Century and in 1999 was selected in the same position on the Team of the Millennium.

JACK O'SHEA

Club: St Mary's, Cahirciveen (Kerry) and Leixlip (Kildare)

County: Kerry

Honours: 7 All-Ireland Senior titles (1978, '79, '80, '81, '84, '85, '86); 3 National League titles (1976–77, '81–82, '83–84); 1 All-Ireland Minor title (1975); 3 All-Ireland Under-21s (1975, '76, '77); 4 Railway Cups (1977, '78, '81, '82); 6 All-Stars awards (1980, '81, '82, '83, '84, '85); Footballer of the Year 1980, '81, '84, '85.

On the fourth Sunday of September 1975, when a tall, gangly 17-year-old won an All-Ireland minor football medal with Kerry in Croke Park, most in the crowd realised that a new star was born. But nobody could have predicted the impact Jack O'Shea would have on Gaelic football over the next 15 years.

Not only did his achievements subsequently elevate him into the pantheon of the greats, but his personality made him one of the most popular footballers of all time, even among those upon whom he heaped so much disappointment and despair.

O'Shea, born and reared in Cahirciveen in South Kerry, was a natural athlete who always wanted to be at the centre of the action. His gifts came naturally to him, to such an extent that in his early years he did not pay as much attention to his preparation as he should have. When he came under the guidance of Mick O'Dwyer, however, O'Shea developed into one of the modern superstars.

As well as winning a minor All-

Ireland in 1975, the teenager was also a member of the Kerry U21 team which embarked on a run that would bring them three All-Ireland championships in a row (they were denied a fourth by losing the 1978 final narrowly to Roscommon). O'Shea had begun his career as a full-forward but was quickly moved to midfield, where he would create the legend.

His elevation to senior status came at a crucial period in the creation of a Kerry team now regarded as the greatest of all time. Kerry had been beaten in the All-Ireland final of 1976 and manager O'Dwyer was acutely aware of the need to bring through some new talent. In the National League of 1976–77, which Kerry won, he nurtured O'Shea so that by the time the championship came around the player was ready.

Although Kerry lost the All-Ireland semi-final to Dublin that year, they were on the verge of making history. In 1978, with O'Shea forming a match-winning partnership with Seán Walsh in midfield, Kerry won the first of four consecutive All-Ireland Senior titles. He showed himself to be a brilliant fielder of the ball, with tireless energy which brought him from one end of the field to the other on countless occasions in every game. When others faltered, O'Shea kept running. He would add three further All-Irelands to his collection between 1984 and '86 and continued playing until 1992.

He was selected at midfield in the Team of the Century in 1984.

'The Master': Galway's versatile Seán Purcell

SEÁN PURCELL

Club: Tuam Stars

County: Galway

Honours: 1 All-Ireland Senior title (1956); 6 Connacht Senior titles (1954, '56, '57, '58, '59, ''60); 1 National League title (1957); 3 Railway Cups (1951, '57, '58).

Affectionately known in his native Galway as 'The Master', Purcell achieved nationwide recognition

as one of the most outstanding talents Gaelic football has ever known. Equally at home in defence, midfield or attack, he was regarded as a player who was very much ahead of his time. There was no apparent weakness to his game and while he won only one All-Ireland senior medal, that in no way detracts from the esteem and respect which his magical skills earned him.

Purcell was a native of Tuam, one of the heartlands of football in Galway, and first came to prominence with St Jarlath's College, with whom he won an All-Ireland medal in 1946. Two years later, he played in his first Connacht senior football final but ended up on the losing side as Mayo beat Galway in a replay.

In fact, he didn't win his first Connacht title until 1954, a season in which he gave one of his greatest performances, at full-back against Mayo in the semi-final. Galway led by 2–3 to 0–1 at half-time but Mayo launched a spirited revival in the second half. However, their vaunted attack was repeatedly repelled by Purcell, who stood firm and defiant in front of the Galway goal. In the end, Galway held on for a one-

point win, 2–3 to 1–5. Although he had established a reputation as a full-back of genuine quality, it was felt that his talents would be of more benefit to the team further afield, so he switched to attack and excelled at centre-forward for several years. He was hugely influential in Galway's All-Ireland success in 1956, giving a memorable performance in the 2–13 to 3–7 win over Cork in the final.

He won a National League medal in 1957 and captained the Galway team to victory in the 1959 Connacht final. However, they lost to Kerry in the All-Ireland final. He won one other Connacht medal, with Galway in 1960, and his championship career ended two years later with defeat by Roscommon in the Connacht final.

Purcell won three Railway Cup medals with Connacht in 1951, '57 and '58, a year in which he had the honour of captaining the team to victory over Munster in the final.

A feature of Purcell's career was the relationship he forged with a Tuam Stars colleague, Frank Stockwell. They were known as 'The Terrible Twins', and worked instinctively off each other, caus-

ing all sorts of problems for defences. Both were deadly finishers but while Stockwell was a specialist attacker, Purcell's ability to improvise in any position marked him apart from all others. However, the consensus among the experts is that he was at his best at centre-forward, where he controlled the attacking channels with a natural expertise which suggests he would have been a success in any field sport.

In 1984, Purcell was chosen at centre-forward for the Football Team of the Century, which was chosen to mark the GAA's centenary celebrations. He also was selected in the Football Team of the Millennium in 1999.

Purcell's wide range of skills have convinced many experts that he was, in fact, the greatest footballer of all time; and while that is obviously a theory which can never be put to a practical test, it speaks volumes for the esteem in which the great Tuam player is held.

As well as contributing so much to Galway, he also played a major role in the many triumphs enjoyed by Tuam Stars, and picked up ten senior county championship medals.

MIKE SHEEHY

Club: Austin Stacks

County: Kerry

Honours: 8 All-Ireland senior titles (1975, '78, '79, '80, '81, '84, '85, '86); 11 Munster senior titles (1975, '76, '77, '78, '79, '80, '81, '82, '84, '85, '86); 2 All-Ireland U21 titles (1973, '75); 4 National League titles (1974, '77, '82, '84); 4 Railway Cup titles (1976, '77, '78,'81); 7 All-Star Awards (1976, '78, '79, '81, '82, '84, '86); Footballer of the Year (1979).

Three minutes from half-time in the 1978 All-Ireland football final, an amazing opportunity presented itself to Mike Sheehy. Dublin goalkeeper Paddy Cullen had come off his line to clear the ball but was adjudged to have fouled Kerry wing-forward Ger Power.

Sheehy, Kerry's deadly free-taker, took the ball, glanced towards goal and saw the opening. With Cullen off his line, Sheehy tried an audacious chip for goal. Cullen sensed the danger and began to back-pedal frantically but Sheehy's delicate lob floated over his head and nestled in the Dublin net to put Kerry ahead, 2–3 to 0–7.

It was one of the cheekiest goals ever scored at Croke Park and it had an amazing impact on the game. Dublin, the defending All-Ireland champions, seemed paralysed by its audacity and they never functioned properly in the second half, eventually losing by 17 points, 5–11 to 0–9.

Sheehy's goal is still talked about but the conclusions remain the same. He was the only player at the time – or quite possibly ever since – who was capable of executing such a brilliant finish. But then Sheehy was special, a truly wonderful talent who combined a sharp mind with a beautiful touch and nerves of steel.

Had he been born into a soccer environment, Sheehy would almost certainly have been a huge international star. Southampton were interested in signing him early in his Gaelic football career but his heart was in Kerry, in particular his native Tralee, so he turned down the chance to try his luck on English soccer fields. His exciting talents first exploded on to the senior scene in autumn 1973 when he made his debut with Kerry at the age of 19. Fifteen years later he played his final game, having won eight All-Ireland senior medals.

His career coincided with Kerry's greatest era. Indeed, his genius contributed enormously to making it so, because not only was he consistently accurate from frees, but he also possessed the instinctive knack of always being in the right place at the appropriate time. In soccer parlance, he was an out-and-out striker, a goal-poacher of the highest calibre.

Examples of his scoring feats dec-

Mike Sheehy's scoring genius wrecked many defences during Kerry's glory years, from 1975 to 1986

orate the pages of Kerry football history. He scored 3–3 against Derry in the 1976 All-Ireland semi-final, 2–8 against Waterford and 2–5 against Cork in the 1978 Munster championship. By 1979, his scoring average was seven points per game, topped by a magnificent 3–5 return against Monaghan in the All-Ireland semi-final and 2–6 against Dublin in the final.

His high strike rate continued right up to his retirement in 1988 following a serious knee injury. He had battled injury for most of his career but played on through the pain barrier. At times it was virtually unbearable but he carried on, as if oblivious to it all.

One of the great disappointments of his amazing career came in 1982 when he missed a penalty in the All-Ireland final against Offaly. This was a special game for Kerry, who were bidding to become the first county to win five consecutive All-

Ireland senior finals. After leading for most of the way, they were caught by a late goal and lost by a point.

Two years later, they regained the All-Ireland crown and retained it in 1985 and 1986. Sheehy captained Kerry in 1987 but they lost the Munster final to Cork and, a year later, he finally had to concede to the ravages of time as his knee problems increased. The curtain was finally drawn on the career of one of Gaelic football's greatest talents.

4

THE LEGENDS OF HURLING

Kilkenny legend D J Carey surges through the Galway defence

Nothing can quite stir the passions like debates on the great hurling men who have dominated summer Sundays in Ireland for over 100 years. Tales of epic feats abound as the deeds of outstanding players are recalled and relived. Christy Ring, Mick Mackey and Nicky Rackard may have passed away, but the memory of their excellence lives on, while modern-day heroes such as D J Carey and Brian Whelahan are building legends which will endure long after they have given up the game.

No player in the modern era has captured the imagination of the Irish public to the same extent as D J Carey. For a decade he has dominated the headlines, his every move a subject for discussion throughout the land. He is the first modern hurling superstar who can capture front-page headlines as well as those on the sports pages.

Although a star since he was a teenager, Carey has managed to maintain his modesty and geniality, a fact which has endeared him even more to an admiring public. He was born in 1970 in Gowran, and his love for hurling and sport in general was obvious at an early stage. His granduncle was Paddy Phelan, regarded as one of Kilkenny's greatest-ever hurlers.

The young D J played hurling, football and handball throughout his youth. Had he been born in a county with a stronger football tradition he could have become a star at that game, and still professes a great love for it. But Kilkenny has always been hurling country and family members and local officials always encouraged him. It was at St Kieran's College that he fine-tuned his natural skills. Teachers noted his outstanding qualities when he was only 13. His stickwork, the delicacy of his play, his vision, were noticeable even at that early stage. Later, as he developed speed, especially over 10 or 15 yards, he evolved into the complete forward. His mother tells stories of D J arriving home from school and spending hours hitting the ball against the gable end of the house or going out to the field to practice his free-taking. His brothers Martin, Jack and Kieran were also keen hurlers and would later gain representative honours with Kilkenny. His sister Catriona was a talented Camogie player and became a highly-respected hockey player.

Carey believes his successes as a young handballer also improved his hurling because it trained his eyes and his hands.

Although regarded as one of the great score-getters of the game, it was not always as a forward that D J starred. He played as a goalkeeper for both his club and for the county, and made his senior debut for Kilkenny as a goalkeeper in 1989. It was a temporary measure, and before long he was released for attacking duties.

Success came very early for Carey. He won All-Ireland Colleges titles with St Kieran's in 1988 and '89, an All-Ireland minor medal with Kilkenny in 1988 and an Under-21 medal in 1990. Also in 1990 he won his first medal as a senior when he was a member of the team which won the National League.

A year later he played in his first All-Ireland final when Kilkenny lost to Tipperary. He suffered the one serious injury of his career when playing for his club in the Kilkenny intermediate final. An accidental blow to the head knocked him unconscious and forced him out of the game for six months to ensure a full recovery. It was time well spent, because in September 1992 Carey collected his first senior championship when Kilkenny beat Cork in the final by 3–10 to 1–12. He added another in 1993 when they beat Galway by five points in the final, 2–17 to 1–15. In the semi-final that summer against Antrim he scored one of the greatest goals seen in Croke Park when he doubled on a cross from the left corner; the ball came back off the crossbar but he reacted instinctively to strike the rebound into the top of the net.

His star status was assured despite the fact that Kilkenny went through what was, for them, a barren period over the next few seasons. Off the field, however, the demands of the game were having an effect on both his business and family life. Such were the pressures of stardom that Carey announced his retirement in 1998. It was front-page news for days and prompted national radio and TV debates. When he was persuaded to change his mind the hurling world celebrated.

It was not an easy comeback, as Kilkenny lost the All-Ireland finals of 1998 and 1999; but Carey's status as a legend of the game was rubber-stamped when he played a brilliant role in the final of 2000, as Kilkenny easily beat Offaly.

Before the final there had been a few negative comments about his place in the game, with spurious arguments that until he delivered a big performance in an All-Ireland final he could not take his place among the legends.

All summer he had been indicating that his form was better than ever, scoring decisive goals in the Leinster final against Offaly and in the All-Ireland semi-final against Galway. Then, after only a few minutes played in the All-Ireland final, he lit up Croke Park with one of his trademark goals and shortly afterwards he added another to set up one of the most one-sided finals of the modern era.

Carey has won numerous national handball titles and in recent times has taken up golf. He now plays to a very low handicap and he could yet play competitively on the amateur scene in Ireland.

D J Carey in artistic pose

Tipperary's Jimmy Doyle: a hurling artist of true stature

JOHN CONNOLLY ✕

Club: Castlegar

County: Galway

Honours: 1 All-Ireland Senior
title (1980); 1 National League
title (1974–75); 1 Railway Cup
(1980); 2 All-Stars (1971, '79).

The name of John Connolly is synonymous with the glorious resur-
gence of Galway as a hurling
superpower during the late 1970s
and early 1980s after almost six

decades in the doldrums. The family name became one of the most
famous in the game and big John
represented the power and the passion that brought Galway back to
the top table.

John was born in 1948 in Leitir
Mor in the Connemara Gaeltacht,
with little hurling tradition in the
Connolly blood. But when John
was aged five the family moved to
Castlegar, an area just outside Galway
city, situated beside the famous
Galway racecourse at Ballybrit.

His father had often listened to

the radio, fascinated by a game
which would later become such an
integral part of the Connolly lifestyle.
Over the next few years of young
John's life he would cycle into
Galway on Sundays to watch hurling games.

The Castlegar playing fields were
just beside the new family home
and John and his five brothers spent
hours in the evenings and at weekends playing football and hurling.
John was talented in both games
and represented Galway at under-
age level in football as well as hurl-

ing in the mid-1960s.

He also enjoyed boxing and was
Connacht junior light-welterweight
champion, coached by Chick Gillen,
who gained fame as coach to Irish
boxing Olympian Francie Barrett
in 1996.

Connolly's greatest love was hurling and he made his senior championship debut for Galway in 1967,
against Clare. Galway played in the
Munster championship through the
1960s with little success, but new
attitudes and greater organisation
in the mid-1970s would bear fruit.

John was captain in 1975 and a highly-influential midfielder when Galway beat Tipperary to claim the National League title. It was an important breakthrough, and finally John Connolly's strength and hurling skill were displayed on the biggest stage of all.

Four years later they reached both the National League and All-Ireland finals but lost both. In 1980, however, with John Connolly at full-forward, they won the county's first All-Ireland title since 1923, beating Limerick in the final. It was a highly emotional experience for the man who had given so much to Galway and to hurling. His brother Joe was the team captain and Michael was at midfield. John retired after that game but was persuaded to return for the 1981 final, but Galway were narrowly beaten by Offaly in the All-Ireland final.

Castlegar had also won the All-Ireland club title in 1980, so when John Connolly retired he had won everything it was possible to win.

JIMMY DOYLE

Club: Thurles Sarsfields

County: Tipperary

Honours: 6 All-Ireland Seniors titles (1958, '61, '62, '64, '65, '71); 6 National League titles (1956–57, '58–59, '59–60, '60–61, '64–65, '67–68); 7 Railway Cups (1958, '59, '60, '61, '63, '69, '70); 3 All-Ireland Minors (1955, '56, '57).

Strangely, the career of a player whose peers regarded him as the greatest forward in the game began and ended as a goalkeeper. Jimmy Doyle was goalkeeper on the Tipperary minor team which lost the All-Ireland final of 1954 (when he was just 14) and played his last senior game for Tipperary in the Munster championship of 1973 against Waterford, as stand-in goalkeeper.

Goalkeeping was part of a rich hurling tradition in the Doyle house-hold in Thurles, into which Jimmy was born in 1940. His father Gerry was substitute goalkeeper on the Tipperary teams that won the All-Ireland championships of 1937 and 1945. His uncle Tommy was one of the famous names of the 1940s with Tipperary, and the young Jimmy was strongly influenced by both these men.

He was a pure hurling artist – quick, stylish, with a great eye and strong, quick hands. His scoring ability was to be seen very early in his career when he hit 2–8 in the All-Ireland minor final of 1955 and 2–3 in the final of 1956 on his way to three minor titles in a row.

He won his first All-Ireland senior title at the tender age of 18 when Tipperary beat Galway in the final, and would add five more titles before he retired. Each one was memorable, although the final of 1961 was probably the most dramatic from his point of view. He suffered a broken ankle in the Munster final against Cork but continued to play on. Afterwards doctors ordered him to rest but he kept on, hoping he would be fit for the final. A few days before the game he was told not to risk permanently damaging the ankle and that he should not start. But Jimmy insisted on travelling to Dublin and had pain-killing injections before the game and at half-time. His leg was numb all through the game, but he still managed to score nine of Tipperary's 16 points as they beat Dublin.

Doyle was Tipperary's captain in 1962 and 1965 when they beat Wexford in both finals. In between he had also won a championship in 1964, against Kilkenny.

Some Tipperary observers will suggest that had Doyle not suffered so many injuries they would have won at least one if not two more titles, such was his influence. He was coming up to the end of his career and recovering from another injury when he gained his sixth and final medal, going on as a substitute in the 1971 final. Doyle carved out a reputation as one of the most stylish players in the history of the game.

John Doyle: swashbuckling

JOHN DOYLE

Club: Holycross

County: Tipperary

Honours: 8 All-Ireland Senior titles (1949, '50, '51, '58, '61, '62, '64, '65); 11 National League titles (1948-49, '49-50, '51-52, '53-54, '54-55, '56-57, '58-59, '59-60, '60-61, '63-64, '64-65); 8 Railway Cups (1951, '52, '53, '55, '57, '58, '60, '63); 1 All-Ireland Minor (1947).

In 19 seasons as a hurler at the highest level John Doyle never missed a championship match for Tipperary and never had to leave the field because of injury. He equalled Christy Ring's record of eight All-Ireland medals and entered into hurling's hall of fame.

Born in Holycross, Co. Tipperary, in 1930, John Doyle was regarded as one of the most dynamic players of his time. Defenders of the period had tended to be less expansive than their forward counterparts. Their roles were seen as dour, always negative. Doyle changed all that and was the first of the swashbuckling defenders in hurling.

He was big in physique and big in personality. Doyle relished the 'hard' reputation gained by the Tipperary defenders, especially later in his career. His partnership in the full back line from 1958 onwards with Mick Maher and Kieran Carey became known as Hell's Kitchen, and many believe it was Doyle who came up with the name.

But his contemporaries warn that it would be a mistake to judge him as a hard player alone. He was tough, but team-mates recall the wonderful stickwork that got him out of difficult situations, while his speed over short distances often surprised his opponents.

Doyle had won an All-Ireland minor medal in 1947 and was just 19 in 1949 when he was selected on the Tipperary senior team. They reached the All-Ireland final where they beat Laois. They would go on to win three consecutive titles and John Doyle would not lose in championship hurling until the Munster final of 1952, when Tipperary were beaten by Cork.

With three championships won, Doyle seemed destined for many more. But Tipperary's fortunes dipped in the following years and Doyle considered retiring. Now running the large family farm, he found the demands of hurling at the highest level were becoming too much.

However, for the 1958 championship the Tipperary selectors prevailed on him to play one more year. He was chosen in a new position of left half-back and his career surged. Tipperary won the Munster title for the first time since 1951 and in the All-Ireland semi-final Doyle produced one of his greatest performances, against Kilkenny.

He continued playing with Tipperary until 1967, the move to left corner-back coming in the early 1960s. He did have a chance to win a record ninth All-Ireland medal and surpass Ring's achievements but was denied by Kilkenny in the 1967 final. He afterwards retired from inter-county hurling.

His profile remained high. He became a member of the Irish senate and maintained a close interest in the GAA, holding a number of posts at local and national level. His son Michael provided John with some of his proudest moments in the game when scoring two goals in extra time of the Munster final replay of 1987 against Cork as Tipperary ended a 16-year wait for a provincial title.

Eddie Keher: a scoring machine

Keher won his second All-Ireland in 1967 and was Kilkenny's captain when they won the 1969 title. Ironically, his greatest individual display in an All-Ireland final came in 1971 when Kilkenny lost to Tipperary by 5–14 to 5–17. This final was one of five played over 80 minutes and Keher scored a remarkable 2–11. This remained a record until 1989, when Nicky English scored 2–12 against Antrim.

In 1972 Keher continued his scoring streak. He scored 17 times in the All-Ireland semi-final when Kilkenny beat Galway by 5–28 to 3–7, and then hit 2–6 as Kilkenny won the All-Ireland final against Cork by 3–24 to 5–11. Kilkenny had trailed by eight points in the second half but turned it around in the last quarter in spectacular style, scoring 2–9 without reply to win by seven points.

Injury forced Keher to miss the 1973 final and his absence is seen as a major cause for Kilkenny's defeat by Limerick. A year later, this stylish forward was back in action as Kilkenny regained the title.

Mick Mackey: all-time great

EDDIE KEHER ✕

Club: The Rower, Inistioge

County: Kilkenny

Honours: 6 All-Ireland Senior titles (1963, '67, '69, '72, '74, '75); 3 National League titles (1961–62, '65–66, '75–76); 9 Railway Cups (1964, '65, '67, '71, '72, '73, '74, '75, '77); 5 All Star awards (1971, '72, '73, '74, '75).

For a man without any identifiable hurling pedigree, Eddie Keher emerged from Kilkenny in the late 1950s as a rising young star who would go on to create scoring records that are still regarded with awe in the modern game.

He was born in 1941: his father Stephen was a native of Roscommon and a member of An Garda Siochana who was posted to Kilkenny and played football for the county. Eddie's mother was a native of Kilkenny whose family were not noted as hurling people, but she did show a love for the game during Eddie's formative years and both parents provided great encouragement when he attended St Kieran's College in Kilkenny.

From an early stage it was clear Eddie had special talent. Even in his teenage years he showed a willingness to practice that would serve him well in his senior career. Quickly noticed, he was chosen on the Kilkenny minor team in 1956, when he was only 15. In all he played in four minor championships, losing in two All-Ireland finals to Tipperary.

He holds the unique distinction of playing in both the All-Ireland minor and senior finals in a single year. He played in the All-Ireland minor final of 1959 and was then brought on to the Kilkenny senior panel and made an appearance as a substitute in the All-Ireland final replay against Waterford, which Kilkenny lost.

He won his first major honour with Kilkenny when they captured the National League in 1962. However, it was the following year that his reputation soared when Kilkenny won the All-Ireland title. They beat Waterford by 4–17 to 6–8 and Keher scored 14 points, ten of them from frees.

His free-taking would become a feature of the game over the next decade. Keher practised three or four nights a week. He analysed his technique, sought advice from other players and tried to perfect his action so that a high percentage of frees taken would be converted.

MICK MACKEY ✕

Club: Ahane

County: Limerick

Honours: 3 All-Ireland Senior titles (1934, '36, '40); 5 National League titles (1933-4, '34-35, '35-36, '36-37, '37-38); 8 Railway Cups (1934, '35, '37, '38, '39, '40, '43, '45).

They called him 'The Playboy of the Southern World'. Mick Mackey was the most charismatic star of his time, a physically-imposing figure who was ebullient in presence and of whom observers always remarked that he had a smile on his face, on and off the field.

From a very strong GAA background, he shared many of his greatest triumphs on the field with his blonde-haired brother John. Their great-grandfather Anthony was the first treasurer of the GAA's Central Council. Their grandfather Mick played for Limerick and their father John 'Tyler' Mackey won Munster championships in 1910 and 1911 and was regarded as one of the best players of his generation.

Mick made his senior debut for Limerick in the National League series of 1930 and for the next 17 years enjoyed a magnificent career as Limerick became established as a major hurling power. Mackey's bustling style, his relishing of the physical challenge and his joy in running at defences made him a crowd-pleaser and favourite. The bigger the occasion, the more relaxed he appeared to be, and this endeared him to the supporters even more.

Mackey's Limerick team first emerged as serious contenders in 1933 when they reached the National League final and the All-Ireland final, losing to Kilkenny in both games. A year later, however, they became the dominant team in the country. They won the first of five consecutive league titles and then went on to complete the double and capture the All-Ireland championship after a replay in the final against Dublin.

The Limerick team developed a rivalry with Kilkenny that would produce some memorable games. It was on those occasions that Mackey was at his best and he gained enormous respect in Kilkenny, as well as in Cork, where he developed a great friendship with Christy Ring.

In 1935 Kilkenny stopped Limerick from retaining their All-Ireland title. Mackey was team captain in 1936 and was an inspiring

leader. There are many observers of the period who regarded Mackey's display against Tipperary in the Munster final at Thurles as one of the greatest ever seen.

Limerick had toured America earlier in the year, during which time Mackey suffered a badly-injured knee. Anticipating that the injury might receive some unwelcome attention from his opponents in the Munster final, Mackey wore a heavy bandage – on the healthy knee. The ruse worked: Mackey went on to score a massive five goals and three points as Limerick won by 8–5 to 4–6. The All-Ireland final attracted a record attendance for the time, 51,235, as Mackey led Limerick to glory. Once again Kilkenny were Mackey's and Limerick's opponents, but this game was unlike others that had gone before. Limerick were at the height of their powers and Mackey was determined to fulfil an ambition of lifting the All-Ireland trophy. Only one point had separated them a year earlier but Limerick won the 1936 final in convincing style by 5–6 to 1–5.

It had been a long, hard year and their efforts in competition and on the US tour would take a toll. They lost their titles in the 1937 Munster final against Tipperary, despite what contemporary reports described as the Herculean efforts of Mackey.

It would be three years before they would return to the All-Ireland podium, with Mackey again as captain. The success was greeted with even greater enthusiasm in Limerick because it was feared that the team had reached the end of its natural life. In the final it was Kilkenny who again provided the opposition, and they were in a position of strength until Mackey was moved to midfield, where he began to dominate. Limerick won by 3–7 to 1–7.

He was also a good footballer and represented Limerick, without achieving title success. At club level with Ahane he won 15 county senior hurling championships and five county football championships. When his playing career with Limerick ended in 1947, after he

Lory Meagher (left): a sensational talent

made an appearance as a substitute in the championship against Clare, Mackey served in a variety of positions in the GAA until his death in 1982. The Mackey Stand at the Gaelic Grounds in Limerick is named in his honour.

LORY MEAGHER ⚔		
Club: Tullaroan		
County: Kilkenny		
Honours: 3 All-Ireland Senior titles (1932, '33, '35); 1 National League title (1932-33); 2 Railway Cups (1927, '33).		

Lorenzo Ignatius Meagher was one of the first great stars of hurling. Born in 1899 into a family that was immersed in both nationalist politics and in the fledgling GAA, Lory developed a passion for the game in his youth and tales are told of hours and hours spent practising the skills of the game beside the family home.

His father, Henry Joseph, had been involved in the founding of the GAA in 1884 and had maintained a very close relationship with the early leaders. He had actively encouraged his sons to become involved in the national games and Lory's brothers Willie and Henry would play alongside him in the

1926 All-Ireland final which Kilkenny lost to Cork, while another brother, Frank, also played for Kilkenny before emigrating to Australia.

Unlike his father, Lory was a reserved character. Throughout his playing career and much later he shunned the limelight. While his achievements on the field became the stuff of folklore during his lifetime, he kept a low profile and rarely granted an interview despite the persistence of the prominent journalists of the time. The late Pádraig Puirséal, one of the most respected GAA writers of all, said of Meagher, 'I have not seen the equal of his artistry or watched a more supreme stylist. When the mood was on him Meagher was a veritable magician.'

Although he had become a revered figure in Kilkenny during the 1920s, it was in the 1930s, when his career should have been coming to an end, that Meagher rose to national prominence. It took three games to decide the All-Ireland final of 1931 between Kilkenny and Cork. Although Cork eventually won the title, this is remembered as Meagher's championship. He had been magnificent in the drawn game but it was in the first replay that Meagher produced one of his greatest performances. A week before the second replay, though, news spread throughout the country that because of damaged ribs Meagher would not be able to play. It created a sensation, and such was the esteem in which Meagher was held by then that the title was virtually conceded to Cork.

A year later, however, he won the first of his three All-Ireland medals when Kilkenny beat Clare in the final. In 1933 he won virtually everything that was on offer. The year began with Kilkenny winning the National League and Meagher was also a member of the Leinster team that won the Railway Cup. In September he captured his second All-Ireland medal when Kilkenny beat Limerick.

Many observers of the time regard the 1935 final as his greatest hour. He was reaching the end of his

Wexford wonders: brothers Bobby and Nicky Rackard

career and Limerick were hot favourites to win the All-Ireland. On a day when weather conditions were described as dreadful, with incessant rain and wind before and during the game, Meagher gave an outstanding exhibition from midfield to help secure the championship for Kilkenny. It was one of his proudest moments, he admitted later, because he was also the team's captain.

Meagher died in 1973 but his memory lives on in Tullaroan. In 1994 the Lory Meagher Heritage Centre was opened on the site of his home and is a very popular attraction for locals and tourists.

NICKY RACKARD

Club: Rathnure

County: Wexford

Honours: 2 All-Ireland Senior titles (1955, '56); 1 Railway Cup (1956); 1 National League title (1955–56).

When Nicky Rackard trudged disconsolately from Croke Park on the evening of 5 September 1954, he believed that the chance of realising a cherished dream had been lost. Wexford had just been beaten by Cork in the All-Ireland final and at the age of 32 Rackard felt his time had come to depart from the county scene.

A record crowd of 84,856 had packed the GAA headquarters to follow the fortunes of a Wexford team which had captured the imag-

ination of a nation. Despite the disappointment and Rackard's pessimism, the great story of Wexford hurling was only beginning to unfold.

Rackard had grown up in Rathnure, the eldest of five boys, at a time when Wexford hurling was at a low ebb. In fact, throughout the 1940s when his career both as a hurler and footballer with the county began, it was with the bigger ball that he might have expected to enjoy some success.

Though Wexford struggled on the hurling fields, Rackard shone brightly as a midfielder and centre half-forward.

Though his legendary status would be gained as a powerful full-forward, he moved to that position only late in his career when his speed was going.

He had learned his skills and developed his power as a boy in Rathnure and at the famous hurling nursery of St Kieran's College. He continued to develop as a veterinary student in Dublin, although his studies did interfere with his training.

It was his move to full forward that coincided with the rise of Wexford.

In 1949 Wexford had suffered a humiliating defeat by Kilkenny in the championship, but there were better times to come.

In 1950, with Nicky alternating between full-forward and centre-forward, they reached the Leinster final, where they lost to Kilkenny. The breakthrough was not too far away.

In 1951, with Nicky as team cap-

tain, Wexford won the Leinster championship for the first time since 1918. Four Rackard brothers played on the team that beat Laois – Jimmy, Bobby, Billy and Nicky. Though they lost to Tipperary in the All-Ireland final, hurling fever swept through the county and Nicky Rackard became a household name.

The All-Ireland final of 1954 was a bitter disappointment, although regarded as one of the greatest in history.

Wexford lost to Cork by two points, but it would not be the end for the team nor for Nicky Rackard. In 1955 they returned to the All-Ireland final and beat Galway comfortably.

They felt the need to add another title, beating Munster opposition in the final: and in 1956 they did so, in a memorable final in which Nicky Rackard stamped his personal mark on the game. Christy Ring was going for his ninth medal and had a goal-bound shot brilliantly saved by Art Foley. The ball came straight down the field and Rackard scored one of his special goals. He brought his playing career to an end the following year.

Rackard faced a long and difficult battle with alcoholism when his playing days ended, but it was another battle he won, and he became a counsellor for hundreds of people all over the country until his death at the age of 53 in 1975.

CHRISTY RING

Club: Glen Rovers

County: Cork

Honours: 8 All-Ireland Senior titles (1941, '42, '43, '44, '46, '52, '53, '54); 4 National League titles (1939–40, '40–41, '47–48, '52, '53); 18 Railway Cups (1942, '43, '44, '45, '46, '48, '49, '50, '51, '52, '53, '55, '57, '58, '59, '60, '61, '63); 2 All-Ireland Minors (1937, '38).

Opposite: Christy Ring: the greatest hurler of all time?

Millennium man: Brian Whelahan was chosen on the greatest team of all time

He was only eight years old when the folk of the little village of Cloyne first noticed there was something different about him. The cut-down hurley seemed like an extension of his little arms. In the Cloyne Street League of 1928, little Nicholas Christopher Ring took his first steps towards sporting immortality. Four decades later, when he finally stopped playing, Ring had collected every honour in the game, broken all records and earned the accolade of the greatest hurler who ever played.

The second-youngest of five children born to Nicholas and Mary Ring in 1920, Christy Ring's philosophy was developed early in life. He once wrote, 'Hurling has always been a way of life with me. It was never my ambition to play the game for the sake of winning All-Ireland medals or breaking records but to perfect the art as well as possible.'

Although his father died when Christy was very young, he had instilled in his sons a deep love for hurling. The back garden of their home in Cloyne adjoined the local hurling field and Christy would spend much of his youth with his brothers Paddy and Willie, perfecting their skills.

After a successful under-age career, during which he won two All-Ireland minor medals, Ring was promoted to senior status for Cork in 1939 at the age of 19. A year later he made his debut in the championship and learned some tough lessons. He survived a pitch invasion in the replay of the Munster final against Limerick, which Limerick won, and realised the need to establish a physical presence in championship hurling.

He was part of the Cork team which won four All-Ireland championships in a row between 1941 and 1944, adding a fifth title in 1946. While his reputation grew slowly during those early years, it was from the mid-1940s on that the legend of Christy Ring spread nationally.

Because he was relatively small in stature, Ring worked very hard on building up his body strength. He felt that such strength was needed to allow him to compete at the highest level and to use the special skills that he had with the hurley. He also had great speed, which would prove to be a big advantage.

Ring was Cork's captain in 1946 when they won the All-Ireland final by beating Kilkenny. It was the day his reputation as the best hurler of his time was cemented and he became a marked man. But his strength, speed and skill meant that he was a match for any opponent. As he built up his collection of honours, the legends grew. In the 1953 Munster final against Tipperary he scored a point to level the game. Moments later he was back on the Cork goal line saving a net-bound shot. In 1954 he collected a record eighth All-Ireland medal (still matched only by John Doyle of Tipperary).

He played in just one more final, in 1956, when Wexford denied him his ninth medal; but the remarkable story went on and on. He was 46 years old when Cork reached the All-Ireland final in 1966, 27 years after he had first played for his county. Such was his form for Glen Rovers that there was a huge demand in Cork, supported by the national newspapers, for Ring to be recalled. However, it was Ring himself who dampened the enthusiasm by indicating he did not believe that he should play.

He played for Glen Rovers in Cork city from 1941 to 1967. After retiring from playing, he enjoyed coaching and was a selector for the Cork team which won three All-Ireland championships in a row between 1976 and 1978. He died in 1979 but his memory lives on in Cloyne and Cork, where a new bridge over the River Lee is named after this legendary sportsman.

BRIAN WHELAHAN ✕

Club: Birr

County: Offaly

Honours: 2 All-Ireland Senior titles (1994, '98); 1 National League title (1990–91); 1 Railway Cup (1998); 2 All-Ireland Minors (1987, '89); 3 All-Stars (1992, '95, '98).

Brian Whelahan's selection on the Hurling Team of the Millennium in 2000, the only player from the modern era to gain inclusion, speaks volumes about the impact the Offaly player has had in his 12 years in the top flight. Although generally regarded as a defender, he has also starred in attack and picked up his 1998 All-Star award while serving as a full-forward.

Born into a hurling family, he first came to prominence when just 16 years old as a member of the first Offaly minor team to win the All-Ireland championship in 1987.

The Whelahan boys – his brothers Simon and Barry would join him on the Offaly team in later years – had the advantage of having one of the game's most successful coaches as their father.

Pat Joe played for Offaly when the county was struggling below the top flight but fulfilled a significant role in bringing on a new generation of players in the late 1970s and early 1980s. He was also manager of the Offaly team in 1989 when they lost to Antrim in the All-Ireland semi-final.

Despite that disappointment for the elder Whelahan, 1989 was a special year for Brian.

He added a second All-Ireland minor medal to his collection and was then a member of the Under-21 team which lost narrowly to Tipperary in the All-Ireland final. He was also called into the senior panel at the end of the year, and expectations were high that he would be a major player in the years to come. So it proved.

Despite his youth, Whelahan adapted very quickly to the pace of the game at the highest level. His cool demeanour was a major advantage. He never seemed to feel any pressure, simply using his sublime skills to get him out of tricky situations. The bigger the game, the better he played.

In his first full season of 1990–91 he played at left half-back on the team which won the National League.

In 1994, in one of the most dramatic finals in modern history, Whelahan won his first All-Ireland senior medal. Offaly scored 2–6 in the final five minutes of the game to break Limerick hearts.

Whelahan is regarded as the most complete defender of the modern era, able to play in any of the three positions on the half-back line with equal aplomb and authority. However, he will be best remembered for his performance in the 1998 All-Ireland final when he was switched to the attack against Kilkenny.

Stricken with 'flu, he was clearly struggling in defence. In a high-risk strategy the team manager, Michael Bond, switched Whelahan to full-forward. He displayed his great skills, strength and vision when he scored 1–6, the goal coming just three minutes from the end of normal time.

Whelahan's status as a modern hero with the Offaly supporters was sealed after that victory. He is a straight-talking, candid individual who shows little interest in the trappings of his fame, and has always maintained that his first love is his club Birr, with whom he has enjoyed spectacular success, including two All-Ireland club championships in 1995 and 1998.

5

THE GREAT DUAL PLAYERS

The winner of six successive All-Ireland titles from 1941–46, Jack Lynch leads Cork into action against Dublin in the 1942 All-Ireland Hurling Final

Other than being governed by the same Association, there are no practical links between hurling and Gaelic Football. Indeed, they are so fundamentally different that, from time to time, there have been calls for the setting-up of separate organisations to administer them at national level. Some counties already have separate Football and Hurling Boards to run their affairs under the general supervision of the County Boards. However, on a general basis, hurling and football remain under the control of the GAA's parent body, using the same administrative structures, competitions and disciplinary systems.

Since the foundation of the GAA, many clubs have run both hurling and football teams, which made the dual play-er phenomenon inevitable. It started before the end of the 19th century when W J Spain won All-Ireland hurling and football medals in the space of two years. Unusually, he achieved that feat with two different counties, Limerick and Tipperary. The growth of the dual play-er phenomenon gathered pace in the 1940s when Cork's Jack Lynch, who would later become Taoiseach in a Fianna Fáil

Government, won six All-Ireland medals – five for hurling, one for football – in six consecutive seasons.

The dual player has always been a prominent feature of Cork GAA. Since the 1970s Ray Cummins, Denis Coughlan, Brian Murphy, Jimmy Barry-Murphy, Teddy McCarthy and Denis Walsh have won All-Ireland medals in both hurling and football while Dinny Allen, Brian Corcoran and Sean Óg O hAilpin have also excelled in both codes.

Dual players are not as common in other counties, largely because hurling and football draw from different areas. That is very much the case in Galway and Offaly, both of which are strong in both codes. However, Offaly's Liam Currams became something of an exception in 1981 when he played in both the All-Ireland football and hurling finals. Dublin, Down, Derry, Wexford and Tipperary have all produced some outstanding dual players over the years.

Given the growing pressures on modern GAA players, it looks certain that the dual player phenomenon will fade away in time. Intense training and competition schedules have made it increasingly difficult for players to perform at the highest level in both hurling and football. The trend in more recent times has been to start out as a dual player before later concentrating on either hurling or football.

Jimmy Barry-Murphy: an expert finisher in both hurling and football, pictured here in 1983

DINNY ALLEN (CORK)

A wonderfully versatile sportsman, Allen holds the distinction of winning two All-Ireland senior football medals and a Munster senior hurling championship medal. He was also a highly-talented soccer player and won an FAI Cup medal with Cork Hibernians in 1973. He was later approached by Brian Clough, who wanted him to join Nottingham Forest: however, the deal broke down. Although best-known as a Gaelic footballer, he was also an excellent hurler and played a major part in Cork's Munster final success in 1975 when they beat Limerick by 3–14 to 0–12. He also played in the 1975 All-Ireland semi-final against Galway,

but Cork lost by two points.

He first played senior football for Cork in 1972, when he was 20 years old. His involvement with soccer didn't endear him to a section of the GAA fraternity in Cork and he missed out on an All-Ireland medal opportunity in 1973. However, he was later restored to the Cork squad. Most of his career coincided with Kerry's dominance, limiting his opportunities to showcase his talents on the All-Ireland stage. However, when Cork finally took control in Munster in the late 1980s Allen was still a vital cog in the machine, and in 1989 achieved his great ambition when he led the side to All-Ireland and National League honours. He won a second All-Ireland medal a year later aged 38 and a football All-Star award as a centre-forward in 1980. He also

won three All-Ireland club football medals with Nemo Rangers.

JIMMY BARRY-MURPHY (CORK)

One of the true dual star heroes, he exploded on to the GAA landscape in the early 1970s when he won All-Ireland minor hurling (1971) and football (1972) medals. His genius in front of goal brought him to the notice of the Cork senior selectors and he made an immediate impact with the footballers in 1973 as they marched impressively to All-Ireland glory. It was Cork's first football title since 1945 and Barry-Murphy's contribution to a special year was immense. In the final against Galway, he scored

67

two great goals as Cork amassed an impressive tally of 3–17. His laid-back style belied an inner cunning which took him to the epicentre of the main action well ahead of his markers; and while he won only one All-Ireland football medal, he has gone down in history as one of the game's deadliest finishers. He was a particularly good goal-scorer and was always prepared to shoot for goal rather than take the safer option of knocking over points.

Although he was equally good in both codes he developed a preference for hurling, partly because defenders were not as negative as their football counterparts. He later opted out of inter-county football completely to concentrate on hurling. He won five All-Ireland senior hurling medals, in 1976, '77, '78, '84 and '86, while also featuring in the Cork teams which lost the 1982 and 1983 All-Ireland finals.

He won three hurling National League medals, one football National League medal and four Railway Cup football medals, and was honoured on seven occasion by the All-Star selectors. He was chosen for the All-Star football team in 1973 and 1974 and won a place on the hurling team in 1976, '77, '78, '83 and '86. He also won four All-Ireland club medals with St. Finbarr's, two each for hurling and for football.

He ceased playing in 1987 but returned to the game as a manager in the 1990s, guiding Cork hurlers to an All-Ireland senior hurling title in 1999.

DERRY BECKETT (CORK)

A member of the exclusive club which has won All-Ireland senior hurling and football championship medals, he played at left full-forward on the Cork hurling team which won the title in 1942, beating Dublin by 2–14 to 3–4 in the final. He made a solid contribution to their win, scoring a crucial goal. Three years later he was back on the winners' podium with Cork footballers, who won the All-Ireland

title. By a curious coincidence, Beckett also played at left full-forward for Cork footballers. Cork's All-Ireland final win in 1945 was achieved against Cavan, whom they beat by 2–5 to 0–7 for their first All-Ireland football title since 1911.

GREG BLANEY (DOWN)

Born in 1963, he shone as a colleges player with St. Colman's, Newry. He progressed to the Down senior football and hurling teams aged 19 and went on to give great service over many years. He won his first Ulster senior football medal in 1981 when Down beat Armagh in the final and two years later helped Down to a National League crown.

Down didn't win another Ulster title until 1991 and this time they built on that success by going on to beat Meath in a dramatic All-Ireland final. Blaney had a great season at centre-forward, orchestrating the Down attack in their glory run through Ulster and on to All-Ireland victory. Three years later, he was equally influential when Down again won the All-Ireland title, beating Dublin in the final. Down hurling has not been anywhere near as successful as its football counterpart but did have some glory days, and Blaney was involved in one of them: he played at centre-forward on the team which beat Antrim in the 1992 Ulster final. He was a very talented hurler and would have achieved much more success had he been playing in a county where the game was stronger. He won All-Star football awards in 1983, 1991 and 1994.

FRANK BURKE (DUBLIN)

A native of Kildare, he switched to Dublin at an early age and enjoyed a great career with them. It lasted from 1917 to 1923, during which he played in nine All-Ireland senior finals. He played in five successive football finals

(1920–24) and three successive hurling deciders (1919–21). He won his first All-Ireland senior medal as a hurler in 1917 when Dublin beat Tipperary in the final. Three years later he won a second All-Ireland hurling medal and, in 1921, won the first of his three All-Ireland football medals when Dublin beat Mayo in the final. He again featured on the Dublin team which beat Galway in the 1922 football final and they completed the three-in-a-row in 1923, when they beat Kerry in the final. He

holds the rare distinction of losing an All-Ireland football final and winning an All-Ireland hurling title in the same year (1920), only to reverse the trend in 1921 when he won a football medal but lost in the All-Ireland hurling final.

TOMMY CAREW (KILDARE)

Although Kildare is predominantly a football county, it has also

Cork dual player Brian Corcoran surges clear of a challenge from Tipperary's Liam Cahill

BRIAN CORCORAN
(CORK)

He first came to prominence in 1991, playing an important role as a full-back of real stature when Cork won the All-Ireland minor football crown. He figured in Cork minor hurling teams which lost All-Ireland finals in 1988 and 1990. He made his senior hurling championship debut as an 18-year-old in 1992 and produced a series of memorable performances as Cork beat Tipperary, the defending All-Ireland champions, Limerick and Down to reach the All-Ireland final against Kilkenny. Corcoran gave another superb exhibition of corner-back play in the final but it wasn't enough to save his side from defeat. He was chosen as the 1992 Hurler of the Year, one of the rare occasions on which the honour didn't go to a player from the All-Ireland-winning side.

He captained Cork to victory over Wexford in the 1993 National Hurling League final and also played a significant role in the county's march to the All-Ireland football final against Derry. Corcoran played at left full-back but it turned out to be another bad day as Cork were beaten by 1–14 to 2–8. He picked up Munster football championship medals in 1993, '94 and '95, and added a hurling National League title to his haul in 1998 when Cork beat Waterford in the final. A year later, Corcoran finally achieved his life-long ambition when Cork won the All-Ireland hurling title for the first time in nine years, beating Kilkenny by a point in the final. He opted out of the football scene after the 1998 championship to concentrate totally on hurling.

DENIS COUGHLAN
(CORK)

Born in 1945, he played club hurling with Glen Rovers and football with the St. Nicholas club. He captured two Cork county football

produced some excellent hurlers. Carew certainly falls into that category and it is generally recognised that had he been born in a strong hurling county he would undoubtedly have won major championship honours.

Born in 1945, he played his club hurling with Coill Dhubh and his club football with Clane, with whom he collected four county championship medals. In addition, Carew also picked up one county hurling championship medal.

He played senior inter-county hurling and football for 15 years between 1965 and 1980. He was at right half-forward on the Kildare team which won the county's first All-Ireland U21 football title in 1965. He also won two more Leinster U21 championship medals.

Kildare's success rate was not matched at senior level and Carew had the unfortunate experience of playing on six teams which lost Leinster finals, in 1966, '69, '71, '72, '75 and '78. He was also a member of the Kildare team which lost the 1968 National League final to Down. He didn't enjoy much luck on the interprovincial football scene either, having been at full-forward on the Leinster team which lost the 1972 Railway Cup football final to Munster in a replay.

He won an All-Ireland junior hurling championship medal in 1962 and also captured two All-Ireland senior hurling 'B' medals in 1974 and 1980. He played for the Leinster inter-provincial side in the Railway Cup on a few occasions.

championship medals and five Cork hurling championships. He also won two All-Ireland club hurling medals with Glen Rovers in 1972 and 1977. He played on the Cork team which lost the 1965 All-Ireland U21 football final to Kildare and his luck was also out when he captained Cork into the 1967 senior All-Ireland football final against Meath, only to lose by three points. He won his first senior All-Ireland medal in 1970 as a sub on the hurling panel and three years later he won an All-Ireland football medal as a midfielder of real stature on the team which beat Galway in the final. It was to be his only senior All-Ireland football championship success but he went on to enjoy some great days with the hurlers, winning three more All-Ireland medals in 1976, '77 and '78. He picked up four hurling National League medals, in 1970, '72, '74 and '80, and won four All-Star hurling awards in 1972, '76, '77 and '78. He was chosen as Hurler of the Year in 1977.

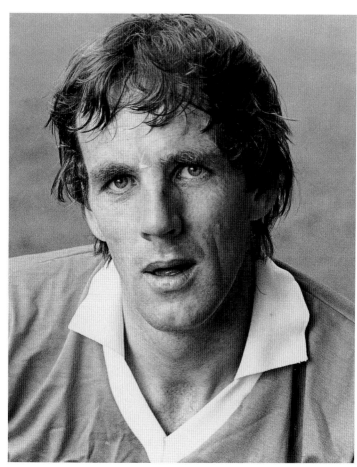

Ray Cummins: a big man for the big occasion in hurling and football

RAY CUMMINS (CORK)

A full-forward of outstanding ability in both hurling and football, he enjoyed a long and fruitful career with club and county. Born in 1949, he made his first major impact as a minor in 1966 when Cork reached the All-Ireland hurling final, where they lost to Wexford. Cummins was at left half-back on that Cork team, a position he also occupied in the U21 team which won the All-Ireland title in 1968. They retained it a year later, but by then Cummins had moved to full-forward.

He won his first All-Ireland senior hurling medal in 1970 and, three years later, collected his only All-Ireland senior football medal when Cork beat Galway in the final. He became the first Corkman for 28 years to win both All-Ireland senior hurling and football medals as a member of the starting teams. Cork retained the Munster football title a year later but lost the All-

Ireland semi-final to Dublin, and it would be nine years before they regained the provincial crown. While Cork's football fortunes dipped, the hurlers embarked on a glorious run which saw them win three consecutive All-Ireland finals in 1976, '77 and '78. Cummins played an important role in all three, especially in 1976 when he captained the team. He achieved a rare distinction in 1972 when he won Railway Cup medals with Munster in both hurling and football. He won five All-Star awards (three for hurling, in 1971, '72 and '77, two for football in 1971 and '73) and had the unique honour of becoming the first player chosen as both a hurling and football All-Star in the same year (1971). He enjoyed big successes with his club Blackrock, too, winning All-Ireland hurling medals in 1972, '74 and '79. In 1999, he was selected for the hurling Team of the Millennium.

LIAM CURRAMS (OFFALY)

While Offaly have enjoyed lots of success in both hurling and football, there has been very little overlapping in terms of players. Hurling and football are drawn from different parts of the county, which gives them largely separate identities. Liam Currams was one of the few players to cross the boundaries, and did so with remarkable style and success in the early 1980s.

Born in January 1961, it was clear from an early stage that he was a special talent and by the time he was 20, he had played in All-Ireland senior hurling and football finals in the same year. The 1981 season provided Currams with lifetime memories. He was at midfield on the Offaly hurling team which made a dramatic comeback to beat Galway in the All-Ireland final. It was Offaly's

first All-Ireland hurling win and, in a fascinating coincidence, they had also qualified for the football final, which was played two weeks later. Currams was at left half-back on the football team but he was unfortunately denied the honour of winning two senior medals in the same year when Kerry beat Offaly by seven points.

However, a year later he reached the summit of his ambitions when Offaly gained revenge on Kerry in amazing circumstances, snatching victory in the final minute and thereby preventing Kerry winning their fifth consecutive All-Ireland football title. Currams won All-Star awards in 1981 (hurling) and 1982 (football).

PAT DUNNY (KILDARE)

The only Kildare player ever to win Railway Cup hurling and football medals with Leinster, Dunny was a gifted performer in both codes and would have had a far higher medal haul had he been playing with a stronger county. The Raheens club man won an All-Ireland junior hurling medal as a 17-year-old in 1962 when Kildare defeated London in the final.

In 1966 he captained Kildare to another All-Ireland junior hurling success and, in the same season, was a star performer when Kildare won the All-Ireland intermediate final, beating Cork by a point in an exciting game. His football career also had its peaks. In 1965, he captained the Kildare U21 team to victory in the All-Ireland final, where they beat Cork. This was Kildare's only All-Ireland win in this grade. Although he never won Leinster senior medals, he was at the heart of Kildare's gallant efforts for many years. He was a regular on the Leinster interprovincial teams, winning four Railway Cup hurling medals in 1971, '72, '74 and '75 and a football medal in 1974. When he retired from playing he went into administration and served Kildare as a selector and county official.

Liam Currams (left) was the first Offaly man to play in All-Ireland hurling and football finals in a single year

DES 'SNITCHIE' FERGUSON (DUBLIN)

His senior hurling and football careers spanned the years from 1949 to 1964, during which he won two All-Ireland senior football medals with Dublin in 1958 and 1963, when they beat Derry and Galway respectively. He also played on the Dublin team which lost the 1955 All-Ireland final to Kerry. He played as a forward in football but as a defender in hurling. He was at right half-back on the Dublin team which lost the 1952 All-Ireland hurling final to Cork and was at right corner-back on the team which went down to Tipperary by a point in the 1961 final. He won two Railway Cup hurling medals with Leinster in 1956 and 1962. His son, Terry, won two All-Ireland senior football medals with Meath in 1987 and 1988.

DES FOLEY (DUBLIN)

Born in 1940 into a famous sporting family, he made his first major impact on the county football scene playing for Dublin minors as a 16-year-old in 1956, and captained them to success in the 1958 All-Ireland minor final, where they beat Mayo.

Three years later, he experienced the hurling big time when Dublin beat Wexford in the Leinster senior final and qualified for the All-Ireland final against Tipperary. Des Foley was at midfield on the Dublin team while his brother, Lar, was at right corner-back. It was a great occasion for the Foley brothers but Tipperary spoiled the party, beating Dublin by a point, 0–16 to 1–12 – one of the few occasions when a team lost an All-Ireland final without conceding a goal.

On St.Patrick's Day 1962 Des set a record by playing for Leinster hurlers and footballers on the same afternoon in the Railway Cup finals at Croke Park. Leinster beat Munster in the hurling final and ousted Ulster in football to ensure Foley a place in the history books.

A year later, Foley enjoyed another memorable triumph when he captained Dublin to victory in the All-Ireland senior football final, beating Galway by 1–9 to 0–10. He went on to win two more Railway Cup hurling medals in 1964–65. He was a member of the famous St. Vincent's club in north Dublin, with whom he excelled in both hurling and football for many years.

LAR FOLEY (DUBLIN)

An older brother of Des Foley, who had a marvellous dual career with Dublin, Lar was an equally gifted hurler and footballer. Whereas Des played mainly at midfield, with the occasional foray into attack, Lar spent most of his career at corner-back where his tigerish qualities were equally effective in both codes. He led Dublin to success in the 1956 All-Ireland minor football final, when they easily beat Leitrim. He made his senior football debut with Dublin in 1957 and a year later, at the age of 19, he won his first All-Ireland senior football medal when Dublin beat Derry by

six points in the final. He won a second All-Ireland football medal in 1963.

In 1961, he was at left full-back on the Dublin hurling team which lost the All-Ireland final to Tipperary by one point, 0–16 to 1–12. Foley had the unfortunate experience of being sent off that day: it would be all of 35 years before another player was sent off in an All-Ireland hurling final (Wexford's Eamonn Scallan in 1996). Foley won Railway Cup hurling medals with Leinster in 1962 and 1964 and also enjoyed many club successes with St. Vincent's. He managed the Dublin hurling side in the late 1980s and early 1990s.

PIERCE GRACE (KILKENNY & DUBLIN)

From Tullaroan, Co. Kilkenny, Grace won his first All-Ireland medal as a footballer on the Dublin side which beat Cork by 0–5 to 0–4 in the 1906 final. Dublin retained the All-Ireland crown a year later, with Grace again making a major contribution to their 0–6 to 0–2 win over Cork.

He won three All-Ireland senior hurling medals with Kilkenny in 1911, '12 and '13. Grace featured on all three teams. It was the only time in Kilkenny's history that the club won three All-Ireland senior finals in a row.

MICK HOLDEN (DUBLIN)

One of the Gaelic Games' great characters, he brought a sense of flair and fun to both hurling and football. His main successes came with Dublin footballers. He won Leinster and All-Ireland senior football medals in 1983 and added a Leinster medal in 1984. He was at his defiant best at right full-back in the 1983 All-Ireland final when Dublin, who had three men sent off, beat Galway by two points. He showed the same battling

'Babs' Keating fought many battles with 'Fan' Larkin and Pat Henderson

round flamboyance and swagger made him one of the big attractions of his time. He later managed Tipperary hurlers to All-Ireland success in 1989 and 1991 (see *The Great Managers*).

JACK LYNCH (CORK)

One of the most charismatic figures in GAA history, Lynch achieved greatness on the hurling and football fields before entering politics, a sphere in which he also excelled. He served two terms as Taoiseach in a Fianna Fáil Government, in 1966–73 and 1977–79, but had achieved fame long before his rise up the political ladder, having been a GAA hero in the 1940s.

Born in 1917, he played his club hurling with the famous Glen Rovers, with whom he won 10 county championship medals, and football with St. Nicholas. He also played with the Civil Service club in Dublin for a time. He first played senior hurling with Cork in 1935 and was on the team which won four successive All-Ireland titles in 1941, '42, '43 and '44, beating Dublin (three times) and Antrim. A beautifully-balanced player, he presided at midfield with elegant authority and was a particularly proud winner in 1942 as he was captain of the team.

In 1945, he was at right corner-forward on the Cork football team which beat Cavan in the All-Ireland final. It was the first time since 1911 Cork had won the football title. A year later, he was back on the winners' podium again as Cork hurlers won another All-Ireland title, earning Lynch the historic distinction of winning All-Ireland senior medals in six successive years. Cork also reached the 1947 All-Ireland hurling final but lost to Kilkenny.

Apart from his All-Ireland trophy haul, Lynch also won three National League hurling medals and three Railway Cup medals with Munster. He was selected at mid-

field on the centenary hurling team which was chosen in 1984 as part of the GAA's celebrations to mark its 100th birthday, and was also at midfield on the hurling Team of the Millennium chosen in 1999.

PADDY MACKEY (WEXFORD)

He won an All-Ireland senior hurling medal in 1910 with the Castlebridge side which represented Wexford in the championship. He then went on to play for Wexford footballers and figured prominently on the four teams which won consecutive All-Ireland titles in 1915–18, one of ten Wexford players who played in all four finals. His haul of five All-Ireland medals (four for football, one hurling) was the largest won by any player until the 1940s when it was surpassed by another dual star, Cork's Jack Lynch.

TEDDY McCARTHY (CORK)

He has gone down in the GAA history for a very special reason. In 1990, he became the first player in the 106-year history of the GAA to win All-Ireland senior hurling and football medals in the same season. It was a truly amazing achievement by the versatile Glanmire man, and one which ensures that his name will always be remembered in the annals of Gaelic Games.

Born in 1965, he made his first major impression on the inter-county scene in 1983 when he played at centre-forward on the Cork minor football team which reached the All-Ireland final, where they lost to Derry by 0–8 to 1–3. He didn't have to wait long for an All-Ireland medal, however, as he came on as a sub in the 1984 U21 football final and helped Cork to beat Mayo. That was the start of a glorious treble for McCarthy, who played a central part

qualities during his hurling career with Dublin but they never managed to make the Leinster championship breakthrough.

MICHAEL 'BABS' KEATING (TIPPERARY)

Affectionately known as 'Babs', his talents were apparent from an early age with his club Ballybacon-Grange. Born in 1944, he first played for Tipperary minor hurlers as a 16-year-old in 1960. They reached the All-Ireland final but were well-beaten by Kilkenny. Tipperary also lost the 1961 and 1962 minor finals to Kilkenny so, by the age of 18, Keating had bad memories of three All-Ireland finals.

His luck would change, however, and he would go on to enjoy remarkable successes on the hurling fields. While his achievements in football were more modest, that was due mainly to the fact that Tipperary were not a great power

in the game. In 1963, he won an All-Ireland intermediate hurling medal and a year later won both All-Ireland senior and U21 medals in the same season.

Tipperary beat Kilkenny in the senior final and easily accounted for Wexford in the inaugural All-Ireland U21 championship decider. Keating played in four more All-Ireland senior finals, winning two more medals in 1965 and 1971 and losing in 1967 and 1968. He won five Munster senior hurling medals and also picked up two Railway Cup medals with Munster in 1968 and 1970. His prowess as a footballer made him an automatic choice on the Tipperary team for 13 years and also earned him regular call-ups to the Munster interprovincial side, with whom he won a Railway Cup medal in 1972. A year earlier, he was chosen at centre half-forward on the inaugural All-Stars hurling team and also won the Hurler of the Year Award.

He was a deadly finisher in both hurling and football and his all-

72

Teddy McCarthy: first to win All-Ireland double in a single season

as Cork retained the All-Ireland U21 football titles in 1985 and 1986.

His reputation continued to grow in both hurling and football and he was drafted into the senior hurling team for the 1986 All-Ireland final against Galway. He showed remarkable maturity in his first major senior test and slotted in comfortably at right half-forward as Cork beat a highly-fancied Galway team. He was promoted to the senior football team the following year and developed into one of the most spectacular fielders in the history of the game. His ability to soar above opposition and colleagues alike made him the ideal midfielder and he went on to play in five All-Ireland finals (including a draw in 1998) in the 1987–90 period. Cork lost to Meath in 1987 and 1988 (after a replay) but won their first All-Ireland title for 16 years in 1989 when they beat Mayo in the final. In 1990 Cork beat Galway in the All-Ireland hurling final, giving McCarthy the opportunity to claim

a place in history if the footballers could beat Meath in the football decider. They duly achieved it (0–11 to 0–9) with McCarthy contributing enormously in midfield. He won a National League football medal in 1989 and added a hurling League medal in 1993. He also played in the 1993 All-Ireland football final against Derry, but Cork were beaten by 1–14 to 2–8. He was chosen as the Footballer of the Year in 1989, a year in which he also won an All-Star award.

LEONARD McGRATH (GALWAY)

The only Galway player to win All-Ireland senior medals in both hurling and football, McGrath was born in the village of Leitrim and was on the Galway team which won the county's first All-Ireland hurling title, beating Limerick in the 1923

final. Galway didn't win another All-Ireland title until 1980. Two years later McGrath was on the Galway football team which won the county's first All-Ireland title.

KIERAN McKEEVER (DERRY)

The 2000 Ulster senior championship final was an emotional occasion for McKeever, who ensured himself of a place in Derry history by adding a provincial hurling medal to the two he had already won in football. McKeever had won Ulster football medals in 1993 and 1998 but the hurling medal eluded him until 2000, when Derry put on a great performance to beat Antrim by a point in the final, 4–8 to 0–19. It was their first Ulster hurling win since 1908. Derry's hurlers had been overshadowed by their footballers, who made the 1990s the most successful decade in their history by winning an All-Ireland senior football title, two Ulster crowns and three National League titles. Derry's All-Ireland final win over Cork in 1993 was especially significant as it was the first time that they had ever won the senior title. McKeever, a tight-marking corner-back with a steely resolve, played an influential role in all Derry football's successes in the 1990s and started the new decade with another football National League win, prior to making the big breakthrough in the Ulster hurling championship. He was nominated for All-Star selection in both football and hurling in 2000 and was selected at right full-back on the football team.

BRIAN MURPHY (CORK)

A versatile hurling and football defender who could fit in anywhere in the full-back line, Murphy earned an impressive reputation during a long and fruitful career. He won his first All-Ireland medal as a minor

footballer in 1969 and a year later an All-Ireland minor hurling title. He won All-Ireland U21 medals in 1971 (football and hurling) and 1973 (hurling). He progressed quickly to the Cork senior teams and was at left full-back on the football team which beat Galway in the 1973 football final. Three years later he was at right full-back on the Cork hurling team which won the All-Ireland final, making him the first player in GAA history to win All-Ireland medals at minor, U21 and senior level in both sports.

He was on the Cork team which

Kieran McKeever

won three consecutive All-Ireland hurling finals in 1976, '77 and '78, and also featured on three losing All-Ireland final teams in 1972, 1982 and 1983. He won three Railway Cup football medals and one hurling medal with Munster. He became the first player to win two All-Star awards in hurling and football. He won All-Star hurling awards in 1979 and 1981 and football awards in 1973 and 1976. A tenacious defender, he imposed his will on opposing forwards. He was by no means a flashy player but was highly-effective in a quiet, determined manner. The fact he survived so long at the highest level in both hurling and football speaks volumes for his all-round ability.

GEORGE O'CONNOR (WEXFORD)

Although best-known as a hurling midfielder of outstanding ability, he was also an extremely accomplished footballer prior to his decision to concentrate exclusively on hurling. From Piercestown, he made his inter-county debut in hurling and football in 1979 and played for 11 different teams – including club and county – in just one season, an incredible feat. Many shrewd judges believe he was a better footballer than a hurler but, because of Wexford's relatively poor strike rate in football, it was almost inevitable he would concentrate on hurling.

He played in two Leinster football semi-finals but it was as a hurler that he really shone. Wexford weren't a particularly lucky side for most of O'Connor's career and he played on four teams which lost Leinster senior finals, in 1981, '84, '88 and '93. He was also on five teams which lost National League finals in 1982, '84, '90, '91 and '93. The 1993 League final defeat was particularly painful as Wexford twice drew with Cork before losing the second replay. It was beginning to look as if he would end his career without the most prized possession of all, the All-Ireland senior medal, but Wexford's big break came in 1996 when they beat Kilkenny, Dublin, Offaly, Galway and Limerick to take the Liam McCarthy Cup for the first time since 1968. O'Connor, dubbed the 'uncrowned king of Wexford hurling' by manager Liam Griffin, had finally become the proud holder of an All-Ireland medal, and nobody deserved it more.

He also won All-Star awards in 1981 (centre-forward) and 1988 (midfield).

A modern-day dual star: Cork's Séan O hAilpín is a solid anchor in defence at both hurling and football

SÉAN O hAILPÍN (CORK)

One of the top modern-day dual players, O hAilpín made his first breakthrough when he won Munster and All-Ireland minor hurling medals in 1995. He went on to win three successive Munster U21 hurling medals in 1996, '97 and '98 and captured two All-Ireland medals in 1997–98. He also won a hurling National League medal in 1998. He enjoyed a remarkable season in 1999 when playing at left half-back

for the senior hurlers and at full-back for the footballers. The hurlers beat Waterford and Clare to win the Munster final for the first time since 1990 and later went on to add the All-Ireland crown with a one-point win over Kilkenny in the final. The footballers beat Kerry in the Munster final and qualified to play Meath in the All-Ireland final, but lost by three points.

O hAilpín brings a swashbuckling swagger to everything he does. Strong under the high ball in hurling, he is also a great striker of the

ball. His anticipation of play in both hurling and football makes him a special talent and an invaluable part of the Cork set-up.

SEAN O'KENNEDY (WEXFORD)

He was on the Castlebridge team which represented Wexford in the 1910 All-Ireland hurling championship, where they beat Limerick in the final. O'Kennedy later played football for Wexford and won three consecutive All-Ireland medals in 1915, '16 and '17. He was also captain for those three successes.

W J SPAIN
(LIMERICK & DUBLIN)

Born in Nenagh, Co. Tipperary, he was the first man in the history of the GAA to win All-Ireland senior medals in both hurling and football, doing so with two different counties. He played in the Limerick Commercials side which won the inaugural All-Ireland football final in 1887, beating Louth Young Irelands. Two years later, he helped Kickhams of Dublin to victory over Clare in the All-Ireland football final.

DENIS WALSH (CORK)

He holds two All-Ireland senior medals from the same year but, unlike colleague Teddy McCarthy, did not play on both the Cork hurling and football teams which won the titles in 1990. He was at full-back on the hurling team and was on the football squad but did not get into the starting 15.

He first came to prominence by winning three successive All-Ireland U21 football medals with Cork in 1984, '85 and '86. He also tasted All-Ireland senior hurling glory in 1986, playing at left half-back on the team which beat Galway in the final. He won a Munster senior football championship in 1987 and played at left full-back on the team which lost to Meath in the All-Ireland final. He was at full-back again a year later when Cork drew with Meath in the All-Ireland football final but was replaced by Stephen O'Brien for the replay, which Cork lost. He was on the subs' bench when Cork won consecutive All-Ireland football finals in 1989-90. A player of great poise, Walsh proved himself to be an extremely valuable asset to both the Cork hurling and football squads for a number of years. He won a football National League medal as a sub in 1989 and added a hurling League medal to his trophy cabinet in 1993.

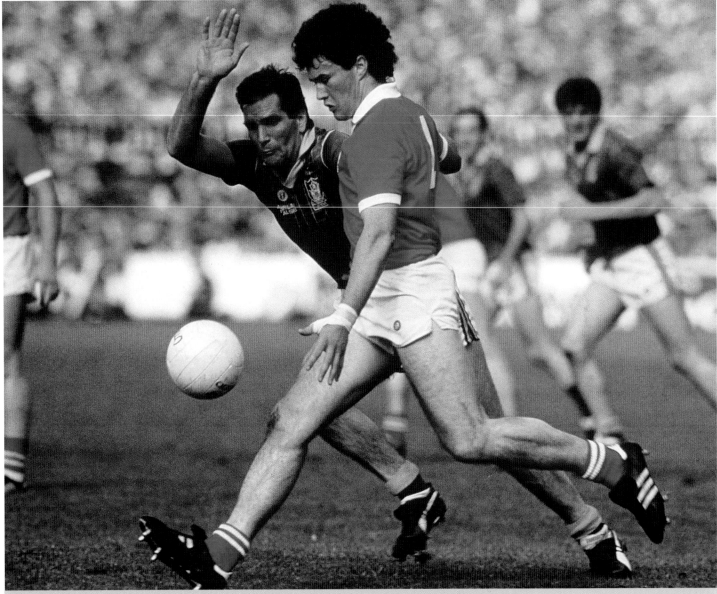

Cork dual ace Denis Walsh gets in his clearance despite the attacking hand of Meath's Joe Cassells

6

THE A–Z OF GREAT PLAYERS

Tony Boyle, high-scoring forward with Donegal in the 1990s, is confronted by Derry's Seán Martin Lockhart in the 1998 Ulster final

FOOTBALLERS

Gaelic football is a game which requires a wide range of physical skills as well as a sharp, agile mind. For well over 100 years, the great players have shown their talents throughout the length and breadth of Ireland and , in some cases, far beyond their native shores. Thousands of gifted performers have given wonderful entertainment to countless thousands of spectators, including the following top 100 who provide enduring testimony to all that is special about the game.

LIAM AUSTIN
(Down)

It was ironic that Austin didn't reach the highest peak of a 15-year inter-county career until his final season in 1991, when he won an All-Ireland senior football medal, coming on as a sub in the final against Meath. He was 33 years old at the time and didn't play for Down again. It was fitting that the Rostrevor giant – he was 6'5" tall – should win an All-Ireland medal, as he had given remarkable service to Down since his senior debut in 1976. He won Ulster championship medals in 1978 and 1981 and was chosen at mid-field on the All-Stars team in 1983. A consistent performer with Ulster for years, he won Railway Cup medals in 1979, '80, '83 and '84.

JIMMY BARRY-MURPHY (Cork)
See The Great Dual Players

GREG BLANEY (Down)
See The Great Dual Players

EDDIE BOYLE (Louth)

Inducted into the Texaco Hall of Fame in 1990, Eddie Boyle from the Cooley Kickhams club holds the unique distinction of being the only Louth player to feature on five winning Leinster Railway Cup teams. He won those medals in 1935, '39, '40, '44 and '45. During a career in which he gained a reputation as one of the greatest ever full-backs, he won county championship medals in his native county in 1935 and 1937 and won a Dublin championship title in 1947 with Seán McDermott's club. In 1943 he enjoyed his greatest success when helping Louth win their first Leinster championship in 31 years. Such is his standing in the game that, in 1984, he was selected at full back on the Team of the Century, for players who never won an All-Ireland senior medal.

TONY BOYLE (Donegal)

From Dungloe, Tony Boyle was full-forward on the team that won Donegal's first All-Ireland senior football title in 1992, when they beat Dublin in the final. A natural-ly-gifted footballer, he faced a con-stant battle against injuries. The early part of his career was disrupted by a knee problem and later he recovered from a career-threaten-ing back injury. Boyle had won-derful balance and was equally comfortable off the left or right foot. He was the central figure in Donegal's highly-successful peri-od during the early- to mid-1990s. Had he been fully fit, it is argued, Donegal would have won at least one of the three National League finals in which they were defeated by Dublin (1992–93) and Derry (1994–95, 1995–96). He was select-ed as an All-Star in 1992.

AIDAN BRADY (Roscommon)

Born into a well-known football family from Elphin in 1928, goal-keeper Aidan was gripped by a deep passion for the game at an early age. He furthered his education at St Jarlath's College in Tuam and had begun playing regularly for Roscommon seniors by the end of the 1940s. He won four Connacht championship medals with Roscommon in 1952, '53, '61 and '62 and played in his only All-Ireland final in '62, when Roscommon lost to Kerry. He won a Railway Cup medal with Connacht in 1958 and was chosen for an Ireland selection to play the Combined Universities in a repre-sentative game in 1960. In 1984 he was chosen on the Team of the Century for players who never won an All-Ireland medal. He achieved fame away from sport as a horti-culturist and was Director of the Botanic Gardens in Dublin.

PHIL BRADY (Cavan)

Known as 'The Gunner' Brady, Phil from Mullahoran won three All-Ireland medals with Cavan in their glory days. He was at midfield on the team which beat Kerry in the All-Ireland final played at the Polo Grounds in New York in 1947. A

A man for all seasons: Kerry's Paddy 'Bawn' Brosnan

year later he manned the same posi-tion as Cavan successfully defend-ed their title, beating Mayo in the final, and in 1952 he played at full-back on the team that beat Cork after a replay. A player of immense power, he gained a huge following in Cavan for his spirited style of football. He won five county cham-pionships with Mullahoran and a club championship in Cork, where he worked as a member of An Garda Siochána.

PADDY 'BAWN' BROSNAN (Kerry)

In a 17-year inter-county career with Kerry, the fisherman and pub-lican from Dingle won every hon-our possible in the game and gained a reputation as one of the strongest footballers of his generation. Known just as 'The Bawn' he won three All-Ireland championships in 1940, '41 and '46 and was captain of the team beaten in 1944 by Roscommon. He won 13 Munster senior championships and was a winner of three Railway Cup medals with Munster. Although primarily remembered as a defender, Brosnan actually began his career as a for-ward and didn't switch back into defence until the 1946 champi-onship, when he played in the left corner-back position. Paddy 'Bawn' Brosnan remained as a defender with Kerry for the rest of his illus-trious career.

Tyrone's Peter Canavan was one of the best finishers of his generation

WILLIE BRYAN (Offaly)

Willie Bryan's performance at mid-field for Offaly in the All-Ireland final replay of 1972 against Kerry is regarded as one of the greatest in the history of Gaelic Football. Facing the legendary Mick O'Connell, Bryan produced a majestic display of high fielding and accurate distribution to help Offaly retain a title they had won for the first time a year earlier. Bryan was also captain of the team. He had first emerged as a special talent in 1964 when he was a member of the Offaly team which won the All-Ireland minor title. He was in midfield on the team that lost the 1969 All-Ireland final. They reached the final again in 1971 and won the championship when beating Galway. He was honoured as an All-Star in the inaugural year of the scheme in 1971 and won a second award in 1972. In that year he was also named Texaco Footballer of the Year.

TOM BURKE (Mayo)

Tom Burke is regarded as the man who popularised the goalkeeping position in Gaelic football in the 1930s because of his athleticism and shot-stopping ability. He was goalkeeper on the Mayo team that reached the 1932 All-Ireland final, losing to Kerry, and an influential player on the team that won Mayo's first All-Ireland senior title in 1936, beating Laois in the final. His reputation soared as Mayo won six successive National League titles between 1934 and '39. He also won Railway Cup medals with Connacht in 1934, '36, '37 and '38.

PETER CANAVAN (Tyrone)

Although on the losing team when Tyrone were beaten by Dublin in the 1995 All-Ireland final, Peter Canavan's display is regarded as one of the best ever seen in a major championship game. He scored 0–11 of Tyrone's total of 0–12 (to Dublin's 1–10) and almost earned a replay, but his last-minute point was disallowed. Small in stature, Canavan is one of the finest footballers of his time. He has wonderful balance, can kick equally well with both feet, has superb vision and possesses an abundance of courage. He was a member of the Tyrone team which lost the All-Ireland U21 final of 1990 to Kerry but then led the county to consecutive U21 titles in 1991 and 1992. He was an All-Star in 1994, '95 and '96, and was the GAA Writers' Footballer of the Year in 1995.

PÁDRAIG CARNEY (Mayo)

'The Flying Doctor', as he became known throughout the country, Pádraig Carney's value to Mayo was such that he was flown home from his base in the United States for the 1954 National League semi-final and final. However, it was worth the effort, because Mayo won the title. It was Carney's second league medal, having also been on the winning team in 1949. One of the great midfielders of all time, he was also very effective at centre-forward. Carney was on the Mayo team which lost the 1948 All-Ireland final by one point to Cavan, but which would gain compensation in 1950 and '51 when they beat Louth and Meath respectively to win the championships. Carney was outstanding in both finals. His clashes with Galway's Seán Purcell have gone down as among the greatest duels in the history of the game. He won one Railway Cup medal, in 1951.

BILL CASEY (Kerry)

One of the most powerful centre half-backs ever to have played the game, Bill Casey appeared in his first All-Ireland senior final in 1938 when Kerry lost to Galway in a replay. A year later, he won the first of four championships when Kerry beat Meath in the All-Ireland final. He added his other three medals in 1940, '41 and '46 and was also a member of the team beaten by Cavan in the 1947 All-Ireland final at the New York Polo Grounds. He won a Railway Cup medal in 1940 with Munster. His nephew Brian Mullins later won four All-Ireland championships with Dublin.

WILLIE CASEY (Mayo)

Although he never had the opportunity of playing in an All-Ireland final Willie Casey, a right full-back of real quality, was one of the most highly-respected players of the 1950s. He won only one Connacht championship in 1955 when Mayo beat Roscommon by 3–11 to 1–3. They subsequently lost to Dublin in an All-Ireland semi-final replay. He showed his style on the big stage with the Connacht teams which won the Railway Cup in 1957 and '58. He won a National League medal in 1954 and was chosen on the Team of the Century in 1984 for players who never won an All-Ireland medal.

ENDA COLLERAN (Galway)

A member of Galway's famous three-in-a-row All-Ireland championship-winning team of 1964, '65 and '66, Colleran was also captain of the team in 1965 and '66. Born in Moylough, Enda showed great promise from an early age and reached his first major milestone by winning an All-Ireland minor championship with Galway in 1960, playing at right half back. When he started playing at senior level, right corner-

Enda Colleran won three All-Ireland medals with Galway in the 1960s

A match-turning save from Paddy Cullen in the 1974 All-Ireland final against Galway

SIMON DEIGNAN (Cavan)

One of an elite group who won All-Ireland championship medals and later refereed All-Ireland finals, Simon Deignan played in five All-Ireland finals and was on the winning side in the 1947 final against Kerry, which was played at the New York Polo Grounds. He won another All-Ireland title in 1948 when Cavan beat Mayo. He was on the losing side in 1943, '45 and '49 but won Railway Cup medals with Munster in 1942, '43 and '47. Deignan began refereeing as his playing days ended and was in charge of the 1950 All-Ireland final between Mayo and Louth, the '54 final between Meath and Kerry and the '58 final between Dublin and Derry.

back became his position and it was there that he won all his major honours in Galway's greatest-ever era. In 1967 he was captain of the Connacht team which won the Railway Cup. Colleran was chosen on the Team of the Century in 1984. After his career ended he became a well-known TV analyst and remains closely involved in the game.

MATT CONNOR (Offaly)
See The Legends of Gaelic Football

RAY CUMMINS (Cork)
See The Great Dual Players

PADDY CULLEN (Dublin)

As Dublin emerged from a barren period in the mid-1970s to win three All-Ireland championships in 1974, '76 and '77, goalkeeper Paddy Cullen epitomised the county's new spirit. Strong and athletic, he was one of the most agile goalkeepers to be found in the game anywhere. In the 1974 All-Ireland final against Galway Cullen played a vital role in securing victory for Dublin when saving a penalty from Liam Sammon. A four-times All-Star award-winner, he was a central figure in the 1978 final when Kerry's Mike

Sheehy scored a controversial goal from a free while Cullen was chasing back to his goal after conceding the free. Cullen became the manager of the Dublin team in 1990 and served in that post for three seasons, winning the National League in 1991 and reaching the All-Ireland final in 1992 when Dublin lost to Donegal.

JOHNNY CULLOTY (Kerry)

When Johnny Culloty from Killarney won his first All-Ireland senior football medal in 1955 he played at right full-forward against Dublin. His career then underwent an extremely dramatic change of course and he won four more All-Ireland championships as Kerry's goalkeeper: in 1959, 1962, 1969 (when he acted as captain) and 1970. He was only 17 years old when he first played senior football for Kerry, having come to attention as a forward with the minor team which reached the All-Ireland final in 1954. He played in nine All-Ireland senior finals for Kerry and won five National League medals, all as goalkeeper, in 1959, '61, '63, '69 and '71. Culloty also played hurling for Kerry for almost two decades.

BILL DELANEY (Laois)

From Stradbally, Bill Delaney won four Leinster Senior Championship medals with Laois in 1936, '37, '38 and '46. His brothers Jack, Tom and Matt also played on the 1936 team which lost the All-Ireland final to Mayo. He was a member of the Railway Cup-winning Leinster teams of 1935, '39 (as captain), '40, '44 and '45. He was still playing inter-county football when he refereed the drawn All-Ireland final of 1946 between Kerry and Roscommon, and he also took charge of the 1951 final between Mayo and Meath.

PADDY DOHERTY (Down)

As Down emerged in 1960 to become the first team from the Six Counties of Northern Ireland to win the All-Ireland senior football championship, Paddy Doherty was carving out a reputation as one of the most incisive forwards of his generation. This left-footed wing forward scored 1–5 in the All-Ireland final of 1960 against Kerry as Down won by 2–10 to 0–8. Doherty was team captain in 1961 when Down retained their title by beating Offaly, and he added a third medal in 1968 when Down again beat Kerry in the final. In his hugely-successful career he also won three National League medals, seven Ulster championships and seven Railway Cup medals with Ulster.

MICHAEL DONNELLAN (Galway)
See The Famous GAA Families

AIDAN DOYLE (Wexford)

Regarded as one of the great score-getters in the early years of the last century, he played in a remarkable seven successive All-Ireland finals between 1913 and 1918, including a replay against Kerry in 1914. Doyle was on the Wexford team which dominated the All-Ireland series from 1915 to '18, winning four consecutive championships.

PAUL DOYLE (Kildare)

Doyle, from Caragh, is one of only two Kildare players (with Mick Buckley) to have won three All-Ireland senior football championship medals. He was only 19 when he played at left half-forward on the Caragh team which represented Kildare and beat a Galway selection in the 1919 All-Ireland final 2–5 to 0–1. Eight years later he added a second medal when Kildare beat Kerry by 0–5 to 0–3 and his third a year later when they beat Cavan 2–6 to 2–5. A very stylish player, he won Railway Cup medals with Leinster in 1928, '29 and '30.

TOMMY DRUMM (Dublin)

One of the most stylish defenders ever to play for Dublin, Tommy Drumm made his championship debut in 1976 and went on to win his first All-Ireland medal at right half back when Dublin beat Kerry in the final. He added a second medal a year later when Dublin beat

Armagh in the final. On the losing Dublin teams in the 1978 and '79 finals, Drumm was Dublin's captain and inspirational centre-back when they beat Galway in the 1983 All-Ireland final. He won four All-Star awards in 1977, '78, '79 and '83, and was Texaco Footballer of the Year in 1983.

JOHN 'TULL' DUNNE (Galway)

A player, administrator and coach of great distinction, Dunne, a native of Ballinasloe, became one of the most recognisable figures in Gaelic football. As a player, he won an All-Ireland Junior football championship in 1931. Three years later he was right half-forward on the Galway team which won the All-Ireland senior championship final, beating Dublin by 3–5 to 1–9. In 1938 he was captain when Galway won the title again, this time beating Kerry after a replay. He also played in three other finals, losing in 1933, '40 and '41. He later achieved fame as a coach and was in charge of the Galway team which won three All-Ireland championships in 1964, '65 and '66. His son Cyril was right half-forward on the team. A noted administrator, 'Tull' served as Galway football secretary and Central Council delegate for many years.

DERMOT EARLEY (Roscommon)

One of the most popular figures in the modern history of football, Dermot Earley had an historic start to his career with Roscommon. In 1966, he became the first player to represent his county at minor (U18), U21 and senior grades in the one year. He was at midfield on the U21 team which won the All-Ireland championship, beating Kildare in the final. He was only 18 years old in 1967 when he played in the Railway Cup competition, coming on as a substitute in the final in which Connacht beat Ulster. Alternating between midfield and

the half-forward line, he won his first Connacht senior medal in 1972 and would add four more with the Roscommon team which dominated the province from 1977 to 1980.

He won a National League medal in 1979 and was on the team which lost the All-Ireland final to Kerry in 1980. His brother Paul also played for Roscommon during the 1980s.

Dermot Earley (senior): a Roscommon hero for many years

Dermot won two All-Star awards in 1974 and '79. He served as team manager for both Roscommon and Kildare. His son Dermot has won two Leinster senior championship medals with Kildare.

JOHN EGAN (Kerry)

A member of the great Kerry team of the 1970s and 1980s, John Egan earned a reputation among his peers as one of the most complete inside forwards of the era. Although his contribution was often overshadowed by other illustrious colleagues, Egan's speed and strength created many of the great scores for the Kerry forward line. He was a member of the Kerry minor team which reached the All-Ireland final in 1970 and lost to Galway. Three years later he won an All-Ireland U21 medal when Kerry beat Mayo. By then he had already made his senior debut. Having won a National League medal in 1974, he was on the senior team which won the All-Ireland championship in 1975. He added four more championships between 1978 and 1981 and was team captain when their bid for a record fifth consecutive title was foiled by Offaly in 1982. He won his sixth All-Ireland medal in 1984 and retired at the end of the season. An All-Star on four occasions – 1975, '76, '77 and '81 – he has enjoyed success as a coach at club level in Cork city, where he works as a member of An Garda Siochána.

SHEA FAHY (Kildare and Cork)

A native of Kildare, Fahy played under-age and senior football for the county before transferring in 1987 to Cork, where he was based as an Army officer. He was on the Cork team, alongside another Kildare native, Larry Tompkins, when they lost the All-Ireland finals of 1987 and '88 to Meath. Midfielder Fahy played a huge part in reversing the losing trend as Cork beat Mayo in

Maurice Fitzgerald's grace and style earned him a reputation as one of Kerry's greatest forwards

the 1989 final and defended their title in 1990 when they beat Meath in the final. His performances in the 1990 championship won him the Footballer of the Year award and he also added a second All-Star award to the one presented in 1988. He played in the 1993 All-Ireland final, which Cork lost to Derry, before ending his career.

MAURICE FITZGERALD (Kerry)

From Cahirciveen in South Kerry, Maurice Fitzgerald grew up in an atmosphere dominated by football. His father Ned had played for Kerry and a close family friend was the legendary Mick O'Connell. It was clear from an early age that Maurice had a special talent. He made his senior championship debut for Kerry in 1988 at the age of 18 and scored 0–10 in the Munster final against Cork. It was not enough for Kerry to win the game but it earned the teenager his first All-Star award. He won his first Munster championship

in 1991 but had to wait until 1997 for his first All-Ireland triumph. His performance in the All-Ireland final against Mayo is regarded as one of the finest individual contributions ever at that level. He added a second championship in 2000 when Kerry beat Galway after a replay. A National League winner in 1997, he was honoured with further All-Star awards in 1996 and '97 and was Footballer of the Year in 1997.

SEAN FLANAGAN (Mayo)

Born in Ballyhaunis in Mayo, later moving to Ballaghaderreen, he was educated at St Jarlath's College in Tuam and studied law at University College, Dublin, with whom he won a Sigerson Cup medal in 1943. He was at left full-back on the Mayo team which lost the 1948 All-Ireland final to Cavan. In 1950 he was appointed Mayo captain and took an active role in team training and match preparations. He led the county to successive All-Ireland cham-

pionship successes in 1950 and '51. In 1951 he was also elected to Dáil Éireann and served as a Government minister in two administrations. His son Dermot, also a defender, was a highly-accomplished performer with Mayo in the 1980s and 1990s. Séan was selected at left full-back on the Team of the Millennium.

BERNARD FLYNN (Meath)

Though small in stature, Bernard Flynn's ball-winning capacity, speed and scoring ability made him one of the outstanding corner forwards of the 1980s and early 1990s. Part of the prolific forward line which also included Colm O'Rourke and Brian Stafford, Flynn won two All-Ireland championships in 1987 and '88 and was a beaten finalist in 1990 and '91. He was an All-Star award-winner in '87 and '91 and won National League medals in 1988, '90 and '94.

DES FOLEY (Dublin)
See The Great Dual Players.

OLLIE FREANEY (Dublin)

Born in 1929, Ollie Freaney was a member of the famous St Vincent's club which dominated the Dublin scene during the 1940s and '50s, winning 13 county senior championships, and of the Dublin minor team which lost the 1946 All-Ireland minor final to Kerry. He made his senior debut for Dublin in 1949 and became one of the game's leading marksmen over the next 11 years. He played in the 1955 All-Ireland final when Dublin lost to Kerry. Three years later, however, he collected a coveted All-Ireland medal when Dublin beat Derry by 2–12 to 1–9. He won five Railway Cup medals with Leinster in 1952, '53, '54, '55 and '59 and three National Leagues in 1953, '55 and '58.

Martin Furlong to the rescue against Eoin Liston in the 1982 Offaly-Kerry All-Ireland final

MARTIN FURLONG (Offaly)

One of the greatest goalkeepers of all time, Martin Furlong played senior football for Offaly from 1965 to 1983. He won an All-Ireland

A deadly finisher, Bernard Flynn won two All-Ireland medals with Meath in 1987-88

minor medal in 1964 and holds the distinction of being the only member of all three Offaly teams to win All-Ireland senior championships in 1971, '72 and '82. A superb shot-stopper with a great awareness of when to come off his line, he was also consistently accurate with his kick-outs. Furlong won four All-Star awards in 1972, '81, '82 and '83 and was the Texaco Footballer of the Year in 1982, one of only two goalkeepers (Billy Morgan of Cork being the other) to receive this accolade.

CHARLIE GALLAGHER (Cavan)

The name Charlie Gallagher was a regular feature at the top of the scoring charts during the 1960s. The Cavan wing forward was prolific throughout his career and topped the charts in both 1965, when he scored a total of 123 points in competitive games, and in 1967, when he scored 109 points. Gallagher was hugely popular with Cavan supporters as he helped the county to three Ulster championships in

1964, '67 and '69. He won four Railway Cup medals with Ulster in 1964, '65, '66 and '68. Selected on the Team of the Century for players who never won an All-Ireland, Gallagher died tragically in a drowning accident in 1989.

JOHNNY GERAGHTY (Galway)

One of the greatest goalkeepers of all time, Johnny Geraghty, a native of Kilkerrin, won an All-Ireland Colleges medal with St Jarlath's, Tuam in 1960 and was a member of the University College Galway team which won the Sigerson Cup in 1963. Geraghty became Galway's regular goalkeeper in 1964 and was a member of the team which won three All-Ireland medals in a row in 1964, '65 and '66, keeping a clean sheet in all three finals while conceding only one goal in three semi-finals. He won a National League medal in 1965 and a Railway Cup medal with Connacht in 1967. A wonderfully-agile keeper, he attracted the interest of Manchester United. Regarded as well ahead of

his time, his style and vigour ensured him a permanent place in the annals of the greats.

TREVOR GILES (Meath)

One of the most gifted players of the modern era, Trevor Giles grew up in the football stronghold of Skryne in Meath where his idols, Colm O'Rourke and Liam Hayes, would become club team-mates. He won an All-Ireland minor medal in 1992 when Meath beat Armagh and a year later was elevated to senior status, winning a National League medal in 1993–94. He also won an All-Ireland under-21 medal in 1993. By 1996 he was one of the key players on the Meath team which won the All-Ireland senior championship, beating Mayo after a replay. He was again hugely influential when Mayo won the 1999 championship, defeating Cork in the final. Named as an All-Star in 1996, '97 and '99, Giles was chosen as both Footballer of the Year and the GAA Writers' Player of the Year in 1999.

On the run: Meath midfielder Liam Hayes outpaces Dublin's Paul Clarke in 1991's Leinster championship saga

JIMMY HANNIFFY (Longford)

In Longford football's glorious era of the mid-1960s, Jimmy Hanniffy was an outstanding wing-forward. He had won two All-Ireland Colleges medals with St Mel's, Longford in 1962 and '63, first played senior football for Longford in 1965, and in the 1965–66 season was part of the team which won Longford's only national senior title, the National League. In 1968 they won their first Leinster senior championship and were narrowly beaten in the All-Ireland semi-final by Kerry, 2–13 to 2–11.

LIAM HAYES (Meath)

This big, strong and very athletic midfielder was born in 1962 in Carlow but the family moved to Meath when he was young. He first played senior football for Meath in 1981 and was a member of the team which won the Centenary Cup in 1984. He won a Leinster championship medal in 1986 and was a key member of the team which won the All-Ireland titles in 1987 and '88. He also played in the finals of 1990 and 1991 when Meath lost to Cork and Down respectively. In all he won five Leinster championships (1986, '87, '88, '90 and '91) and two National Leagues, in 1988 and 1990. He was chosen as an All-Star in 1988 and retired in 1992, when he wrote the acclaimed autobiography *Out Of Our Skins*, a revealing account of his career.

KEVIN HEFFERNAN (Dublin)
See The Legends of Gaelic Football

JACK HIGGINS (Kildare)

Jack Higgins played in seven All-Ireland finals for Kildare, including a replay in 1926, and was a winner on two occasions, in 1927 against Kerry and in 1928 against Cavan. Higgins was the centre half-back and regarded as one of the most influential players of that era. A natural leader, he captained Leinster to Railway Cup success in 1930 and '32 and was also a winner in 1928, '29 and '33.

MICK HIGGINS (Cavan)

One of the greatest centre-forwards in the history of the game, Higgins was a star during Cavan's glory years in the 1940s and '50s. Born in New York in 1922, he played for Cavan from 1942 to 1953 and won seven Ulster senior championships. He was a member of the Cavan teams beaten in the All-Ireland finals of 1943 and '45, returned to the city of his birth for the 1947 All-Ireland final which was played at the New York Polo Grounds and collected his first All-Ireland title when Cavan beat Kerry. He won a second medal in 1948 when Cavan triumphed over Mayo and was the team captain when he collected his third medal in 1952. A Railway Cup medal-winner in 1947 and '50, Higgins later became a successful coach. He was honoured with an All-Time All-Star award in 1987 and inducted into the Texaco Hall of Fame in 1992.

EUGENE HUGHES (Monaghan)

Known to football followers all over the country as 'Nudie', Hughes is one of only five players to have won All-Star awards as a forward and a back. He won three All-Star awards in all, one as a right full-back in 1979 and two as a left full-forward in 1985 and '88. From Castleblayney, Hughes was an inspirational figure on the Monaghan team which won the Ulster championship in 1979. It was the first time in 41 years that the county had won the title. He added two more provincial championships in 1985 and '88, was a member of the team which won the National League in 1985, and won three Railway Cup medals with Ulster in 1980, '83 and '84.

MICKEY KEARINS (Sligo)

One of the greatest marksmen the game has ever seen, Mickey Kearins was football's most prolific scorer during a career with Sligo which lasted for an astonishing 17 seasons, from 1961 to 1977. During that period he played in the Railway Cup series no fewer than 13 times and won two medals with Connacht in 1967 and 1969. Born in Dromad in 1943, Kearins played minor football for Sligo in 1960 and was promoted to senior status a year later. He played in the Connacht finals of 1965 (they lost to Galway) and 1971 (losing to Galway again, this time after a replay). But in 1975 Kearins played some wonderful football to help Sligo win their first provincial title since 1928. He was chosen as an All-Star in 1971 and was selected on the Team of the Century for players who never won an All-Ireland medal.

JIMMY KEAVENEY (Dublin)

Born in 1945, Jimmy Keaveney was a dual player at minor and under-21 level with Dublin. He made his senior championship debut in 1964 and was a member of the Leinster championship-winning team of 1965. In 1972, with Dublin's fortunes at a low ebb, he retired from the inter-county game but continued playing at club level with St Vincent's. Coaxed out of retirement in 1974 by Kevin Heffernan, he became a crucial member of the Dublin teams which won the All-Ireland championship in 1974, 1976 and 1977. In the 1977 final he scored 2–6 as Dublin beat Armagh by 5–12 to 3–6. A great finisher, he was equally accurate from frees and general play. He won Footballer of the Year awards in 1976 and '77 and was the recipient of three All-Star awards in 1974, '77 and '78.

'Nudie' Hughes won All-Star awards as both a defender and attacker

DONAL KEENAN (Roscommon)

A winner of county championship medals in his native Roscommon with Elphin and in Dublin with UCD, Donal Keenan was left half-forward on the Roscommon teams which won the county's only All-Ireland senior championships in 1943 and '44. A respected rugby player for UCD, he concentrated on Gaelic football and became one of the era's most successful free-takers. He was on the Roscommon team which lost the 1946 All-Ireland final to Kerry after a replay. After his playing career ended he became involved in administration and coaching and served as president of the GAA from 1973 to 1976.

Robbie Kelleher won four
All-Star awards in the 1970s

JOHN KEENAN
(Galway)

From the famous Dunmore McHales club, Keenan was one of the most opportunist forwards in the game during the 1960s. He played in four All-Ireland senior finals, in 1963, '64, '65 and '66, winning the latter three in what was the greatest-ever era for Galway football. He also won a National League medal in 1965 and was at left full-forward on the Connacht teams which won the Railway Cup finals in 1967 and 1969. Although Keenan was at his best as a corner-forward, he was also effective in midfield. However, he is best remembered for his accuracy, even from the most acute of angles.

ROBBIE KELLEHER
(Dublin)

One of the key players in the Dublin team created by Kevin Heffernan which exploded on to the football scene in the 1970s, corner-back Kelleher was both intelligent and tenacious, crowning his career with three All-Ireland championship successes in 1974, '76 and '77. He also played in the finals of '75 and '78, won two National League medals in 1976 and '78 and was an All-Star in 1974, '75, '77 and '78.

PADDY KENNEDY
(Kerry)

For style, strength and fielding ability, there were few players to match Paddy Kennedy, the great Kerry midfielder of the 1940s. From Annascaul in the west of the county, Kennedy was a member of the Kerry team which won three All-Ireland senior championships in a row, in 1939, '40 and '41. In 1946 he added a fourth medal to his haul as captain when Kerry beat Roscommon by 2–8 to 0–10 in the All-Ireland final replay. He was a losing finalist in 1938, '44 and '47. Kennedy also won Railway Cup medals with Munster in 1946 and in 1948.

TIM KENNELLY
(Kerry)

A centre half-back of great stature, his strength and durability earned him the nickname 'The Horse'. Born in 1954 in Listowel, he won an All-Ireland under-21 medal with Kerry in 1973 and made his senior debut in 1974. Kennelly won five All-Ireland championships, in 1975, '78, '79, '80 and '81, and was chosen as man of the match in the finals of 1980 and '81. He was an All-Star in 1979 and '80, won four Railway Cup medals and captained Munster to success in 1982. His son Noel won an All-Ireland senior medal in 2000 and a second son,

Tadhg, is playing Australian Rules football.

JOE KEOHANE
(Kerry)

His reputation as one of the more durable full-backs ever to wear the No. 3 jersey conceals the fact that he was one of the finest footballers of his generation. In the catch-and-kick game he had few peers and earned enormous respect from team-mates and opponents. He was still a minor when he won the first of five All-Ireland senior championships in 1937, when Kerry beat Cavan in a replay. His other four championship successes came in 1939, '40, '41 and '46. He was a losing finalist in 1944, '47 and '48. In a career lasting from 1937 to 1948, he won ten Munster championships and was on the Munster teams which won the Railway Cup in 1941 and 1948. He retained a passionate interest in football after his playing days ended, and was a team selector during the glory years of Kerry football between 1975 and 1986.

JOE KERNAN
(Armagh)

Joe Kernan's career as a player and coach has spanned four decades. Hailing from Crossmaglen in South Armagh, he was a member of the Armagh team which reached the All-Ireland final in 1977 where they lost to Dublin. Strong and powerful, Kernan was a very versatile player who was comfortable in a variety of positions. He won three Ulster championships in 1977, '80 and '82, and was an All-Star in 1977 and '82. As a coach he guided Crossmaglen Rangers to three All-Ireland Club championships in 1997, '99 and 2000.

TOM LANGAN
(Mayo)

Full-forward has always been one of the glamour positions in Gaelic football, so selection at No. 14 in the Team of the Millennium underlines the status Langan earned during a glorious career. The high points came in 1951 and 1952 when his excellence was crucial to Mayo's double All-Ireland success. His goal-scoring ability, allied to his uncanny knack of placing himself at the heart of the action, made him a consistent scourge of rival defences. As well as two All-Ireland medals, he also won a Railway Cup medal with Connacht in 1951.

JOE LENNON
(Down)

His prowess was first noted when

Armagh's Joe Kernan: an outstanding player before excelling as a coach

Down's Mickey Linden, one of the longest-serving players in the history of football

he was a student at St Colman's College in Newry. After playing for Down minors, he made his senior debut in 1952. An influential member of the trail-blazing Down team which won the county's first All-Ireland senior championship in 1960, he won a second medal, again as a midfielder, when they retained the title a year later. In 1968 he was captain and left half-back on the team which beat Kerry in the All-Ireland final. Lennon also won three National League titles and four Railway Cup medals with Ulster. He coached at both schools and inter-county level and has written

several books on Gaelic football.

SEAMUS LEYDON (Galway)

A free-running, exciting component in the highly-successful Galway team which won three All-Ireland titles in a row, in 1964, '65 and '66, Leydon, from Dunmore, was a bravura performer, taking on rival defences with a blend of blistering speed and fancy footwork. An All-Ireland minor winner in 1960, his emergence as a senior star was a mere formality. As well as three All-Ireland

medals, in 1964, '65 and '66, he also added a National League medal (1965) and Railway Cup medals with Connacht in 1967 and 1969 to his collection. He was chosen for the All-Stars team in 1971.

MICKEY LINDEN (Down)

Standing 5' 10", Linden gave away inches to many opponents but his speed, allied to superb balance and a keen eye for goal, made him one of the great forwards of his generation. He was 28 when Down re-

emerged as a major force and won the Ulster and All-Ireland championships of 1991, beating Meath in the final by 1–16 to 1–14. Three years later Linden collected a second medal when Down beat Dublin in the final by 1–12 to 0–13. He won one All-Star award at right full-forward in 1994, and Railway Cup medals in 1992, '95 and '98.

EOIN LISTON (Kerry)

After winning an All-Ireland U-21 medal in 1977, he was promoted to senior status by the Kerry manager, Mick O'Dwyer, for the National League of 1977–78. His goal-scoring exploits earned him the nickname 'The Bomber'. At 6'5", Liston was the ideal target-man. He was also an inventive playmaker and created many chances for his colleagues. In 1978, Liston scored three goals in the All-Ireland final against Dublin as Kerry won by 5–11 to 0–9. He won further All-Ireland medals in '79, '80, '81, '84, '85 and '86, won four All-Star awards in 1980, '81, '82 and '84 and was in the Ireland squad for the International Rules tour to Australia in 1986.

SEAN LOWRY (Offaly)
See The Famous GAA Families

MICK LYONS (Meath)

From the Summerhill club, Mick Lyons was one of the great fullbacks. Powerfully-built, a good athlete with a natural football instinct, he was a major figure with Meath for many years. He first played for the county in 1979 and was on the team which won the Centenary Cup in 1984. He won his first Leinster senior championship medal in 1986, and in the following year he won his first All-Ireland medal when captaining Meath to victory over Cork in the final, adding another medal the following year. He also played in the finals of 1990 and '91, losing to Cork and Down respectively. His brother Pádraig played alongside him for many years. Mick won National League medals in 1988 and '90 and was an All-Star in 1984 and '86. He later served as a Meath selector.

PAUDIE LYNCH (Kerry)

From Beaufort, Paudie Lynch has the distinction of winning three All-Star awards during his distinguished career, all in different positions. He was honoured in 1974 at

Galway's Mattie McDonagh is the only Connacht man to have won four All-Ireland football titles

midfield, '78 at left half-back and '81 at left full-back. He was a member of the Kerry minor team which lost the All-Ireland final in 1970 and of the U21 and senior teams which lost the finals of 1972. In 1975 he won his first All-Ireland senior medal when Kerry beat Dublin and he added four more as Kerry dominated the championship from 1978 to '81. He also played in the finals of 1976 and '82. His brother Brendan won All-Ireland medals in 1969, '70 and '75.

JAMES AND DAN McCARTAN
(Down) See The Famous GAA Families

MATTIE McDONAGH (Galway)

From Ballygar, Mattie McDonagh is the sole Connacht footballer to hold four All-Ireland senior championship medals. He was only 19 years old in 1956 when he played at midfield on the team which beat Cork in the final. He had moved to centre half-forward by 1963 when Galway were beaten in the final by Dublin and held that position with

distinction in 1964, '65 and '66 when Galway won three All-Ireland finals in a row. He also won National League medals in 1957 and 1965 and was a member of the Connacht team which won the Railway Cup in 1958. He also holds the unique distinction of playing minor football for Galway and minor hurling for Roscommon in the same year, 1953, as his club was deemed to be in Roscommon for hurling purposes. He was honoured as Footballer of the Year in 1966.

BRIAN McENIFF (Donegal)

He first came to prominence as a member of the Donegal minor team from 1959 to 1961. He emigrated first to New York before moving to Canada. Returning home to help in the family business, he resumed his career with Donegal and was player-manager when the county won its first Ulster senior championship in 1972. He was an All-Star at right half-back in '72. Donegal regained the Ulster title in 1974. McEniff then turned to coaching

and guided Donegal to the Ulster title in 1983, '90 and '92. In '92 he was the brains behind the successful march to the county's first All-Ireland senior title. He won Railway Cup medals as a player in 1970 and 1971 and later managed the side to several interprovincial titles. He was appointed manager of the Irish International Rules team in 2000.

PACKIE McGARTY (Leitrim)

Mention Leitrim football and followers all over the country will name Packie McGarty. He never played in the All-Ireland series and never even won a Connacht championship, but he was one of the most respected and popular players of his generation. A forward of outstanding ability, with great balance, a burst of speed and uncanny accuracy, he played in four consecutive Connacht finals from 1957 to 1960 but was beaten on each occasion by Galway. In 1963, a McGarty-inspired Leitrim reached another provincial decider and again Galway stood in the way of an elusive title. McGarty won two Railway Cup medals in 1957 and '58 with Connacht and was a popular choice on the Team of the Century, for players who never won an All-Ireland title.

PETER McGINNITY (Fermanagh)

He never won a major honour with Fermanagh but earned a reputation as one of the outstanding players of the 1970s and 1980s. Tall and strong, he was a powerful presence in midfield from an early age. He was only 16 when he played U21 football for Fermanagh in 1970, helping them to the All-Ireland final where they lost to Cork. McGinnity was also on the team the following year when Fermanagh again lost in the final. He also reached an All-Ireland final at club level with Belfast team St John's but they lost the 1978 decider to Thomond College, Limerick. McGinnity played in one Ulster final in 1982 when Fermanagh lost to Armagh. He won Railway Cup medals with Ulster in 1979,

Peter McGinnity: a great player of the 1970s and 1980s

'80 (as captain), '83 (as captain) and '84, and was an All-Star in 1982.

FRANK McGUIGAN (Tyrone)

A member of the Tyrone minor team which was beaten in the All-Ireland final of 1972 by Cork, McGuigan was regarded as one of the most skilful footballers of all time. In that year he went on as a sub in the Ulster senior final which Tyrone lost to Donegal. A year later, at the age of 19, he was Tyrone's captain when they won the Ulster championship, beating Down in the final by 3–13 to 1–11. Injury and a spell living in the United States curbed his career, but he was at full-forward on the Tyrone team in 1984 which won the Ulster title, beating Armagh by 0–15 to 1–7 with McGuigan scoring 0–12. He was selected as an All-Star in 1984.

MARTIN McHUGH (Donegal)

Known as 'The Wee Man' because of his slight stature, Martin McHugh was one of the most talented footballers of the 1980s and 1990s. He made his senior debut for Donegal in 1980 and embarked on a remarkable career in which he became an attacker of immense substance and style. He won an All-Ireland U21 medal in 1982 and ten years later was a major influence on the Donegal team which won the All-Ireland senior championship for the first time. Honoured as an All-Star in 1983 and '92, he was Texaco Footballer of the Year in '92 and coached Cavan to the Ulster championship in 1997. His brother James was a team-mate on the successful Donegal team of 1992.

JIM McKEEVER (Derry)

When the first national Sportstar of the Year awards were introduced in 1958, sponsored by Caltex and

Donegal's 'Wee Man', Martin McHugh, won an All-Ireland medal in 1992

later Texaco, Jim McKeever was the unanimous choice as Footballer of the Year. He had been Derry's captain that year in the county's first appearance in an All-Ireland final. They lost to Dublin by 1–9 to 2–12 but the defeat, however, did not tarnish the reputation of the multi-talented midfielder. Born in 1931, McKeever played at minor level for both Antrim and Derry but played all his senior football with the latter in a career which extended from 1948 to 1962. Derry reached the Ulster finals of 1955 and 1957 but did not achieve the big breakthrough until 1958 when they beat Down in the final. McKeever won two Railway Cup medals with Ulster in 1956 and 1960. He became a highly-respected coach and was involved with Derry teams at all levels, including senior. In 1984 he was selected at midfield on the Team of the Century, which was made up of players who never won an All-Ireland medal.

JOHN McKNIGHT (Armagh)

Playing at left corner-back on the Armagh team which won the All-Ireland minor championship in 1949 by beating Kerry in the final, John McKnight never won a senior All-Ireland title, which was a most unfortunate fate for such an outstanding talent. The closest he managed to come to achieving that honour was when Armagh reached the final in 1953: however, they then went on to lose by four points at the hands of Kerry with a scoreline of 1–6 to 0–13. As regards other awards, McKnight won one Railway Cup medal with Ulster in 1956. While a law student at University College, Dublin, he also won two Sigerson Cup medals, in 1953 and 1955, on the latter occasion playing alongside his brother Felix. John was chosen for the Team of the Century for players who never won an All-Ireland senior medal.

Bobby Miller (Laois) excelled as both a player and a coach

years' outstanding service, mainly in midfield. Laois failed to make the championship breakthrough but Miller's consistent excellence brought him nationwide acclaim. He won a Railway Cup medal with Leinster in 1974. On his retirement he took up management and enjoyed phenomenal success with Éire Óg, Carlow, whom he guided to three Leinster titles in 1993, '94 and '96.

PADDY MOCLAIR (Mayo)

One of the great characters of Gaelic Football, Paddy Moclair was a member of the Mayo team which won six National League titles in succession from 1934 to 1939, captaining the team to the last two victories. A full-forward, he is regarded as the first to play a roving game and influenced generations of players who followed. He was a member of the Mayo team beaten in the All-Ireland final of 1932 by Kerry. Four years later Moclair and Mayo

won the county's first All-Ireland senior championship by beating Laois 4–11 to 0–5 in the final. He won four Railway Cup medals with Connacht in 1934, '36, '37 and '38. In 1982 he was honoured as an All-Time All-Star.

BILLY MORGAN (Cork)

From the Nemo Rangers club in Cork city, Billy Morgan was the first goalkeeper to be chosen as Footballer of the Year when he received the honour in 1973. That was the year in which he won his only All-Ireland senior championship medal when he captained Cork to success, beating Galway in the final. Morgan played in the All-Ireland under-21 final of 1965 which Cork lost to Kildare. He became senior goalkeeper the following year and was on the team beaten by Meath in the All-Ireland final of 1967. He won two All-Ireland club championships in 1973

TONY McMANUS (Roscommon)

He never won an All-Ireland senior championship, but Tony McManus was regarded as one of the greatest forwards of his generation. With his club, Clann na nGael, he played in five All-Ireland finals in the 1980s and '90s but never won a title. He won three Sigerson Cup medals with UCD and six Connacht senior championships with Roscommon, in 1977, '78, '79, '80, '90 and '91. He played in the All-Ireland final of 1980 when Roscommon lost to Kerry. A winner of a National League medal in 1979, he was an All-Star in 1989. His brother Eamon shared in most of his triumphs with Roscommon.

TONY McTAGUE (Offaly)

Central to Offaly's arrival as an All-Ireland football power in the early

1970s was their flame-haired marksman Tony McTague. His uncanny accuracy from frees and from play was a highlight of their All-Ireland senior championship successes in 1971 when they beat Galway by 1–14 to 2–8 and in 1972 when they beat Kerry in a replay 1–19 to 0–13. McTague was the centre-forward on the Offaly minor team which won the All-Ireland championship in 1964 and played senior football with the county for 11 years, winning four Leinster championships. He was selected as an All-Star in 1971 and '72.

BOBBY MILLER (Laois)

Born in Timahoe, he showed promise from an early age and by the time he was 18 years old had won two Leinster minor championship medals with Laois, in 1966 and 1967. Two years later he won a Leinster U21 medal and was promoted to the senior team, where he gave many

Goalkeeper, manager, motivator – Billy Morgan

and '79, won four Railway Cup medals with Munster in 1972, '75, '77 and '78 and was the All-Star goalkeeper in 1973. Morgan coached and managed Cork, guiding them to the All-Ireland championship in 1989 and '90. They also reached the finals of 1987, '88 and '93 and won a National League in 1989.

SÉAMUS MOYNIHAN (Kerry)

Moynihan was still only 19 when he was called into the Kerry senior team in 1992 and received a baptism of fire when they were shocked in the Munster final against Clare. Moynihan had been an outstanding minor in the team which reached the 1990 All-Ireland final, losing to Meath. He won his first Munster senior championship medal in 1996 and his reputation was growing quickly. By 1997 his influence was huge and he won his first All-Ireland medal when Kerry beat Mayo in the final. It was in 2000, however, that he proved his true greatness. Used as an emergency full-back – he is more suited to the half-back line – Moynihan gave a series of stunning displays as Kerry won the championship. That year he was chosen as Footballer of the Year and was also named the GAA Writers' Player of the Year.

Séamus Moynihan of Kerry was Footballer of the Year in 2000

EUGENE MULLIGAN (Offaly)

During Offaly's emergence as a major footballing power in the 1960s and '70s, Eugene Mulligan was a major player. A wing-back of great elegance, he was on the minor team which won the 1964 All-Ireland championship and played in the All-Ireland final of 1969 when Offaly lost to Kerry. In 1971 he was a major inspiration behind Offaly's first All-Ireland senior success when they beat Galway by 1–14 to 2–8 in the final: voted Footballer of the Year that season, he was an automatic choice at right

half-back on the first All-Star team. He added a second All-Ireland medal in 1972 when Offaly beat Kerry in the final.

BRIAN MULLINS (Dublin)

Only 19 years old when Kevin Heffernan made him a central figure in the Dublin team of 1974, the tall, blonde-haired Mullins would become one of the best-known players of all time. A spectacular fielder with superb passing ability, he won All-Ireland championships in 1974, '76, '77 and '83. He fought back after being seriously injured in a car accident to regain his form, winning All-Star awards in 1976 and '77. Mullins, whose determination and power were an inspiration to his colleagues, also won an

All-Ireland club championship with St Vincent's in 1976. Later he was joint manager of Dublin and also managed Derry, winning an Ulster championship in 1998.

BRIAN MURPHY (Cork)
See The Great Dual Players

SEAN MURPHY (Kerry)

One of the most celebrated players of the 1950s, Sean Murphy was chosen as Footballer of the Year in 1959. He enjoyed early success when, as a teenager, he had won All-Ireland Junior (1949) and Minor (1950) championships, and collected his first All-Ireland senior medal in 1953 when Kerry beat Armagh by 0–13 to 1–6. By 1955 he was a regular at right half-back

and won his second championship when Kerry beat Dublin in the final. But it was his performance in the 1959 All-Ireland final which earned him the greatest accolades. He was outstanding as Kerry beat Galway by 3–7 to 1–4. Murphy also played in the finals of 1954 and 1960 when Kerry were beaten by Meath and Down respectively.

TOMMY MURPHY (Laois)

Known as 'The Boy Wonder', Murphy was born in Graiguecullen, Co. Laois, in 1921 and at the age of 16 made his debut with Laois in a season in which they won the first of three successive Leinster championships. A natural footballer who brought great style to the game, he became popular with supporters all

Dublin's Brian Mullins is pursued by Offaly's Richie Connor in a Leinster championship clash

Despite the fact that Wicklow never seriously challenged for major honours, Kevin O'Brien was recognised as one of the country's most skilful and inventive footballers during the 1980s and '90s. He never contested a major inter-county final other than a 'B' championship, but did win an All-Ireland club championship with Baltinglass in 1990. He won Railway Cup medals with Leinster in 1987 and 1996 and was a member of the International Rules panel in 1990. He was the first Wicklow player to be selected as an All-Star when chosen at full-forward in 1990.

PADDY O'BRIEN (Meath)

Chosen at full-back on the Team of the Century in 1984, Paddy O'Brien was one of football's most powerful figures during the late 1940s and early 1950s. Regarded as being among the finest fielders in the game, O'Brien was a star of the Meath team which won the county's first All-Ireland championship in 1949, beating Cavan by 1–10 to 1–6. He was still wearing the No. 3 jersey when Meath won a second title in 1954. O'Brien won three other Leinster championships in 1947, '51 and '52, was a National League winner in 1951 and collected three Railway Cup medals with Leinster in 1953, '54 and '55, on the latter occasion as captain.

over the country and in the USA, where he toured in 1938. He won Railway Cup medals with Leinster in 1940 and '45, and in 1946 his fourth Leinster championship medal, when Laois beat Kildare by 0–11 to 1–6, Murphy scoring eight of the Laois points. Murphy, who died in 1985, was chosen for the Team of the Millennium at midfield.

JIMMY MURRAY (Roscommon)
See The Legends of Gaelic Football

CHARLIE NELLIGAN (Kerry)

From Castleisland in North Kerry, Charlie Nelligan won an All-Ireland minor championship in 1975 and was a member of the under-21 team which won three All-Ireland titles in a row between 1975 and 1977. He became Kerry's regular goal-keeper at senior level in 1978, taking over from Paud O'Mahony, and went on to win seven All-Ireland senior championships in 1978, '79, '80, '81, '84, '85 and '86. He also won an All-Ireland club championship with Castleisland Desmonds in 1985. An All-Star in 1980 and '86, Nelligan also played soccer for Home Farm.

MARTIN NEWELL (Galway)

At left half-back on the great Galway team which won three successive All-Ireland finals in 1964, '65 and '66, Martin Newell was a supreme footballing stylist who brought a high level of efficiency to all aspects of his game. He enjoyed a particularly outstanding season in 1965 when he won All-Ireland and National League medals and crowned

the double triumph by being chosen as Footballer of the Year. As well as always carrying out his defensive duties with tidiness and efficiency Newell was also a very accurate kicker of the ball, and launched many attacks with carefully-placed deliveries to his forward colleagues. A class performer in every way.

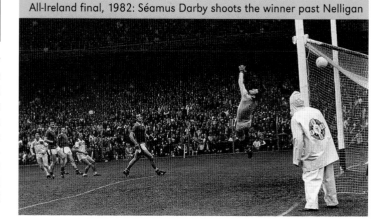
All-Ireland final, 1982: Séamus Darby shoots the winner past Nelligan

Martin O'Connell celebrates Meath's All-Ireland win in 1996

MARTIN O'CONNELL
(Meath)

The only player from the modern era to be selected on the Team of the Millennium, the athletic O'Connell made his debut as a senior with Meath in 1982 and was still a major figure when they won the All-Ireland championship in 1996. It was O'Connell's third All-Ireland medal, having played at left half-back on the successful teams of 1987 and '88. Although he did have a brief stint as a forward with Meath, it was as a wing-back that he carved out a reputation as one of the finest footballers of his generation. Deceptively quick, he always looked extremely composed even on the biggest occasions. A winner of four All-Star awards – in 1988, '90, '91 and '96 – he was also cho-

SÉAN O'CONNELL (Derry)

Throughout the late 1960s and early 1970s, Séan O'Connell was hailed as one of the most exciting forwards in Gaelic Football. Playing at either full-forward or left full-forward, he was the tormentor of defenders throughout Ulster as Derry won the Ulster championship in 1970, '75 and '76. While they never won the All-Ireland championship during his career, O'Connell's reputation was unblemished. He won four Railway Cup medals with Ulster in 1966, '68, '70 and '71. O'Connell was named right half-forward on the Team of the Century for players who never won an All-Ireland medal.

MICK O'DWYER (Kerry)
See The Legends of Gaelic Football

DAN O'KEEFFE (Kerry)

Although born in Cork, Dan O'Keeffe (known as Danno) played all his football for Kerry and was chosen as goalkeeper on the football Team of the Millennium in 1999. He won an All-Ireland junior championship with Kerry in 1930 and that proved to be the springboard for an extraordinary career. He won seven All-Ireland senior championships in 1931, '32, '37, '39, '40, '41 and '46, and was a losing finalist on three occasions in 1938, '44 and '47. Between 1931 and 1948 he won 15 Munster senior championships. He was captain of the Munster team which won the Railway Cup in 1941 and added a second inter-provincial title in 1948.

JOHN O'KEEFFE (Kerry)

One of the most elegant footballers of all time, John O'Keeffe was an outstanding midfielder and centre-back before being switched to full back. Born in Tralee in 1951, he was a member of the Kerry panel which won the All-Ireland championship in 1969. He won six championships as a member of the starting 15, in 1970, '75, '78, '79, '80 and '81, and played in three other finals, in '72, '76 and '82. O'Keeffe won six National League medals and five All-Star awards, in 1973, '75, '76, '78 and '79, and collected seven Railway Cup medals, six with Munster and one with the Combined Universities in 1973. He won two All-Ireland club championships, with UCD in 1974 and with Austin Stacks of Tralee in 1977, when he was captain.

SEAN O'KENNEDY (Wexford)

From New Ross, Sean O'Kennedy holds the unique distinction in Gaelic football of being the only man to captain a team to three consecutive All-Ireland victories. He was centre half-forward on the Wexford team which won the championship in 1915, '16 and '17 but missed the fourth victory in 1918. His brother Gus was a member of all four teams. Sean was regarded as a

Rivals John O'Keeffe and Jimmy Keaveney fought many duels in the 1970s

sen as Footballer of the Year in 1996 after a series of exceptional performances at left corner-back, and collected three National League medals in 1988, '90 and '94.

MICK O'CONNELL (Kerry)
See The Legends of Gaelic Football

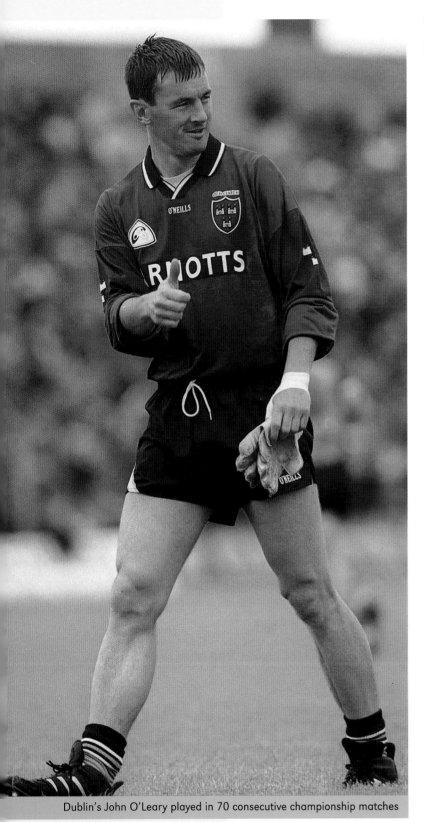

Dublin's John O'Leary played in 70 consecutive championship matches

natural leader who also took a role in preparing the team. Renowned for the length of his fisted pass, O'Kennedy was also one of the pioneers of the hand pass.

JOHN O'LEARY (Dublin)

There was a 12-year break between his two All-Ireland senior successes, but in the interval John O'Leary became one of the most celebrated footballers in the game. A goalkeeper of outstanding athleticism, he won an All-Ireland minor championship in 1979 when Dublin beat Kerry and made his senior championship debut in the Leinster final of 1980, a surprise late addition to the team to play Offaly. Although Dublin lost, O'Leary had begun a 17-year career which would bring him All-Ireland glory in 1983, when Dublin beat Galway, and in 1995, when he led them to victory against Tyrone. He won three Railway Cup medals with Leinster in 1985, '86, '87 and three National League medals in 1987, '91 and '93. He was an All-Star in 1984, '85, '93, '94 and '95, and represented Ireland in the International Rules series in 1984, '86 and '87 (as captain).

BOB O'MALLEY (Meath)

Known variously as Bob, Bobby and Robbie, he was the outstanding corner-back of the 1980s. Born in 1965, he made his senior championship debut for Meath in 1983. He played on the team which won the special Centenary Cup competition in 1984 and won his first Leinster senior championship medal in 1986. In 1987 he was at right corner-back on the team that beat Cork in the All-Ireland final and they repeated the feat the following year. O'Malley's contribution was recognised when he was named Footballer of the Year in 1988. An All-Star in 1987, '88 and '90 and led Ireland's team in the International Rules series in Australia in 1990.

GERRY O'MALLEY (Roscommon)

In a career which spanned three decades, from the late 1940s to the early 1960s, Gerry O'Malley became one of the most popular figures in football. He won four Connacht championships with Roscommon in 1952, '53, '61 and '62, but never an All-Ireland championship. At 33, he was an inspiring captain when Roscommon reached the 1962 final but his dreams were dashed as Kerry won by 1–12 to 1–6. He won Railway Cup medals with Connacht in 1951, '57 and '58. A talented hurler, he played with Roscommon in that code for many years.

SEAN O'NEILL (Down)
See The Legends of Gaelic Football

GERRY O'REILLY (Wicklow)

It is a measure of the talent of Gerry O'Reilly that he played in a county which achieved no major success but carved out a personal reputation as one of the outstanding wingbacks to have played the game. During his career with Wicklow in the 1950s he never even got the opportunity to play in a Leinster final. With his province Leinster, however, he was able to compete with the best footballers and won three Railway Cup medals in succession in 1952, '53 and '54. O'Reilly was chosen on the Team of the Century for players who never won a senior All-Ireland medal.

JOHN JOE O'REILLY (Cavan)
See The Legends of Gaelic Football

COLM O'ROURKE (Meath)

From the Skryne club in Meath, Colm O'Rourke played senior football for Meath when only 19 years old in 1976. Despite the county's lack of success over the next ten years, O'Rourke built up a reputation as one of the most talented forwards in the game. He won his first Leinster senior championship in 1986 and was a key figure on the team which won the All-Ireland championships of 1987 and '88.

Colm O'Rourke is chaired off the pitch after another Meath success

JEROME O'SHEA (Kerry)

Popularly known as 'Aeroplane' because of the height he could jump and his fielding ability, O'Shea is regarded as one of the greatest midfielders of all time. He was on the Killarney team which represented Kerry in the All-Ireland championship in 1913 when they beat Wexford's Raparees by 2–2 to 0–3. A year later they retained the title by beating another Wexford team, Blues and Whites, by 2–3 to 0–6. He also played on the losing team in the 1915 final.

GER POWER (Kerry)

His father Jackie won All-Ireland hurling medals with Limerick but it was as a Gaelic footballer of outstanding athleticism that Ger Power made his mark on the nation's sporting history. He won eight All-Ireland senior championships with Kerry between 1975 and 1986 and was captain of the team which won the title in 1980. A player of great versatility, he played at wing-back and wing-forward. Power, who was born

in 1952 in Limerick, won an All-Ireland under-21 medal in 1973 and collected four National League medals and six Railway cup medals. He was an All-Star in 1975 (left half-back), '76 (left half back), '78 (right half-forward), '79 (right half-forward), '80 (right half-forward) and '86 (left full-forward).

PADDY PRENDERGAST (Mayo)

In the development of Mayo as a major force in the 1950s, the arrival of Paddy Prendergast as a full-back of great stature was a critical element. Traditionally the full-back's role was to protect the edge of the square but, while Prendergast was a powerful man and a great fielder, he was also extremely athletic and regularly moved away from his position to cover roving forwards. He played at full-back on the team which lost the 1948 All-Ireland final but won two championships in 1950 and '51. Prendergast also won National League medals in 1949 and '54 and a Railway Cup medal with Connacht in 1951.

SEÁN PURCELL (Galway)
See The Legends of Gaelic Football

He won National League titles in 1986, '90 and '94 and was honoured as an All-Star in 1983, '88 and '91. He was chosen as Footballer of the Year in 1991. He managed the successful Ireland team in the International Rules series in Australia in 1999.

PÁIDÍ Ó SÉ (Kerry)

The joint record holder with eight All-Ireland medals, Páidí Ó Sé had an outstanding career in the 1970s and 1980s. Born in 1955 in West Kerry, he played minor football for Kerry for four years before making

his senior debut in 1974. By 1987 he had won 11 Munster championships. He collected his All-Ireland senior haul in 1975, '78, '79, '80, '81, '84, '85 and '86. (His teammates Denis 'Ogie' Moran, Pat Spillane, Ger Power and Mike Sheehy share the record). In all his finals he conceded just one point to his immediate opponent (to David Hickey of Dublin in 1976). He won five successive All-Star awards from 1981 to '85. He is also a highly-successful coach and was team manager when Kerry won the All-Ireland championships of 1997 and 2000.

JACK O'SHEA (Kerry)
See The Legends of Gaelic Football

Páidí Ó Sé: star footballer who became a top manager

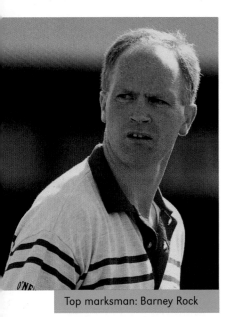

Top marksman: Barney Rock

BARNEY ROCK
(Dublin)

Scorer of one of the most famous goals in an All-Ireland final when he lobbed Galway goalkeeper Pádraig Coyne from 50 yards in the 1983 final, Barney Rock was one of the great marksmen of the modern era. Born in 1961, he was a member of the Dublin team which won the All-Ireland minor championship in 1979 and made his senior debut later that year. He played in three All-Ireland finals, winning in 1983 and losing the next two to Kerry. A Railway Cup medal-winner with Leinster, he won National League medals in 1987 and 1991 and was an All-Star in 1983 and '84. He became very involved in coaching when his playing days were over and was Westmeath manager for three years.

MIKE SHEEHY (Kerry)
See The Legends of Gaelic Football

PAT SPILLANE (Kerry)
See The Famous GAA Families

BRIAN STAFFORD
(Meath)

Because of his quiet nature Stafford was a reluctant football star, but under the guidance of Sean Boylan he became a scoring machine for Meath over a nine-year period. From play and from frees he had uncanny accuracy and was central to Meath's successes. He won All-Ireland championships in 1987 and '88 when they beat Cork on both occasions, scoring eight of Meath's 13 points in the final replay of '88. Stafford was also on the teams that lost the finals of '90 and '91. He won National League medals in 1988, 1990 and '94 and was an All-Star in 1987, '88 and '91. He was chosen as Footballer of the Year in 1987.

LARRY STANLEY
(Kildare and Dublin)

One of the great all-round athletes of the early part of the 20th century, Larry Stanley holds the distinction of winning All-Ireland senior championships with two counties and representing Ireland in the Olympic Games. In 1919 Stanley captained the Caragh club which represented Kildare to beat a Galway selection in the All-Ireland final by 2–5 to 0–1. By 1923 he had moved to Dublin and won an All-Ireland with them when they beat Kerry by 1–5 to 1–3. In 1926 he was back with Kildare but they were beaten in the final. He represented Ireland in the high jump at the 1924 Olympic Games in Paris.

FRANK STOCKWELL
(Galway)

Although he became famous through his partnership with Seán Purcell on the Galway teams of the 1950s – they became known as 'The Terrible Twins' – Frankie Stockwell was a brilliant individual footballer. His score of 2–5 in the All-Ireland final of 1956 when Galway beat Cork by 2–13 to 3–7 stands as a record for a 60-minute final. He was also on the Galway team which lost the 1959 All-Ireland final, and won a total of six Connacht senior championships and a National League medal in 1957. He won Railway Cup medals with Connacht in 1957 and '58.

NOEL TIERNEY
(Galway)

Noel Tierney first tasted All-Ireland championship success when he was full-back on the Galway team which won the minor title in 1960, beating Cork in the final. He won his first Connacht senior title in 1963 but Galway lost in the All-Ireland final to Dublin. Over the next three championships Tierney earned a status as one of the greatest full-backs in the history of the game when he played a major part in Galway's three-in-a-row All-Ireland triumphs. He won a National League medal in 1965. A Railway Cup winner with Connacht in 1967 and '69, he was chosen as Footballer of the Year in 1964.

TONY TIGHE
(Cavan)

Born in 1927, Tony Tighe was only 18 years old when he played in his first All-Ireland senior final in 1945. He was right half-forward on the team which travelled to the New York Polo Grounds for the All-Ireland final in which Cavan beat Kerry by 2–11 to 2–7. Tighe was in the same position a year later when Cavan retained their title, beating Mayo in the final by one point, 4–5 to 4–4. By 1952 he had moved to full-forward and won his third All-Ireland medal – one of only four Cavan players to do so – when they beat Meath in the final after a replay, 0–9 to 0–5. He won a Railway Cup medal with Ulster in 1950.

ANTHONY TOHILL
(Derry)

From the Swatragh club, Anthony Tohill was one of the young Irish players recruited by the professional Australian Rules clubs in the early 1990s. A member of the Derry team which won the All-Ireland minor title in 1989, in early 1992 he returned to Ireland and was on the Derry senior team which won the National League. A year later he won his first Ulster senior championship and was an influential figure in midfield as the Derry team won the county's first All-Ireland senior football championship. He won All-Star awards in 1992, '93, '95 and 2000. He won a second Ulster championship in 1998 and collected three more league medals in 1995, 1996 and 2000.

LARRY TOMPKINS
(Kildare and Cork)

Catapulted on to the national stage aged 16 when selected to play for the Kildare seniors in 1979, he played minor and under-21 football in the same year. A brilliantly-gifted footballer, he emigrated to New York and, following a dispute with his native county in the mid-1980s, returned to Ireland to play for Cork. He was a member of the team which lost two All-Ireland finals in 1987 and '88. In 1989 he was centre half-forward on the Cork team which beat Mayo in the All-Ireland final and was captain when they retained the title in 1990. He won a Railway cup medal with Leinster in 1985. An All-Star in 1987, '88 and '89, he coached Cork to win the Munster championship in 1999: they were beaten in the All-Ireland final by Meath.

SEÁN WALSH
(Kerry)

One of the great fielders of the ball, soaring to great heights, Seán Walsh played a huge part in Kerry's successful run in the 1970s and '80s. Having won an All-Ireland minor championship medal in 1975, he went on to collect three All-Ireland under-21 championships in 1975, 1976 and 1977, and came on as a replacement in the 1976 All-Ireland final in which Kerry were beaten by Dublin. By 1978

Larry Tompkins gave outstanding service to both Kildare and Cork

he had formed a midfield partnership with Jack O'Shea which would become the best double-act in the game. They won four championships together between 1978 and '81. In 1984 Walsh was at full-back as Kerry beat Dublin in the final and he collected two more titles as a full-back in 1985 and '86. An All-Star award-winner in 1979 and '81, he also played at full-forward for Kerry. When his playing days ended he filled a prominent role as a team selector.

STEPHEN WHITE (Louth)

One of the outstanding half-backs of the 1950s, Stephen White won the first of his three Leinster championships in 1948 when Louth beat Wexford in the provincial final. White went on to enjoy a highly-successful footballing career which reached its climax when he appeared at left half-back on the team which won the All-Ireland championship in 1957, Louth overcoming Cork by 1–9 to 1–7 in the final. White was a member of the Leinster team which memorably won four Railway Cups in succession between 1952 and 1955. He also had ample opportunity to display his positional versatility when lining out as a forward in 1952 and '53, as a midfielder in 1954 and as a defender in 1955. Stephen White was selected as a member of the Team of the Century in 1984. His son Stefan played for Louth and Monaghan.

HURLERS

Hurling fans are convinced that their sport is the best field game in the world, combining skill and subtlety with power, passion and athleticism to provide a fascinating mix which has thrilled a nation. Although hurling had always lacked an international dimension, there can be no doubt that many of its finest exponents would have prospered on the biggest stage if the opportunity had arisen.

Hurling has produced a long and deep river of outstanding talent. These are the men who, through their skills and personalities, have left an indelible imprint on the ancient game.

CIARAN BARR (Antrim & Dublin)

A big, powerful forward who was very effective under the dropping ball, he had excellent vision and positioning skills. After progressing through the minor and U21 ranks with Antrim, he was promoted to the senior side in 1984 and, four years later, achieved the major distinction of becoming the first Antrim hurler to win an All-Star award. In 1989, he captained Antrim to a memorable All-Ireland semi-final win over Offaly. It was the first time that Antrim had qualified for the All-Ireland final since 1943. They lost the final to Tipperary but it was still a great year for Barr and Antrim. A few years later he transferred to Dublin, and gave them outstanding service too.

JIMMY BARRY-MURPHY (Cork)
See The Great Dual Players

RICHIE & PHIL BENNIS (Limerick)
See The Famous GAA Families

MICK BERMINGHAM (Dublin)

He is the only Dublin player to have won five Railway Cup titles with Leinster, which is proven testament to his outstanding attacking talent. He won his first in 1964 and added

Ciarán Carey hoists the Munster Championship trophy after Limerick's success in 1996

four more in 1965, '71, '72 and '73. He also holds the distinction of being the first Dublin hurler to win an All-Star award, having been honoured in 1971, the inaugural year of the scheme. Dublin's failure to make an impression on the championship meant Bermingham's opportunities to shine on the big summer days were restricted but that in no way takes away from the fact that he was a truly outstanding forward.

JIMMY BROHAN (Cork)

His career coincided with an uncharacteristically barren decade for Cork hurling but that in no way diminished his status as an outstanding corner-back. He was a sub on the Cork team which won the 1954 All-Ireland senior final and went on to play until 1964, a period in which Cork failed to win another All-Ireland title and picked up just one Munster title, in 1956. Although Cork were in a rare depression, Jimmy continued to excel in difficult circumstances. He also showed his talents with Munster, with whom he won five Railway Cup medals in 1957, '59, '60, '61 and '63. Brohan, from Blackrock, later served as a Cork selector. He combined skill, determination and intelligence to make him a defender of unquestionable quality.

JOHN CALLINAN ✕ (Clare)

He made his senior inter-county debut at the age of 18 in 1973 and went on to enjoy a 14-year career which brought him two National League titles in 1977 and 1978. However, he never achieved the great ambition of winning a Munster or All-Ireland title, despite reaching Munster finals in 1974, '77, '78, '81 and '86. A strong-running, intelligent wing-forward/midfielder, Clarecastle clubman Callinan won Railway Cup medals with Munster in 1976, '78 and '81. He was unlucky never to have won championship honours, but his qualities were recognised by the All-Star selectors, who chose him at right half-forward in 1979 and 1981.

DJ CAREY (Kilkenny)
See The Legends of Hurling

CIARÁN CAREY ✕ (Limerick)

He made his senior debut with Limerick in 1988 at the age of 18 and went on to become one of the county's true craftsmen. Carey won a National League medal in 1992, when Limerick beat Tipperary in the final. It was to be the start of a very productive period for Limerick, who won Munster titles in 1994 and 1996. Equally adept in attack, midfield or defence, Carey's most memorable performances were at centre-back, where he combined style and skill with an unrelenting desire to win. His winning point against Clare in the 1996 Munster semi-final, which came after a dashing run upfield, is regarded as one of the best scores of all time.

TED CARROLL ✕ (Kilkenny)

Winner of an All-Ireland Colleges medal with St Kieran's, Kilkenny, in 1957, he played in two losing All-Ireland minor finals with Kilkenny in 1956 and 1957. Carroll, a defender of great composure, progressed to the Kilkenny senior team in 1961 and went on to win three All-Ireland senior medals, in 1963 as a centre-back and as a right corner-back in 1967 and 1969. He also played on three Kilkenny teams which lost All-Ireland finals in 1964, '66 and '71 (sub). He won a National League medal in 1966 and crowned his appearances with Leinster in 1965 when he won a Railway Cup medal. But Carroll's best year was 1969, when a string of outstanding performances in Kilkenny's march to All-Ireland glory earned him the Hurler of the Year Award.

TOM CASHMAN (Cork)
See The Famous GAA Families

TOM CHEASTY ✕ (Waterford)

Born in Ballyduff in 1934, he showed early signs of the brilliance which would later make him an outstanding centre-forward. He was chosen for the Waterford minor team as a 16-year-old and promoted to the senior team at the age of 20 in most unusual circumstances. He went to watch Waterford play Kilkenny in a National League game but was pressed into action due to some withdrawals from the squad. It was the start of a magnificent career, during which he won one All-Ireland medal in 1959, four Railway Cup medals with Munster in 1958, '60, '61 and '63, and three Munster titles in 1957, '59 and '63.

IGGY CLARKE ✕ (Galway)

A wing-back/midfielder of great artistry and skill, Clarke was an influential presence in Galway's re-emergence from the wilderness in the mid-'70s. He won an All-Ireland U21 medal in 1972 and progressed quickly to the senior team at a time when Galway were making rapid progress. They finally made the breakthrough in 1975 when they won the National League title, their first success since 1951. In 1980 Galway won the All-Ireland title for the first time since 1923, and although Clarke missed the game through injury he was chosen for that year's All-Star team. He won three other All-Star awards in 1975, '78, '79 and three Railway Cup medals with Connacht in 1980, '82 and '83.

SEAMUS CLEERE ✕ (Kilkenny)

A highly-effective wing-back who combined style with determination and energy, in 1963 he became the first Kilkenny man to win the Hurler of the Year award. It was the culmination of a brilliant season for the Bennettsbridge man, who had earlier captained Kilkenny to victory over Waterford (4-17 to 6–8) in a remarkably high-scoring All-Ireland final. Cleere won two more All-Ireland medals in 1967 and 1969 (as a sub) and two National League titles in 1962 and 1966. He also won three Railway Cup medals with Leinster in 1964, '65 and '67. He captained the Leinster side in 1964. He retired in 1969, having earlier missed the All-Ireland final victory over Cork due to a knee injury.

SEAN CLOHOSEY ✕ (Kilkenny)

There were no skills or requirements in hurling which he failed to master. A wonderful craftsman, he delighted hurling fans for over a decade in the 1950s and 1960s, during which he won two All-Ireland senior titles. He won the first as a left full-forward in 1957 when Kilkenny beat Waterford and the second as a midfielder when they again beat Waterford in 1963. He captained the Kilkenny team to Leinster title success in 1959 but they lost the All-Ireland final to Waterford. Clohosey also won a National League medal in 1962.

Kilkenny captain Brian Cody raises the McCarthy Cup after 1982's All-Ireland final.

BRIAN CODY (Kilkenny)

Cody was a brilliant colleges player at the famous St Kieran's hurling nursery in Kilkenny, and made his first impression at inter-county level in 1972 as a centre-back on the minor team which won the All-Ireland championship. He won All-Ireland U21 and senior medals in 1974 and 1975 (he was a sub on the senior team in 1974) and went on to collect two more All-Ireland senior titles in 1982 and '83. He captained Kilkenny to their 1982 triumph. He won National League medals in 1976, '82 and '83 and was chosen on the All-Stars teams in 1975 (left corner-back) and 1982 (full-back). Cody won All-Ireland club medals with James Stephens in 1976 and 1982. He took over as Kilkenny manager in 1998, and guided them to All-Ireland glory two years later.

MICHAEL COLEMAN (Galway)

Having won an All-Ireland U21 medal in 1983, he made his first big impression at senior level when he was plucked from relative obscurity to play in the 1988 All-Ireland final. A big, powerful man with endless resolve, he was a major driving force behind Galway in the late 1980s and through most of the 1990s, and although he won only one All-Ireland senior medal (1988), he left a lasting impression on hurling. He won National League medals in 1987, '89 and '96 and Railway Cup medals in 1989, '91 and '94. Coleman, equally effective at midfield or centre-back, won All-Stars awards in 1989, '90 and '95. His older brother, Mattie, was a regular on the Galway football team for several years in the 1980s.

JOHN CONNOLLY (Galway)
See The Legends of Hurling

JOE COONEY (Galway)
See The Famous GAA Families

BRIAN CORCORAN (Cork)
See The Great Dual Players

EUGENE 'EUDIE' COUGHLAN (Cork)

Coughlan, born in 1900, enriched the hurling scene for many years. He was blessed with a high skill level and his attacking prowess earned him country-wide respect. He was especially revered in his native Cork, with whom he won four All-Ireland senior titles in 1926, '28, '29 and '31, being captain on the last occasion. He won National League medals in 1926, the inaugural year of the competition, and in 1930. Coughlan was a regular on the Munster inter-provincial team for several years and won three Railway Cup medals in 1928, '29 and '31. He was a proud member of the famous Blackrock club, and won seven county titles with them.

EUGENE COUGHLAN (Offaly)

Coughlan made his senior debut with Offaly in 1976 at a time when nobody could have had any idea of what lay ahead for the county. They had never won a Leinster or All-Ireland title up to then but all that changed in 1980 when they beat Kilkenny in the Leinster final. A year later they won their first All-Ireland title and added a second four years later. Coughlan was a strong and influential presence at full-back as Offaly wrote new and exciting chapters of their history. As well as winning two All-Ireland medals he also won seven Leinster medals in 1980, '81, '84, '85, '88, '89 and '90. He was named as All-Star full-back in 1984 and again in 1985, when he was also chosen as Hurler of the Year.

GER COUGHLAN (Offaly)

He was an integral part of the Offaly team which ended decades of misery in 1980 when they won the

Eugene Coughlan won All-Ireland medals with Offaly in 1981 and 1985

15. He was a sub for the Kilkenny team which won the 1967 All-Ireland title but played crucial roles as a powerful midfielder in seven All-Ireland victories in 1969, '72, '74, '75, '79, '82 and '83. He also won three National League medals in 1976, '82 and '83 and six Railway Cup medals with Leinster in 1971, '72, '73, '74, '75 and '77. Cummins was chosen as Hurler of the Year in 1983 and won four All-Star awards in 1971, '72, '82 and '83. He completed a remarkable career haul by also winning three All-Ireland club titles with Blackrock of Cork in 1972, '74 and '79.

Multi-talented: Eamonn Cregan

Frank Cummins was an inspiring presence for Kilkenny over three decades

Leinster title for the first time. A year later they made more history when they won their inaugural All-Ireland final, against Galway. Coughlan won a second All-Ireland final in 1985 when they again beat Galway in the final, and he was chosen on the All-Star teams in 1981 and 1985. Small in stature, his natural talent and instinctive ability to make the right decision more than compensated for his lack of height. His uncanny knack of being in the right place to sweep on to the loose ball made him one of the most effective wing-backs of his era.

RAY CUMMINS (Cork)
See The Great Dual Players

EAMONN CREGAN (Limerick) ⚔

Equally at home in defence or attack, Cregan made his senior inter-county debut in 1964 and continued to wear the Limerick colours with distinction until 1983. He was at left full-forward when Limerick won

the National League in 1971 and underlined his versatility by switching to centre-back two years later, anchor of the defence when they won the All-Ireland title. He was at centre-back again in 1974 when Kilkenny gained revenge on Limerick in the All-Ireland final, and by the time Limerick next appeared in the final Cregan was playing in attack. He scored 2–7 against Galway in the 1980 decider but Limerick lost by 2–15 to 3–9. Cregan won three Railway Cup medals with Munster; as a defender in 1968, as a midfielder in 1969 and as a forward in 1981. He also won three All-Star awards, in 1971, '72 and '80, and managed the Offaly team to All-Ireland glory in 1994.

FRANK CUMMINS ⚔ (Kilkenny)

One of hurling's strongest men, his senior career spanned 18 years from 1966 to 1984, during which he won eight All-Ireland medals, seven as a vital member of the starting

Ger Cunningham of Cork was a top goalkeeper for many years

GER CUNNINGHAM (Cork)

He showed early prowess as a soccer player but it was as a hurling goalkeeper that he made such an impressive mark on the sporting landscape. He won All-Ireland medals at every level in an inter-county career which spanned 20 years. He won his first All-Ireland medal as a minor in 1978 and continued to wear the Cork jersey until 1998. Cunningham added another minor medal in 1979 and followed up with an U21 title in 1982. He won the first of his three All-Ireland senior medals in 1984, added two more in 1986 and 1990, won three hurling National League medals in 1981, '93 and '98, and captured three Railway Cup medals with Munster in 1984, '85 and '92. He was Hurler of the Year in 1986.

ANTHONY DALY (Clare)

A natural leader, he captained Clare for eight seasons (1992–99), during which they underwent an amazing transformation. They were beaten by Tipperary and Limerick respectively in the 1993 and '94 Munster finals, but re-launched themselves in 1995 and became the dominant force in hurling for the next three seasons, during which they won two All-Ireland and three Munster titles. Daly's imposing presence at left half-back was hugely significant as Clare set about burying past ghosts. He was a player of immense presence on the field, and an influential figure in the dressing-room. He won two All-Ireland medals in 1995 and 1997 and Munster medals in 1995, '97 and '98. Daly also won two Railway Cup medals with Munster in 1995 and 1996 and won three All-Stars, in 1994 (right full-back), 1995 (left half-back) and 1998 (right half-back).

TOMMY DALY (Clare and Dublin)

A goalkeeper of great stature, he is regarded as a legend in Clare although he won all four of his All-Ireland senior medals with Dublin. Under the rules of the era he had to play for Dublin when he went to live there. He won an All-Ireland junior medal with Clare in 1914 and, on moving to Dublin, quickly became established on the senior team. He won four All-Ireland medals with Dublin in 1917, '20, '24 and '27, and won a Railway Cup medal with Leinster in 1927. A change in the eligibility rules allowed Daly to declare for his native Clare in 1928 and four years later he won a Munster championship medal. He was tragically killed in a road accident in 1936, at the age of 42.

PAT DELANEY (Offaly)

A strapping centre half-back with a flamboyant style, he was a key figure in Offaly's emergence as a major force. In 1980, they made history by winning Offaly's first Leinster senior hurling title and a year later rewrote the history books by winning the All-Ireland title for the first time, beating Galway in the final: Delaney was outstanding, helping Offaly to haul back a seven-point deficit en route to a three-point win. The Kinnity clubman won his second All-Ireland medal along with an All-Star award in 1985 and was chosen as Hurler of the Year in 1981.

LIAM DEVANEY (Tipperary)

A player of outstanding versatility, Borrisoleigh's Devaney gave remarkable service to Tipperary at all levels. He launched his fabulous career by winning consecutive All-Ireland minor medals in 1952 and '53 and was promoted to the senior squad in 1955. Between then and 1968 he played in eight All-Ireland senior finals, winning five; in 1958 (full-forward), '61 (centre-forward), '62 (midfield), '64 (sub centre-forward) and '65 (left half-forward). He also collected eight National League hurling medals in 1955, '57, '59, '60, '61, '64, '65 and '68, and won three Railway Cup medals with Munster in 1961, '63 and '66. Devaney was chosen as Hurler of the Year in 1961.

JOHNNY, BILLY & JOE DOOLEY (Offaly) See The Famous GAA Families

Seánie McMahon and Anthony Daly (centre) hail another Clare triumph

Tony Doran is assured of a place in the affections of all Wexford supporters

the first two of his five All-Ireland finals as a half-forward in 1937 and 1945 before going on to make a significant contribution to Tipperary's three-in-a-row triumph in 1949, '50 and '51 as a half-back. He won three National League medals in 1949, '50 and '52 and featured prominently on the Munster teams who won Railway Cup titles in 1943, '46 and '48. Doyle also enjoyed a great club career with Thurles Sarsfields, winning seven county titles.

NOEL DRUMGOOLE (Dublin)

Regarded by many experts as the best full-back never to have won an All-Ireland senior hurling title, the closest Drumgoole went to achieving the ultimate goal was in 1961 when he captained Dublin to Leinster title glory, only to lose to Tipperary by a single point (0–16 to 1–12) in the All-Ireland final. A year later he captained Leinster to the Railway Cup title. A forceful figure, he had all the physical attributes to make an excellent full-back and combined them with an intelligent mental appreciation of the game.

TONY DORAN (Wexford)

The ultimate tribute to Doran's enduring talents as a full-forward is underlined by the fact that he won an All-Ireland club medal with Buffer's Alley at the age of 42. That was in 1989, and a fitting finale to a remarkable career which reached its first peak in 1963 when he won an All-Ireland minor medal with Wexford. In 1965 he won an All-Ireland U21 medal, and he made it a triple success in 1968 when he scored 2–1 as Wexford staged a great comeback to beat Tipperary in the All-Ireland senior final. Doran also won two National League medals in 1967 and 1973 and played for seven Leinster teams who

won Railway Cup titles in 1971, '72, '73, '74, '75, '77 and '79. He was chosen as Hurler of the Year in 1976 and won an All-Star award in the same season.

JIMMY DOYLE (Tipperary)
See The Legends of Hurling

JOHN DOYLE (Tipperary)
See The Legends of Hurling

JOHN JOE DOYLE (Clare)

Affectionately known as 'Goggles' due to the protective cover he applied to the glasses which he always wore while playing hurling, he was regarded as one of the best half-backs of his era. Doyle made his senior inter-

county debut in 1927 but took five years to achieve his great ambition of winning the Munster title, when Clare beat Cork in the final. He was a consistent presence on the Munster team for several seasons and won four consecutive Railway Cup medals in 1928, '29, '30 and '31. He was selected on the Ireland team for the Tailteann Games in 1932. Doyle, a solid anchor for his club, Newmarket-on-Fergus, won six Clare county championship medals.

TOMMY DOYLE (Tipperary)

His senior inter-county career lasted from 1937 to 1953, during which he established a reputation as a player of rare versatility. He won

SEANIE DUGGAN (Galway)

One of the best goalkeepers never to win an All-Ireland medal, Duggan featured on the Galway team for several years. In 1947 he captained Connacht to victory over Munster in the Railway Cup final, and in 1951 he won a National League medal with Galway when they beat New York in the final. Two years later, he experienced All-Ireland heartbreak when Galway lost to Cork in the All-Ireland final and he also was on Connacht teams who lost Railway Cup finals in 1944, '46, '49 and '52. Despite several big-time disappointments he maintained a consistently high standard of goalkeeping, and in 1984 was named on a national team drawn

Tipperary's Nicky English, winner of six All-Star awards in seven years

from players who had never won an All-Ireland senior medal.

JIM ENGLISH (Wexford)

A right half-back of genuine substance, and a member of Wexford teams which played in three consecutive All-Ireland finals in 1954, '55 and '56. Wexford lost the 1954 final to Cork but beat Galway a year later and gained revenge on Cork in 1956 when they won by 2–14 to 2–8 in a great game. English gave a captain's example in 1956, driving his comrades forward in what proved an historic year for Wexford. It was the only time in their history that they won consecutive All-Ireland senior titles. English added a third All-Ireland medal to his haul in 1960 when Wexford beat Tipperary in the final. He won National League medals in 1956 (as captain) and 1958 and collected Railway Cup medals with Leinster in 1956 and 1962.

NICKY ENGLISH (Tipperary)

A player with a wonderful style and swagger, English made an early impact as a minor when Tipperary won the 1980 All-Ireland final, beating Wexford. A year later he was on the Tipperary team which won the All-Ireland U21 final against Kilkenny, and once he settled into the senior team he went on to become one of his generation's most prolific attackers in both the half-forward and full-forward lines. He won All-Ireland senior medals in 1989 and 1991, Munster medals in 1987, '88, '89, '91 and '93, National League medals in 1988 and 1994 and topped up his title haul with two Railway Cup honours, in 1984 and '85. He was Hurler of the Year in 1989 and got six All-Star awards in seven years: 1983, '84, '85, '87, '88 and '89.

LEONARD ENRIGHT (Limerick)

When Pat Hartigan's brilliant career was cut short by an eye injury in 1979, it left Limerick with a massive gap at full-back – soon closed

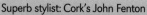
Superb stylist: Cork's John Fenton

by Enright's wonderful presence. He was an imposing defender, who combined strength and determination with a subtle touch and a shrewd mind. Although he never won an All-Ireland senior title, he is assured of a place in the list of great full-backs for his consistent excellence during the 1980s. Enright won Munster titles in 1980 and 1981, and in 1984 and 1985 he won National League medals with Limerick and Railway Cup medals with Munster. He was selected as the All-Stars full-back in 1980, '81 and '83.

LIAM FENNELLY (Kilkenny)
See The Famous GAA Families

JOHN FENTON (Cork)

He won his first All-Ireland medal with the Cork U21 team in 1976, a year in which the county's seniors embarked on the first leg of their triple All-Ireland success. He had to wait until 1984 to win his first All-Ireland senior medal but it holds special memories because that was the GAA's centenary year and he had the honour of captaining the Cork team. Fenton won the 1984 Hurler of the Year award and, two years later, captured another All-Ireland senior title. He also won two National League crowns (1980 and '81), played a prominent part in two Munster Railway Cup final wins (1984 and '85) and was chosen as an All-Star for five consecutive seasons (1983, '84, '85, '86 and '87). He also won an All-Ireland club medal with Midleton in 1988. A midfielder of rare elegance, he was also a consistently accurate free taker from any distance.

JIMMY FINN (Tipperary)

A defender of style and substance, he first came to prominence as a centre-back on the Tipperary minor hurling team which won the All-Ireland title in 1949. He progressed quickly to the senior side and, in 1950, was at right half-back on the team which beat Kilkenny in the All-Ireland final. A year later, Borrisoleigh's Finn achieved an even higher honour when he captained the team to victory over Wexford in the All-Ireland final, clinching the three-in-a-row for Tipperary. He won a third All-Ireland senior medal in 1958 and picked up Railway Cup medals with Munster in 1957 and 1958. His consistent excellence was recalled long after his retirement and, in 1984, he was selected at right half-back on the hurling Team of the Century chosen to mark the GAA's centenary.

PETER FINNERTY (Galway)

A member of the Galway U21 team which won the All-Ireland title in 1983, he was promoted to the senior

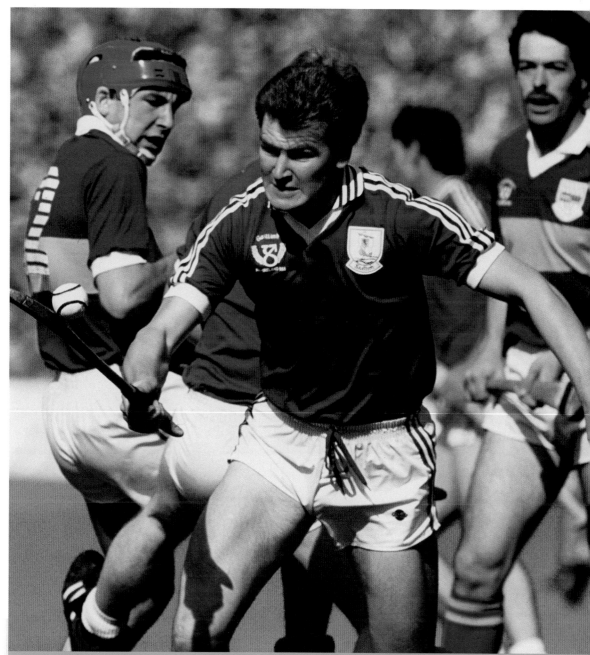
Galway's Peter Finnerty fought many great battles with Tipperary pair John Leahy (left) and Donie O'Connell

squad in 1984 and went on to become one of the best right half-backs in hurling history. Finnerty played in five All-Ireland finals in the next six seasons, winning in 1987 and '88 and losing in 1985, '86 and '90. He also won National League medals in 1987 and 1989, collected four Railway Cup titles with Connacht in 1986, '87, '89 and '91 (as captain) and was chosen as an All-Star in 1985, '86, '87, '88 and '90. Finnerty was a strong, forceful player and an inspirational

figure whose influence was central to Galway's achievements in their greatest era.

DAVY FITZGERALD (Clare)

Fitzgerald stands only 5' 8'' and sceptics initially claimed that he was too small for inter-county hurling, but he took little time in proving them wrong. A brilliant shot-stopper, his natural enthusi-

asm provided a vital part of the inspiration which enabled Clare to emerge as a major force in the mid-1990s. He won All-Ireland medals in 1995 and 1997 and added two Railway Cup medals with Munster to his trophy haul in 1996 and 1997. He also won an All-Ireland club medal with his club, Sixmilebridge, in 1996, and an All-Star award in 1997. As well as being an outstanding goalkeeper, his powerful striking has yielded some priceless goals from frees.

Billy Fitzpatrick captained Kilkenny to an All-Ireland senior title in 1975

BILLY FITZPATRICK (Kilkenny)

In the space of four years (1972–75), Fitzpatrick won All-Ireland medals at Colleges, minor, U21 and senior level. In 1972 he won a minor title for his county and a Colleges one with St Kieran's, Kilkenny, and added two consecutive U21 medals in 1974 and 1975. The first of Fitzpatrick's four All-Ireland senior medals came in 1975 when, as a 21-year-old, he captained the team to success over Galway in the final. Three more All-Ireland medals followed in 1979, '82 and '83 and his honours list also includes three National League medals (1976, '82 and '83), a Railway Cup medal with Leinster (1979) and two All-Star awards (1982 and '83). Fitzpatrick was a deadly finisher both from general play and frees, who averaged six points per game in his prime.

MJ 'INKY' FLAHERTY (Galway)

A half-back of enduring quality, he gave outstanding service to Galway between 1936 and 1953. While equally gifted at Gaelic football and boxing, it was as a hurler of real dynamism that he established a lasting reputation. He won a Railway Cup medal with Connacht in 1947, and four years later captained Galway to a National League title. He retired after Galway lost the 1953 All-Ireland final to Cork but continued to work diligently as a coach and guided Galway to a National League triumph in 1975, a victory which is still regarded as the launch-pad for their subsequent successes at All-Ireland level.

PAT FLEURY (Offaly)

You needed a special brand of defiant courage to fight against years of disappointment in Offaly who up to the end of the 1970s, had never won a Leinster or All-Ireland senior hurling title. Fleury and his colleagues, however, delivered in style in 1980 when they won the Leinster crown in dramatic circumstances. They would go on to become the dominant force in Leinster in the Eighties, winning six provincial titles. However, it was their All-Ireland victories in 1981 and 1985 which really stirred the county's emotions. Fleury was a tenacious corner-back in both triumphs and had the honour of captaining the team in 1985. He won All-Star awards in 1982 and 1984.

AIDAN FOGARTY (Offaly)

When he made his senior inter-county debut in 1976, nobody could have any idea of the change which would take place in Offaly hurling over the next five years. Fogarty, a defender of great stature, played a major part in Offaly's emergence and subsequent consolidation as a superpower. He was at right half-back on the team which made history by winning Offaly's first Leinster title in 1980 and, a year later, they reached another milestone by winning the All-Ireland title for the first time. Four years later Fogarty picked up a second All-Ireland medal, this time as a right full-back. He won a Railway Cup medal with Leinster in 1988, a National League medal in 1991 and was honoured by the All-Star selectors in 1982 and 1989.

SEAN FOLEY (Limerick)

A player of great style and finesse, Foley's ability to lift and strike the ball in one movement made him a delight to watch. He first came to prominence as a teenager when he played minor hurling for Limerick in 1966 and 1967 and his progress to the senior ranks was inevitable. The high point of his career came in 1973 when he played at left half-back on the Limerick team which won the All-Ireland senior title for the first time since 1940. He captained the team to Munster championship success in 1974 but they lost the All-Ireland final to Kilkenny. He won two more Munster titles in 1980 and 1981, having gained a National League medal in 1971. Foley, who was chosen as an All-Star in 1973, also won a Munster club medal with Patrickswell in 1990, at the age of 41.

PAT FOX (Tipperary)

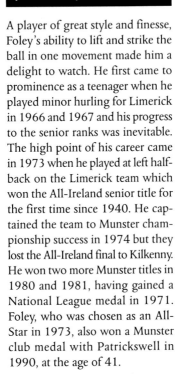

A versatile performer who could fit in anywhere on the Tipperary team. Fox won his first All-Ireland medal at U21 as a midfielder in 1979, and added two more U21 medals to his haul in 1980 and 1981, both as a corner-back. He progressed to the senior side but his career was disrupted by a serious knee injury. He worked extremely hard to regain fitness and by 1987 he was a vital figure in the Tipperary attack when

Pat Fox: a deadly finisher for Tipperary over several seasons

they won their first Munster title since 1971. Fox won All-Ireland senior medals in 1989 and 1991, a season in which he was also named Hurler of the Year and Players' Player of the Year. He won All-Star awards at right corner-forward in 1987, '89 and 1991.

JOSIE GALLAGHER
(Galway)

A native of Gort in Galway's hurling heartland, he was one of the best wing-forwards of his generation. He played for Galway between 1942 and 1954 but this was a period in which his county failed to make any impression on the All-Ireland senior championship. He was on the Galway team which won the National League in 1951 and picked up a Railway Cup medal with Connacht in 1947. In a special promotion in the GAA's centenary year (1984), Gallagher was chosen at right half-forward for the best team never to have won an All-Ireland medal.

MICK GILL
(Galway & Dublin)

Mick Gill created hurling history in 1924 when he became the only player in the history of the GAA to win two All-Ireland senior medals in a single year. To add to his remarkable achievement, he won them with different counties. In September 1924 he was playing for his native Galway when they defeated Limerick in the All-Ireland final. However, that particular game was actually the 1923 championship, which had been delayed. Gill was based in Dublin in 1924 and had to play with them in the championship. In December that year, he helped Dublin to victory over Galway in the All-Ireland final. Gill, an outstanding midfielder, won another All-Ireland medal with Dublin in 1927, captaining them to victory over Cork, having picked up a Railway Cup medal with Leinster earlier in the same year, which was the inaugural year of the inter-provincial competition.

Tight and tenacious: Offaly corner back Martin Hanamy

MARTIN HANAMY (Offaly)

Hanamy, an extraordinarily efficient left full-back, was the most consistently dominant performer in the position for many years. He won his first Leinster senior title in 1998, and though he did not capture his first All-Ireland crown until 1994 it was worth the wait, because he was team captain on a day when Offaly staged a remarkable recovery to beat Limerick in the final. In 1998 he added a second All-Ireland medal to his title haul, which also included a National League medal in 1991. Tight, tenacious and a smart reader of the game, he served Offaly brilliantly and had his talents recognised by the All-Star selectors in 1988, '94 and '98.

PAT HARTIGAN (Limerick)

One of hurling's real giants, Hartigan has gone down in history as a full-back of incredible talent and stature. He played minor hurling for Limerick for four consecutive seasons (1965, '66, '67, '68) and was on the U21 side for six seasons (1966, '67, '68, '69, '70, '71). He was also a highly-accomplished shot putter and represented Ireland on four occasions. He won an All-Ireland senior medal with Limerick in 1973, having won a National League medal two years earlier. He won five consecutive All-Star awards in 1971, '72, '73, '74 and '75 and won Railway Cup medals with Munster in 1976 and 1978. His glorious career was sadly and prematurely ended when he suffered a serious eye injury in 1979, but his exploits prior to that have lived on in hurling folklore.

CONOR HAYES (Galway)

Born in 1958, he captained Galway to an All-Ireland U21 win over Tipperary in 1978, and two years later won the first of his three All-

EAMON GRIMES (Limerick)

From the moment Grimes first put on the Limerick jersey as a minor in 1963, it was clear a special talent had emerged. Three years later he made his Munster senior championship debut aged 19 and, over the next 14 years, would contribute enormously both to Limerick and hurling in general. A crafty midfielder/half-forward, he won his first major honour in 1971 when Limerick won the National League crown. Two years later his career peaked when he captained Limerick to All-Ireland success, their first since 1940. It was a memorable day for the South Liberties clubman, who scored 0–4 of Limerick's 1–21 total in the final against Kilkenny. He won All-Star awards at left half-forward in 1973 and 1975 and was chosen as Hurler of the Year in 1973.

PHIL GRIMES (Waterford)

His senior inter-county career lasted for an amazing 19 seasons (1947–65), during which he built a deserved reputation as a brilliant midfielder whose artistry and guile were admired by colleagues and rivals alike. He captained Waterford to Munster championship success in 1957 but they lost to Kilkenny in the All-Ireland final. However, two years later Grimes was a major presence as the Waterford team won the All-Ireland title by beating Kilkenny in a final replay. He won Railway Cup medals with Munster in 1958 and 1960 and added a National League title in 1963. He also won 12 Waterford county championship medals with Mount Sion, including nine in a row (1953–61).

est level as a wing-back, corner-back and midfielder. Hennesey made an early impression as a minor, winning an All-Ireland medal in 1973, before adding two U21 titles to his trophy collection in 1975 and 1977. He figured prominently on the Kilkenny senior teams which won All-Ireland titles in 1979, '82 and '83, won four National League medals in 1976, '82, '83 and '86 and collected a Railway Cup medal with Leinster in 1979. Hennessy also enjoyed a hugely-successful career with his club James Stephens, winning All-Ireland titles in 1976 and 1982. His remarkable level of consistency earned him five All-Stars awards in 1978 (right half-back), 1979 (midfield), 1983, 1984 (right half-back) and 1987 (right full-back).

Kilkenny's Joe Hennesey: a determined performer with a subtle touch

Conor Hayes, Galway captain in the All-Ireland double of 1987–88

Ireland senior medals when Galway beat Limerick in the final. He experienced All-Ireland final defeats against Offaly and Cork in 1985 and 1986, but over the next three years captained Galway to All-Ireland wins over Kilkenny and Tipperary in 1987 and 1988 and to National League triumphs in 1987 and 1989. Hayes, who won three successive All-Star awards in 1986, '87 and '88 and Railway Cup medals in 1980, '83, '86 and '87, is regarded as one of the game's most assured and intelligent full-backs.

PAT, GER & JOHN HENDERSON (Kilkenny)
See The Famous GAA Families

JOE HENNESSY (Kilkenny)

Small in stature but a wonderfully-gifted craftsman, his versatility enabled him to perform at the high-

History-maker: Pádraig Horan was the first Offaly man to captain the county to All-Ireland hurling glory

A member of the famed Blackrock club, he first made an impression as a minor in 1967 playing at centre-back on the Cork team which beat Wexford in the All-Ireland final. He won All-Ireland U21 medals in 1970 and 1971 and the first of his four All-Ireland senior medals in 1970, lining out at left corner-back on the Cork team which beat Wexford in the final. He added three more All-Ireland medals in 1976, '77 and '78, captured four National League medals in 1970, '74, '80 and '81 and won a Railway Cup medal with Munster in 1978. He captained Blackrock to success in three All-Ireland club finals in 1972, '74 and '79. His consistent excellence earned him All-Star awards in 1974, '77 and '78 and he was chosen as Hurler of the Year in 1978.

GARRETT HOWARD
(Limerick, Tipperary and Dublin)

As well as giving distinguished service to his native Limerick, Howard also performed at the highest level with Tipperary and Dublin in a remarkable career which lasted from 1919 to 1936. He also won five All-Ireland senior hurling medals, three with Limerick in 1921, '34 and '36 and two with Dublin in 1924 and 1927. He won five National League medals, one with Dublin and four with Limerick, and achieved the rare distinction of winning two Railway Cup medals with different provinces. He was on the Leinster team which won the inaugural interprovincial competition in 1927, and in 1931 he won another Railway Cup medal with Munster.

JIM HURLEY
(Cork)

Regarded as one of Cork's best midfielders ever, he was a hugely important figure in the county's four

PÁDRAIG HORAN
(Offaly)

Horan booked his place in history in 1981 when captaining Offaly to their first All-Ireland senior hurling crown, and won a second All-Ireland medal in 1985. He played at full-forward on both occasions, but earlier in his career he was a defender of outstanding talent, having won three consecutive Railway Cup medals at full-back with Leinster in 1973, '74 and '75. After switching to the Offaly attack he developed into a deadly finisher, particularly from frees, where his accuracy from all angles and distances was invaluable. He won an All-Star award in 1985. After his retirement he turned to team management, and led Offaly to their first National League title in 1991.

All-Ireland successes of 1926, '28, '29 and '31. They beat Kilkenny in the 1926 and 1931 finals and accounted for Galway in both 1928 and 1929. It was a glory period for Cork and Hurley's power hurling, allied to his skilful touches, played a major part in ensuring the Leesiders dominated for so long. His consistent excellence brought him to the attention of the Munster selectors and he won three Railway Cup medals in 1928, '30 and '31, beating Leinster in all three finals.

MICK JACOB
(Wexford)

An amazingly versatile performer, he played as a goalkeeper, defender and midfielder for Wexford and lined out as a forward for his club, Oulart-The-Ballagh. He was in goal when Wexford beat Tipperary in the 1965 All-Ireland U21 final and a year later was at midfield when Wexford lost the U21 final to Cork. He won an All-Ireland senior medal as a sub in 1968 but subsequently suffered the disappointment of losing three All-Ireland finals to Cork in 1970, '76 and '77. After playing at midfield in his early days as a senior he switched to centre-back, where he established a fine reputation. He won a National League medal in 1973 and featured on Leinster teams which won Railway Cup titles in 1973, '75 and '77. He was chosen as All-Star centre-back in 1972, '76 and '77.

TONY KEADY
(Galway)

A strong, powerful centre-back, particularly effective under the high ball, he won an All-Ireland U21 medal in 1983 and went on to win All-Ireland senior medals in 1987 and 1988, National League medals in 1987 and 1989 and Railway Cup medals in 1986, '87 and '91. He was at his commanding best in 1988 when Galway beat Tipperary in the All-Ireland final and was later chosen as the Hurler of the Year.

Keady won All-Star awards in 1986 and 1988. In 1989 he was suspended for 12 months for playing without the proper clearance in New York, which cost him a place on Galway's championship team and led to a major row (see *Controversies and Scandals*).

JOHN KEANE
(Waterford)

Although he won only one All-Ireland senior hurling medal, in 1948, Keane's name has gone down in history as one of the greatest players Waterford ever produced. He won an All-Ireland junior medal as a full-back in 1934 at the age of 18 and earned speedy promotion to the senior side. In 1938 he was at centre-back on the Waterford side which won the Munster senior title for the first time, but had to wait ten years before winning an All-Ireland senior medal when Waterford beat Dublin in the final. He played at centre-forward in that final but it was as a defender that he staked his claim to true greatness. Keane, who won seven Railway Cup medals with Munster (1937, '38, '39, '40, '42, '43, '49), was chosen at centre-back on the Hurling Team of the Millennium in 2000.

MICHAEL 'BABS' KEATING
(Tipperary) See The Great Dual Players

EDDIE KEHER (Kilkenny)
See The Legends of Hurling

PADGE KEHOE
(Wexford)

The 1955–60 period was the most successful in the history of Wexford hurling and Kehoe, whose senior career stretched from 1946 to 1962, was an integral part of the glory story. As well as winning Leinster and All-Ireland senior medals in 1955, '56 and '60, he won Leinster championship honours in 1951, '54 and '62. He captained Wexford to the Leinster title in 1954 but suffered the disappointment of losing

Happy days for Offaly: Joachim Kelly and Pádraig Horan celebrate

the All-Ireland final to Cork. However, he was at the heart of Wexford's subsequent surge and they went on to win consecutive All-Ireland titles over the next two seasons, the only time in history that they achieved two-in-a-row. A prolific half-forward, the St Aidan's clubman was hurling's top scorer in 1958, averaging 0–6 per game.

JOACHIM KELLY
(Offaly)

One of the most inspirational midfielders of his era, Kelly was a major driving force as Offaly turned from optimistic triers to sure-footed winners in 1980 when they took the Leinster title for the first time. He was equally-influential when they reached an even higher peak in 1981, winning their first All-Ireland final, and they won a second in 1985. Kelly won seven Leinster titles in 1980, '81, '84, '85, '88,

'89 and '90 and a National League medal in 1991, when Offaly took the title for the first time. He was chosen as an All-Star in 1980 and 1984. A player possessing great power and presence, Kelly was the epitome of the new-found Offaly spirit of his era.

GARY KIRBY
(Limerick)

One of the best players never to win an All-Ireland senior championship medal, he came very close with Limerick in 1994 and 1996, only to be thwarted by Offaly and Wexford respectively in the finals. He won an All-Ireland minor medal in 1984 and maintained the impressive progression towards the senior grade by winning an All-Ireland U21 medal in 1987. Kirby was a constant presence on the Limerick senior team during the 1990s, winning National League medals in

Winning feeling: Galway's Noel Lane was an expert goal-poacher

1992 and 1997 and Munster championship titles in 1994 and 1996. A master sharp-shooter, he was Limerick's top scorer for many years and his consistently high strike rate from frees and general play helped him to win four All-Star awards in 1991, '94, '95 and '96.

NOEL LANE (Galway)

A versatile attacker, he played for Galway for more than ten years, during which they enjoyed record levels of success. He won his first All-Ireland senior medal in 1980 when Galway won the title for the first time since 1923, and he went on to collect two more All-Ireland medals in 1987 and 1988. On both occasions he was a sub in the finals and scored late goals to ensure victory. He also won two National League medals in 1987 and 1989 and added to his title haul by playing a significant role in Connacht's five Railway Cup wins in 1980, '82, '83, '86 and '87. Lane was chosen as an All-Star in 1983 and 1984. Having managed Galway at minor and U21 level, he took over the senior team in 2000.

JIMMY LANGTON (Kilkenny)

He won his first All-Ireland senior medal as a 19-year-old in 1939, when Kilkenny beat Cork in the final. He captained Kilkenny a year later but suffered the disappointment of an All-Ireland defeat against Limerick, and he had to wait until 1947 to win his second All-Ireland medal, when Kilkenny beat Cork in the final. He won eight Leinster senior medals in 1939, '40, '43, '45, '46, '47, '50 and '53. A wingforward of great style and vision, he was a regular on the Leinster inter-provincial team for many years and won Railway Cup medals in 1941 and 1954. He was chosen at right half-forward on the Hurling Team of the Millennium in 2000.

PHIL 'FAN' LARKIN (Kilkenny)
See The Famous GAA Families

SYLVIE LINNANE (Galway)

One of the most colourful characters of his generation, his tigerish defensive qualities made him an invaluable component of the Galway teams which won All-Ireland senior titles in 1980, '87 and '88. He was right half-back in 1980, when Galway won their first All-Ireland title for 57 years, but won his two other titles as a corner-back. He won two National League medals in 1987 and 1989 and collected five Railway Cup titles with Connacht in 1980, '82, '83, '86 and '87. He was chosen on the All-Stars teams in 1985, '86 and '88. A strong, determined player, his fiery style sometimes disguised the fact he was also extremely skilful and an excellent reader of the game.

BRIAN LOHAN (Clare)
See Families GAA Families

FRANCIS LOUGHNANE (Tipperary)

Deadly accurate from frees and general play, the Roscrea sharpshooter created history in 1964 by captaining Tipperary to victory over Wexford in the inaugural All-Ireland U21 final. He was a sub on the Tipperary side which won the 1968 Munster senior final, and three years later reached the peak of his outstanding career by winning an All-Ireland senior title. He won a National League medal in 1979 and played with Munster for several seasons, winning a Railway Cup title in 1976. He enjoyed an outstanding club career with Roscrea and won an All-Ireland title in 1971, the inaugural year of the club championships. Loughnane won successive All-Star awards in 1971, '72 and '73, all at right half-forward.

GER LOUGHNANE (Clare)

Although Loughnane managed Clare to All-Ireland glory in 1995 and 1997, the honour had eluded him as a player during a distinguished 16-year career. Nonetheless, he made a huge impression as a dashing wing-back and corner-back. He won two National League titles in 1977 and 1978 and featured on three Munster squads which won Railway Cup titles in 1976, '78, '81. In 1974 he became the first Clare player to be chosen as an All-Star, and won a second award in 1977. He played on five teams which

Damien Martin, Offaly's keeper during their 1981 All-Ireland win

lost Munster finals in 1974, '77, '78, '81 and '86, but never lost confidence in Clare's ability to make the breakthrough and played a massive role in achieving that as a manager in the Nineties.

JACK LYNCH (Cork)
See The Great Dual Players

JOHN LYONS (Cork)

When John Lyons took over as the Cork team's full-back on a permanent basis at the beginning of 1952, having first played at senior level in 1946, he could have had no idea of the glory days which lay ahead. Over the next five seasons he would play in four All-Ireland finals, winning three-in-a-row in 1952, '53 and '54 and losing one in 1956. Lyons also collected a National League medal in 1953, and meanwhile on the interprovincial scene picked up Railway Cup medals in 1955, '57 and '58. A great reader of the game, Lyons placed great emphasis on trying to outwit his opponents mentally, rather than dominating them physically.

MICK MACKEY (Limerick)
See The Legends of Hurling

STEVE MAHON (Galway)

Galway failed to win an All-Ireland senior title between 1923 and 1980, but in the next eight seasons they enjoyed their most productive spell ever, winning three All-Ireland finals in 1980, '87 and '88. Mahon, a strong midfield anchor in all three successes, also featured on the Galway teams which lost All-Ireland finals in 1979, '81, '85 and '86. He won an All-Ireland U21 medal in 1978, captured Railway Cup honours with Connacht in 1980, '82, '83, '86 and '87, and won All-Star awards in 1981 and 1987.

DAMIEN MARTIN (Offaly)

Martin first played for Offaly in 1964 at a time when the county weren't serious contenders for All-Ireland honours. However, his continued excellence in goal was hugely-influential in raising Offaly's fortunes and they finally made the breakthrough in 1980, winning their first Leinster title by beating great rivals Kilkenny. A year later they reached a new peak by winning the All-Ireland title for the first time. Martin made a huge contribution to both successes and was also in goal when Offaly reached the 1984 All-Ireland final, losing to Cork. He featured on the Leinster team which won the Railway Cup title in 1972 and was chosen for the All-Stars team in 1971.

CHARLIE McCARTHY (Cork)

A diminutive corner-forward with a sharp eye for goal, McCarthy's opportunism in open play, combined with his free-taking expertise, were priceless assets for club and county for many years. He made his first major impact in 1964 when he won an All-Ireland minor medal and added an U21 medal in 1966, a year in which he also captured the first of his five All-Ireland senior medals. He won his second in 1970 and was part of the successful three-in-a-row side in 1976, '77 and '78, captaining Cork in the latter year. He also won four National League medals in 1970, '72, '74 and '80, and was honoured by the All-Star selectors in 1972, '77 and '78. His club career with St Finbarr's also scaled the heights and he won two All-Ireland titles in 1975 and 1978.

GERALD McCARTHY (Cork)

Right from his juvenile days McCarthy was destined to make a huge impact on the hurling scene. A beautifully-balanced performer, he brought supreme elegance to his craft. He first played with Cork seniors as a 17-year-old in 1964 and went on to script several exciting chapters in a hugely-successful story. In 1966 he had the distinction of captaining Cork senior and U21 teams to All-Ireland glory. He went on to win four more All-Ireland senior medals in 1970, '76, '77 and '78 and picked up National League medals in 1969, '70, '72 and '74. He won four Railway Cup medals with Munster in 1969, '70, '76 and '78. Equally at home at midfield or in the half-forward line, he won two All-Ireland club titles with St Finbarr's in 1975 and 1978, and was chosen on the All-Stars team in 1975.

JUSTIN McCARTHY (Cork)

In 1966 he achieved the rare distinction of being chosen as Hurler of the Year at the age of only 21. It was a remarkable season for McCarthy, who as well as playing a major part in Cork's march to the All-Ireland senior crown also captured a U21 medal when Cork beat Wexford at the third attempt in the final. He won Railway Cup medals with Munster in 1968 and '69 but had his career seriously curtailed when he broke a leg in

A giant on the loose: Limerick's Joe McKenna on the prowl against Wexford. George O'Connor (Wexford), another great talent, is on the left

three places in a motorbike accident while on his way to training for the 1969 All-Ireland final against Kilkenny. A strapping midfielder, he won National League and Munster championship medals in 1972, and after his retirement in 1974 he took up coaching, at which he also excelled.

JOHN 'JOBBER' McGRATH (Westmeath)

A player of great substance, he would almost certainly have been one of

the truly big names had he been born in one of the stronger hurling counties. Westmeath's inability to match the superpowers robbed him of an opportunity to adorn the big occasions but he still left an indelible mark on the game by his sheer excellence and consistency in the 1950s and early 1960s. He started as a goalkeeper before switching to the outfield, where he shone in defence and midfield. He won two Division 2 National League medals with Westmeath and crowned his interprovincial career with a Railway Cup medal, won with Leinster in 1956.

PA 'FOWLER' McINERNEY (Clare and Dublin)

His senior inter-county career lasted from 1913 to 1933, during which he won two All-Ireland medals with Clare and Dublin. He won his first medal in 1914 when Clare beat Laois in the All-Ireland final and added a second in the Dublin colours in 1927, when they beat Cork in the final. He also won a Railway Cup medal with Leinster that year and added a National League title to his haul in 1929. He later returned

to Clare and, 18 years after making his first All-Ireland final appearance, played in the 1932 decider. However, Clare lost to Kilkenny, a defeat which in no way took any of the gloss off a fabulous career.

JOE McKENNA (Limerick)

Born in Offaly, with whom he played minor hurling, he later switched to Limerick and developed into an outstanding attacker. He was at left full-forward on the Limerick team which won the 1973 All-Ireland

SEANIE McMAHON (Clare)

The courage of Seanie McMahon in battling on against Cork in the 1995 Munster semi-final despite having sustained an ankle injury typified the spirit which ran through the Clare team as they set out on an exciting adventure which ended with an All-Ireland title triumph – the county's first since 1914. McMahon's brilliant performance at centre-back was a crucial factor in Clare's triumph and he was later chosen as Hurler of the Year. He was a strong, dominating influence, whose accuracy from frees gave an added dimension to Clare's attacking plans. McMahon won a second All-Ireland title in 1997, was chosen as the All-Star centre-back in 1995, '97 and '98 and also collected an All-Ireland club title with St Joseph's (Doora–Barefield) in 1999.

TERENCE McNAUGHTON (Antrim)

Few players gave greater service to inter-county hurling than the man who was affectionately known as 'Sambo'. A player of great versatility, McNaughton also possessed a steely determination to succeed and while Antrim found it difficult to survive against the game's super-powers on a consistent basis, there were days when McNaughton inspired them to produce a defiant stand against the odds. He featured prominently on the Antrim team which beat Offaly in the 1989 All-Ireland semi-final. It was the first time for 46 years that Antrim had qualified for the All-Ireland final. In 1993, McNaughton's excellence earned him a place at midfield on the All-Stars team.

LORY MEAGHER (Kilkenny)
See The Legends of Hurling

title and went on to play in two more finals, in 1974 and 1980, but lost both to Kilkenny and Galway. He built up an impressive reputation as a strapping full-forward whose trademark was consistent goal-scoring. He won Railway Cup medals with Munster in 1976,'78,'81 and '84, and his consistent excellence was reflected in his All-Star award haul. He was honoured in three different positions and collected six awards; in 1974 (right half-forward), 1975 (centre-half-forward), 1978, '79, '80, and '81 (full-forward).

An Antrim hero: Terence 'Sambo' McNaughton won an All-Star award in 1993

On a high: Galway's P J Molloy enjoyed much success in the 1970s and '80s

PADDY MOLLOY
(Offaly)

While never winning a Leinster or All-Ireland medal, he was an outstanding talent at a time when Offaly hurling was struggling to join the elite. He played for Offaly between 1955 and 1971, during which time he proved himself a versatile and ultra-consistent performer in defence, midfield and attack. His only Leinster final appearance was in 1969 when Offaly lost by two points to Kilkenny, 3–9 to 0–16. While Offaly failed to win any championship titles during Molloy's career, his excellence didn't go unnoticed by the Leinster selectors and he was a regular on the team for several seasons. He won two Railway Cup medals with Leinster, in 1965 as a left half-back and in 1967 as a right full-forward.

P J MOLLOY
(Galway)

A gifted wing forward who gave outstanding service to Galway at minor, U21 and senior level for almost 20 years, he played on the Galway minor team which lost the 1970 All-Ireland final but two years later won his first All-Ireland medal when Galway beat Dublin in the 1972 U21 final. He progressed quickly to the senior ranks and played a big part in Galway's National League success in 1975, their first since 1951. Over the next 12 years, he featured in five All-Ireland finals (1975, '80, '85, '86 and '87) during which he won two titles in 1980 and 1987 (sub). He also won five Railway Cup medals with Connacht in 1980, '82, '83, '86 and '87, and picked up a second National League medal in 1987. He won an All-Star award in 1977.

CHRISTY MOYLAN
(Waterford)

Moylan was a key member of the Waterford team which won the county's first All-Ireland senior title in 1948, and hurled at inter-county level for 15 years. An opportunist forward, he scored 1–2 against Dublin in the 1948 final as they swept to victory 6–7 to 4–2. His brilliance made him an automatic choice on the Munster team for several seasons and he won five Railway Cup medals in 1937, '38, '39, '40 and '42. He was also an accomplished footballer.

BRIAN MURPHY (Cork)
See The Great Dual Players

DONIE NEALON
(Tipperary)

He hurled at senior level with Tipperary between 1958 and 1969, during which he won every honour in the game. Success came in his very first year as a senior when he featured at right half-forward as Tipperary beat Galway in the All-Ireland final. He played in seven All-Ireland finals during the 1960s, winning in 1961, '62, '64 and '65. He also won National League medals in 1959, '60, '61, '64, '65 and '68. He was a key member of the Munster side for several seasons, winning Railway Cup medals in 1959, '63, '66 and '68, and was chosen as Hurler of the Year in 1962.

PAT NOLAN
(Wexford)

A goalkeeper of immense stature, his career at senior level spanned 17 years, during which he carved out a great reputation. He won his first All-Ireland senior medal as a sub in 1956. Promotion to the first team followed quickly and he went on to enjoy a remarkable career. He won two more All-Ireland senior medals in 1960 and 1968, when Wexford twice beat Tipperary, and collected three National League medals in 1958, '67 and '73. Nolan played on the Leinster team which won the 1971 Railway Cup final but his interprovincial opportunities were limited because he was vying for the goalkeeping position with another all-time great, Ollie Walsh of Kilkenny.

CHRISTY O'BRIEN
(Laois)

Generally regarded as one of the best hurlers never to have won an All-Ireland senior medal, he was a consistently powerful presence on the Laois senior team for many years. However, their failure to make the breakthrough robbed him of an opportunity to prosper on hurling's big championship days but that in no way detracted from the fact that he was an outstanding forward. His brilliance earned him a place on the Leinster Railway Cup team for several years and he won three interprovincial titles in 1962, '64 and '65, a record for a Laois hurler. He also won five Laois county championship medals with Borris-in-Ossory.

LIAM O'BRIEN
(Kilkenny)

Nicknamed 'Chunky', O'Brien was a familiar presence on the Kilkenny team throughout the 1970s, dur-

Tony O'Sullivan (right) and Martin Naughton of Galway clashed in the 1986 and 1990 All-Ireland finals

ing which he won four All-Ireland titles in 1972, '74, '75 (all as midfielder) and '79 (at left half-forward). He also played on Kilkenny teams which lost All-Ireland finals in 1973 and 1978. He was a regular on the Leinster team for several seasons, picking up Railway Cup medals in 1973, '75 and '77. A dedicated member of the James Stephens club, he won an All-Ireland medal with them in 1976. He was chosen on the All-Stars teams in 1973, '74, '75 (midfield) and '79 (left half-forward). He won the Hurler of the Year award in 1975.

GEORGE O'CONNOR (Wexford)
See The Great Dual Players

JAMES O'CONNOR (Clare) ✕

An exciting runner in the amazing Clare adventure which was launched on a wave of energy and enthusiasm in 1995, he was at midfield on the team who won the All-Ireland final for the first time in 81 years. In 1997, he was at right half-for-

ward when Clare won another All-Ireland title and captured a third All-Ireland medal with his club, St Joseph's (Doora-Barefield) in 1999. He won Railway Cup medals with Munster in 1995 and 1996 and was chosen on the All-Star teams in 1995, '97 and '98. Consistently accurate from frees and general play, O'Connor won Hurler of the Year in 1997.

SEANIE O'LEARY (Cork) ✕

The holder of All-Ireland medals at minor, U21 and senior level, he is best-remembered for his goal-scoring talents and an uncanny knack of always finding his way to the point of action at the right time. He won his first All-Ireland medal as a minor in 1969 and added three U21 medals in 1970, '71, '73. He suffered a disappointment in his first All-Ireland senior final, losing to Kilkenny in 1972, but received more than adequate compensation over the next 12 years, during which he won All-Ireland medals in 1976,

'77, '78 and '84. He also won four National League medals in 1972, '74, '80 and '81. O'Leary was honoured three times by the All-Star selectors, winning awards in 1976, '77 and '84, all at left full-forward.

TONY O'SULLIVAN ✕ (Cork)

He may have been small in stature but his skill, mobility and cleverness made him one of the best attackers of his era. After winning an All-Ireland minor medal in 1979, O'Sullivan progressed quickly through the ranks and played in All-Ireland senior and U21 finals in 1982. Cork won the U21 final but were beaten by Kilkenny in the senior decider. However, this was no more than a temporary setback for O'Sullivan, who went on to win three All-Ireland medals in 1984, '86 and '90. He won a National League medal in 1993 and a Railway Cup title with Munster in 1985. Equally prolific from frees and general play, O'Sullivan's status as an outstanding attacker was empha-

sised by his selection on the five All-Stars teams in 1982, '86, '88, '90 and '92.

PADDY PHELAN ✕ (Kilkenny)

The testament to his brilliance is underlined by the fact that he was chosen at left half-back on the hurling Team of the Millennium in 2000. He won the first of his four All-Ireland senior medals with Kilkenny in 1932 when they beat Clare in the final. He won three more All-Ireland medals in 1933, '35 and '39, and featured on three Kilkenny teams which lost All-Ireland finals in 1931, '36 and '40. He won four Railway Cup medals with Leinster in 1932, '33, '36 and '41. Current Kilkenny star DJ Carey (see The Legends of Hurling), is his grand-nephew.

JACKIE POWER ✕ (Limerick)

An outstanding hurler and footballer, his versatility was further emphasised by his ability to play in a variety of positions in defence and attack. Although he played inter-county football for Limerick, it was as a hurler that he gained national prominence. He hurled for 15 years at the highest level, during which he won All-Ireland medals in 1936 and 1940. He won five consecutive National League titles in 1934, '35, '36, '37 and '38 and starred for Munster when they won seven Railway Cup titles in 1940, '42, '43, '44, '45, '46 and '48. A member of the Ahane club, he won 20 Limerick county championship medals, 15 in hurling, five in football. His son Ger won eight All-Ireland football medals with Kerry between 1975 and 1986.

SEAMUS POWER ✕ (Waterford)

The Mount Sion clubman was a colossus in a variety of positions for Waterford in an inter-county career which lasted for 16 years. He won a Munster senior championship medal in 1957 and two years later went a step further, playing a substantial role in Waterford's All-Ireland triumph when they beat Kilkenny in a replayed final. Although best-known as a midfielder, he was also comfortable in defence and attack and won a National League medal as a corner-forward in 1963. He featured on five Munster teams which won Railway Cup medals in 1955, '58, '59, '60 and '61.

DAN, MARTIN, PAT & JOHN QUIGLEY (Wexford)
See The Famous GAA Families

NICKY RACKARD (Wexford)
See The Legends of Hurling

CHRISTY RING (Cork)
See The Legends of Hurling

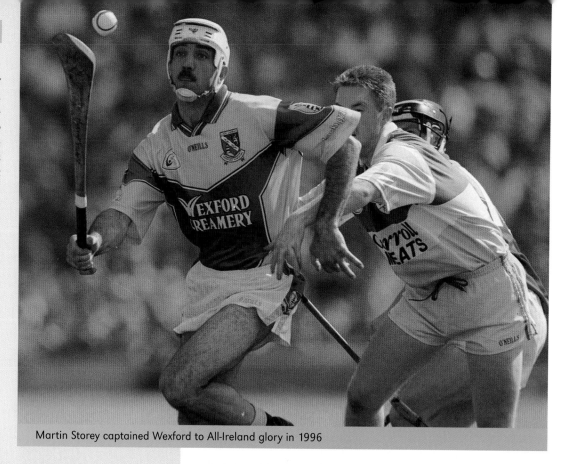

Martin Storey captained Wexford to All-Ireland glory in 1996

MICK ROCHE (Tipperary)

One of the great centre-backs in hurling history, he turned it into an art form, standing strong and proud under the dropping ball before sweeping majestic clearances deep into enemy territory. He won his first All-Ireland title as a midfielder in 1964 on the Tipperary team which won the inaugural U21 final. It was at centre-back that he really made his mark, however, winning three All-Ireland senior titles in 1964, '65 and '71. He suffered heartbreak in both 1967 and 1968 when he captained Tipperary to successive All-Ireland defeats, but the experience in no way dulled his appetite, as he subsequently proved. He won two National League medals in 1965 and 1968, and played a central role in Munster's Railway Cup triumphs in 1966, '68 and '70.

MICK RYAN (Tipperary)

A constant presence at centre-forward on the outstanding

Tipperary team, winners of three consecutive All-Ireland senior titles in 1949, '50 an d '51, beating Laois, Kilkenny and Wexford in the finals. He also won six National League medals in 1949, '50, '52, '54, '55 and '57. A Munster regular for many years, he won five Railway Cup medals and in 1952 played for Ireland against the Combined Universities in a special challenge game.

TIMMY RYAN (Limerick)

One of the small band of Limerick hurlers to have won three All-Ireland senior medals, he played on the teams which captured the titles in 1934, '36 and '40. He won Munster championship medals in 1933 and 1935, five consecutive National Hurling League titles in 1934–38 and Railway Cup medals with Munster in 1934 and 1935, captain on both occasions. A midfielder of real talent, his inter-county career lasted 15 years, while at club level, he won 15 Limerick county championship medals with Ahane.

JOE SALMON (Galway)

He played senior inter-county hurling for 15 years between 1949 and 1964, and although this coincided with a barren period for Galway he established a marvellous reputation as a midfielder of true quality, a status which was recognised in 1984 when he was named on the best team never to have won an All-Ireland medal. He played for three Galway teams which lost All-Ireland senior finals in 1953, '55 and '58, and was also on three losing Connacht Railway Cup sides in 1949, '52 and '55. Salmon, a true stylist, won the admiration of every hurling follower. He played club hurling with Eyrecourt and Liam Mellowes in Galway and with Glen Rovers in Cork, where he won six county championship medals.

PADDY SCANLON (Limerick)

Limerick hurling enjoyed its best-ever run in the 1934–40 period, during which they won three All-Ireland

senior titles. Scanlon played a big part in the latter two triumphs, delivering several outstanding goalkeeping performances en route to Limerick's All-Ireland successes in 1936 and 1940. They beat Kilkenny on both occasions. Scanlon's stature as a goalkeeper made him an automatic first choice on the Munster team for several seasons, and he won Railway Cup medals in 1934, '35, '37, '38 and '40.

NOEL SKEHAN (Kilkenny)

One of the finest goalkeepers of all time, Skehan holds a unique place in hurling as the only player to win nine All-Ireland senior medals. He won three as a sub in 1963, '67 and '69 and six as a player in 1972, '74, '75, '79, '82 and '83. Having been a sub for Ollie Walsh for several years, he took over in goal in 1972 and captained Kilkenny to victory over Cork in the All-Ireland final. He added five more All-Ireland medals in the next 11 years and by the time he retired in 1985 had added three National League titles (1976, '82, '83) and won four Railway Cup medals with Leinster in 1973, '74, '75 and '79. He was Hurler of the Year in 1983 and won seven All-Star awards in 1972, '73, '74, '75, '76, '82 and '83.

JIMMY SMITH (Clare) ✕

One of the best forwards never to have won an All-Ireland medal, his outstanding talents were obvious from an early stage in his home club, Ruan. He played minor hurling for Clare at the age of 14 in 1945 and had the rare distinction of doing so for five consecutive seasons. He progressed to the Clare senior side at the age of 18 and continued to play at the highest level for the next 19 years. His opportunities to shine on the championship scene were limited, however, as Clare appeared in only one Munster final during his career, losing to Limerick in 1955. He enjoyed more success at interprovincial level, winning six Railway Cup medals in 1955, '58, '59, '60, '61 and '63.

SEAN STACK (Clare) ✕

Although he never won an All-Ireland senior championship medal, his name still has gone down in the history books as one of hurling's outstanding centre-backs. A player of immense presence and power, he was unlucky enough to play for four Clare teams which all lost Munster finals, but he enjoyed some glory days too, notably the 1977 and 1978 National League finals which Clare won, beating Kilkenny on both occasions. He captained the team to success in 1978. Stack also won two Railway Cup medals with Munster in 1984 and 1985 and an All-Star award in 1981.

PAT STAKELUM (Tipperary) ✕

For almost a decade he established himself as a half-back of genuine stature, a man who thrived on the biggest of occasions. A member of the Holycross club, with which he won three Tipperary county championship medals, he captained Tipperary to All-Ireland senior glory in 1949. He switched from right half-back to centre-back a year later and was an important anchor as Tipperary retained the All-Ireland title – and he was again at his very best when they made it three-in-a-row in 1951. He won six hurling National League titles in 1949, '50, '52, '54, '55 and '57, and crowned a remarkable career with five Railway Cup medals, won with Munster in 1950, '51, '52, '53 and '55.

MARTIN STOREY (Wexford) ✕

He wore the famous Wexford colours for 23 years, starting on the U14 team in 1977 and ending with the seniors' Leinster championship defeat by Offaly in 2000. He made his senior debut in 1985 and endured many years of disappointment before finally making the breakthrough. He played on Wexford teams which lost four Leinster senior finals in 1988, '92, '93 and '94 and they were also beaten in the National League finals of 1990, '91 and '93. Despite all the setbacks, Storey remained a constant source of inspiration in the Wexford attack with his driving, determined style, and when he was appointed captain for the 1996 season he was well aware it might be his last big chance of glory. It turned into a memorable season as he led Wexford to their first All-Ireland title since 1968. He won All-Star awards in 1993, '96 and '98 and captured Railway Cup medals with Leinster in 1993 and 1998.

TONY WALL (Tipperary) ✕

A member of the famous Thurles Sarsfields club, his feats with club and county ensured him a permanent place in the affections of all hurling lovers.

Ollie Walsh: a star player who became a great manager

An ultra-competent centre-back, his inspirational performances were central in what was a golden era for Tipperary hurling. He won the first of his five All-Ireland senior titles as team captain in 1958. He added four more medals to his haul in 1961, '62, '64 and '65. He won five National League medals in 1959, '60, '61, '64 and '65, and collected five Railway Cup medals with Munster in 1958, '59, '61, '63 and '66. He was chosen as Hurler of the Year in 1958.

OLLIE WALSH (Kilkenny) ✕

He showed early promise as a soccer goalkeeper but his passion for hurling superseded every other ambition and he went on to play in eight All-Ireland senior finals, spanning three decades. A goalkeeper of rare talent, he won his first All-Ireland senior medal in 1957 and added a second in 1963. He won his third in 1967, giving a memorable exhibition against Tipperary in the final, and captured a fourth medal in 1969. He also played on Kilkenny teams which lost All-Ireland finals in 1959, '64, '66 and '71. He won National League medals in 1962 and 1966 and helped Leinster to Railway Cup titles in

1962, '64, '65 and '67. Walsh was chosen as Hurler of the Year in 1967. On his retirement, he took up coaching and was Kilkenny manager when they won All-Ireland senior titles in 1992 and 1993 (see *The Great Managers*). His son, Michael, was in goal for both successes.

NED WHEELER (Wexford) ✕

Wheeler, from the Faythe Harriers club, played senior inter-county hurling with Wexford for 16 years between 1949 and 1965, during which he won three All-Ireland titles. He won the first as a centreforward when Wexford beat Galway in 1955 and was at midfield a year later when Wexford retained the title with a victory over Cork in one of the classic All-Ireland-finals. He was also at midfield when Wexford won their third All-Ireland title in six seasons by beating Tipperary in the 1960 final. Ned also won seven Leinster titles in 1951, '54, '55, '56, '60, '62 and '65, won hurling National League medals in 1956 and 1958 and was a member of Leinster teams which won Railway Cup titles in 1954, '56 and '64.

BRIAN WHELAHAN (Offaly)
See The Legends of Hurling

Since its earliest days, the GAA has always been a family-oriented organisation. The pattern of parents handing on the hurling and football tradition to their sons continues to be one of the GAA's main anchors. There have been many instances of several family members playing together on club and inter-county teams, often at the highest level. In some cases, successive generations have been high achievers, as proved by the Donnellans from Galway and the Larkins from Kilkenny where grandfather, son and grandson have all won All-Ireland senior medals.

THE BENNISES
(Limerick)

As Richie Bennis prepared to take a last-minute '65' in the 1973 Munster hurling final against Tipperary, he knew that the stakes could not have been higher. Miss, and the game would end in a draw: score, and Limerick were in with a great chance of reaching the All-Ireland final for the first time since 1940. Bennis, one of the most consistent free-takers of his era, held his nerve and steered the ball over the bar for the winning point. It was a score which is still fondly remembered in Limerick as the catalyst for a great season which ended with an All-Ireland title success after an easy win over Kilkenny. Richie Bennis, a midfielder/half-forward of genuine pedigree, was accompanied on Limerick's great adventure by his brother Phil, who was at right half-back. They came from a marvellous hurling family in Patrickswell, one of Limerick's true sporting heartlands. The 1973 success lifted the gloom which had hung over Limerick for so long and although they were beaten by Kilkenny in the 1974 All-Ireland final, the memories of the previous year's win are still cherished in the county.

The Bennis family were huge contributors to Limerick and Patrickswell. In 1966 six Bennis brothers – Phil, Richie, Gerry, Pat, Peter and Thomas – were on the Patrickswell team which won the Limerick county title. As well as winning All-Ireland senior medals with Limerick in 1973, Richie and Phil also won National League honours in 1971, and Richie collected an All-Star award at midfield in 1973. Phil managed Limerick in the early 1990s, guiding his county to a National League success in 1992.

Tom Cashman: a member of one of Cork's great hurling families

THE BONNARS (Tipperary)

Sunday, 3 September 1989 was a proud day for the Bonnar family from the famous Cashel King Cormacs club. Tipperary easily beat Antrim to win their 23rd All-Ireland senior hurling final with a team in which three Bonnar brothers made significant contributions. Conal, the youngest of the trio, was at right half-back, Colm was at midfield, while Cormac, the Viking-like warrior, was at full-forward. Two years later all three would win another All-Ireland title when Tipperary beat Kilkenny in the final. The family had another special reason to celebrate in 1991, as they anchored the Cashel King Cormacs club to a Tipperary and Munster club title.

Of Donegal extraction, the Bonnars can be extremely proud of their role in Tipperary hurling. Cormac was at full-back on the U21 team which won the 1980 All-Ireland U21 final, while two years later Colm won an All-Minor medal. Colm was at midfield on the team which won the Munster title for the first time in 16 years in 1987. A year later he won a National League medal and was also a member of the team which reached the All-Ireland final, losing to Galway. Cormac came on as a sub in the final.

By 1989 Colm and Cormac had been joined on the team by Conal for Tipperary's exciting championship adventure. Conal, who also picked up an All-Ireland U21 medal in 1989, was a quick, decisive half-back while Colm brought a measured authority to everything he did. He was equally comfortable at midfield or in the half-backs, while Cormac, a strong, determined full-forward with a great eye for the ball, caused havoc among rival defences.

Colm became the first of the three brothers to win an All-Star award in 1988 while Conal and Cormac won similar awards in 1989 and 1991, making it a rare treble achievement for the family.

THE CASHMANS (Cork)

When Mick Cashman succeeded Dave Creedon as Cork senior hurling goalkeeper in 1956, he can have had no idea of the frustrating days which lay ahead. Up until then, Cork had won 19 All-Ireland titles – including three-in-a-row in 1952, '53 and '54 – so it was reasonable to assume that Cashman would win a medal, probably quite quickly. Everything appeared to be going to plan when Cork reached the 1956 All-Ireland final, but then they lost out to Wexford. Surprisingly, Cork went into decline after that and didn't reach another All-Ireland final until 1966, by which time Cashman had retired. Despite his lack of success with Cork, he proved himself to be one of the top goalkeepers in the country, winning a place on the Munster inter-provincial team for seven consecutive seasons (1957–63) during which he won six Railway Cup medals.

Mick's wife, Anne, was the sister of another famous Cork hurler, Jimmy Brohan, so it seemed natural that the Cashman boys would develop as fine sportsmen – and so it proved. Tom and Jim won every honour in hurling during highly-decorated careers in which skill and sportsmanship were paramount virtues. Tom won All-Ireland minor hurling and football medals in 1974 and added U21 honours two years later. He progressed quickly to the senior side and won four All-Ireland titles (1977, '78, '84 and '86). Equally comfortable among the half-backs or in midfield, he also won National League medals in 1980 and '81 and was chosen on the All-Stars team in 1977, '78 and '83. Younger brother Jim won All-Ireland senior medals in 1986 and 1990 and picked up All-Star awards at centre-back in 1990 and 1991. Between them, Tom and Jim won four Railway Cup medals to bring the family haul to ten. Tom served as a minor and senior selector with Cork in the 1990s and took over as senior manager in 2000.

THE CONNOLLYS (Galway)

When Castlegar became the first Galway club to win the All-Ireland hurling final in June 1980, it represented yet another sporting peak for the Connolly family. Five brothers – Pádraig (full-back), John (centre-back), Joe (centre-forward), Gerry (right full-forward) and Michael (full-forward) – all played key roles in the win over Ballycastle (Antrim) while two more, Tom and Murt, were among the subs.

While that success was the high point of the Connollys' club careers, they also gave outstanding service to Galway and Connacht. John, a strapping performer who was comfortable in a variety of positions from centre-back to full-forward, enjoyed the highest profile of all (see The Legends of Hurling) in a long career during which Galway crossed the great divide from eternal optimists to proven achievers. John was central to that process, battling through several disappointing seasons before finally making a significant breakthrough in 1975 when Galway won the National League for the first time since 1951. John, who was also an accomplished footballer and boxer, was team captain when Galway beat Tipperary in the 1975 hurling league decider. It was the start of a new, exciting era for Galway, who won the All-Ireland final in 1980 with three Connollys – John, Michael and team captain Joe – aboard for a victory which ended a 57-year gap without the title. Another brother, Pádraig, was a sub.

Galway reached the 1981 All-Ireland final but lost to Offaly after which John retired, ending a career in which, as well as his on-field achievements, he also won All-Star awards in 1971 and 1979 and a Hurler of the Year Award in 1980. Joe won an All-Star award in 1980. Between them John, Joe and Michael won nine Railway Cup medals with Connacht. A noted coach, John has been involved with Galway minor and senior teams over the years and is currently a Galway selector.

Style and skill, backed up by a steely determination to succeed, came naturally to the Connolly brothers, who are owed an enormous debt by Galway hurling.

THE CONNORS (Offaly)

Shortly after Christmas 1975, a meeting was held in Walsh Island, Co. Offaly, at which it was decided that the townland would go it alone, having previously been linked with Clonbologue and Bracknagh for GAA purposes. It was to prove a historic decision, as Walsh Island prospered on their own winning six consecutive Offaly county football titles in 1978, '79, '80, '81, '82 and '83 and two Leinster crowns in 1978 and '79. The Connor name featured prominently in those successes while also making a massive contribution to the Offaly team at Leinster and All-Ireland level.

Murt Connor flew the family flag at the highest level in 1971 when playing at left full-forward on the Offaly team which won the All-Ireland title for the first time in history. He won a second All-Ireland medal a year later. Murt was the oldest of five brothers, along with Willie, Richie, Matt and Seamus. All five played on the great Walsh Island team of 1978–83, a period in which Matt (see The Legends of Gaelic Football) established himself as one of the greatest players of all time through his exploits with Offaly. Richie also carved out a brilliant career, leading Offaly to a memorable All-Ireland triumph in 1982 when they staged a great finish to beat Kerry, who were bidding to create history by becoming the first county to win five consecutive All-Ireland senior football titles.

Equally at home in defence or attack, Richie was at centre-back on the 1981 team beaten by Kerry in the All-Ireland final, but a year later he anchored the attack from centre-forward. He won an All-Star award in 1981.

Michael Donnellan: a Galway star whose father and grandfather also won All-Ireland titles

THE DONNELLANS
(Galway)

The Donnellan name has been synonymous with Dunmore and Galway football since 1925 when Mick Donnellan won an All-Ireland senior medal. A player of great stature, he captained Galway to the 1933 All-Ireland final where they lost to Cavan. However, a year later he had the distinction of captaining Connacht to their first Railway Cup interprovincial title.

A football dynasty had been launched. Mick's sons John and Pat followed in their father's illustrious footsteps. In the 1960s they both made major contributions to the most successful period in the history of Galway football, during which they won three consecutive All-Ireland titles in 1964, '65 and '66. John captained the team in 1964 but his joy at beating Kerry in the final was short-lived. His father died while watching the game from the Hogan Stand. John was unaware of the tragedy until after he had been presented with the Sam Maguire Cup. It was a sad end to what should have been a wonderful day for the Donnellan family.

Pat was a sub on the 1964 team but a year later he was at midfield on the Galway team which retained the All-Ireland crown, while John was at right half-back. A year later Pat was again at midfield while John went on as a sub as Galway completed the three-in-a-row with an All-Ireland final win over Meath. They both won National League medals in 1965 and Railway Cup medals with Connacht in 1967. In 1964 John followed his father, who had been a national politician for more than 20 years, into politics, polling 20,920 votes in a by-election. He enjoyed a 25-year career as a Fine Gael TD and served as a junior minister in a coalition government.

Two generations of Donnellans had now made an auspicious contribution to GAA life and, in due course John's sons, Michael and John, would begin to make an impact

Matt and Richie gave outstanding service to Walsh Island and Offaly, as did their first cousins, Liam and Tomás. They were at full-back and midfield respectively on the Offaly team which won the All-Ireland title in 1982, having previously won Leinster titles in 1980 and '81. Tomás won an All-Star award in 1978 while Liam got a similar honour in 1982. The Connor family name has gone down in history as a massive contributor to Offaly in the 1971–82 period, during which the county won three All-Ireland and six Leinster titles.

THE COONEYS
(Galway)

The Sarsfields club base is drawn from 300 houses in the New Inn-Bullaun area of Co. Galway, but for such a tiny area they have achieved an incredible amount of success. None of it would have been possible without the remarkable Cooney family, who provided so much talent and inspiration over many years. Jimmy, a tenacious corner-back, was the first to emerge on the scene in the late 1970s at a time when Galway hurling was building towards an exciting climax. It arrived in 1980, when they won the All-Ireland senior title for the first time since 1923. Jimmy also won a Railway Cup medal with Connacht in 1980 and had his consistent excellence recognised by selection on the All-Star team.

Three years later, his younger brother Joe made his first impact as a star forward on the Galway minor team which won the county's first All-Ireland crown in that grade. A year later, he was promoted to the senior team and was a permanent fixture on the inter-county scene for the next 16 years, during which he built up a reputation as one of the greatest forwards of his generation. He won an All-Ireland U21 medal in 1986, All-Ireland senior medals in 1987 and '88, National League medals in 1987, '89 and '96 and Railway Cup titles with Connacht in 1986, '87, '89 and '91. He won All-Star awards in 1985, '86, '87, '89 and '90 and was chosen as Hurler of the Year in 1987.

While Jimmy and Joe achieved top honours at inter-county level, they also remained fiercely loyal to their club team. Sarsfields won their first Galway title in 1980 but it was in the 1990s that they hit the big time nationally, becoming the first club to win consecutive All-Ireland club titles in 1993 and 1994. Both occasions were major triumphs for the Cooney family. Jimmy was a sub when they made the All-Ireland breakthrough in 1993 but watched with pride as five of his brothers – Pakie, Brendan and Michael, who made up the full-back line, Joe and Peter – played magnificently in the glorious triumph. Pakie had the additional honour of captaining the team. All five were again on the team which retained the All-Ireland crown a year later.

on Galway football. Michael won a Connacht minor medal in 1994 and three years later the brothers played together for the first time on a Galway senior championship team. Galway lost in the first round of the 1997 Connacht championship, but in 1998 they embarked on a great adventure which ended with an All-Ireland win, their first since 1966.

John missed the campaign through injury but Michael was an inspiring figure with his speed, athleticism and finishing skills all key ingredients in Galway's march to the summit. His excellence was subsequently recognised by the All-Star selectors who chose him at right half forward, while he was also named Footballer of the Year. Both John and Michael won Connacht championship medals in 2000 but they were denied All-Ireland glory by Kerry, who beat Galway in the final replay.

THE DONNELLYS (Antrim)

Antrim hurling may have suffered from being situated so far away from the strong power bases in the South of Ireland but it has never lost its sense of pride or identity. Nobody has epitomised that special passion and spirit more than the Donnelly clan from Ballycastle. While their medal haul is much smaller than that of comparable families in the South, their contribution to hurling is equally as important.

Brothers, Eddie, Dessie, Brian and Kevin Donnelly and their first cousins Terence, Séamus and Brendan (all brothers) enjoyed long and productive careers while another cousin, Ronan, continues to carry the family name with distinction at inter-county level.

Eddie, who was regarded as one of the best players of his generation, and Kevin won All-Ireland intermediate medals with Antrim in 1970 and ten years later six Donnellys featured on the Ballycastle team which reached the All-Ireland club final. Kevin, Séamus, Terence,

Billy Dooley, an opportunist forward for several years

Dessie, Brendan and Brian battled bravely to bring the All-Ireland club hurling title to Ulster for the first time but Ballycastle lost out by three points to a Castlegar side, powered by the Connolly brothers.

In 1989 Terence, Dessie and Brian reached the high point of their careers by beating Offaly in the All-Ireland semi-final. It was the first time since 1943 that Antrim had reached the final but they lost out to Tipperary. However, it was still a special year for the Donnellys,

and in particular for Dessie, who was chosen as the All-Star left fullback. The Donnelly family are guaranteed a permanent place in the folklore of Antrim hurling, an honour they richly deserve.

THE DOOLEYS (Offaly)

Clareen may be one of the smallest parishes in Ireland but it has made an enormous impression on

hurling, not just in Offaly but throughout the entire country. It has produced many outstanding craftsmen over the years, but no family has contributed more than the Dooleys.

Between them, the Dooley brothers – Joe, Billy and Johnny – have won seven All-Ireland senior medals in careers which reached the highest peaks over several years. Their uncle Joe played with Offaly in the 1950s but the county was not a major hurling force at the time, so

Johnny Dooley (centre): leader, free-taker and inspiration

unlike his nephews he never got a chance to shine on the big days.

It was all very different by the time Joe, Billy and Johnny arrived on the scene. Offaly had made the Leinster and All-Ireland break-throughs in the early 1980s so when Joe's blossoming career took off in 1984, they were recognised as a powerful force. They reached the 1984 All-Ireland final – Joe's first – but were beaten by Cork. However, a year later Joe won his first All-Ireland medal as a quick, intelligent left corner-forward on the team which beat Galway.

A year later Billy, who is five years younger than Joe, won an All-Ireland minor medal and picked up a second in 1987. Johnny, who is two years younger than Billy, also won an All-Ireland minor medal as a 16-year-old in 1987 and added a second two years later. In 1991 the three brothers won their first national title together when they featured prominently on the Offaly team which won the National League. It was to be the launch of a very successful decade for Offaly and the Dooleys, during which they won two All-Ireland and three Leinster titles.

Both of the All-Ireland victories were of a highly-dramatic nature, with the Dooleys centrally involved in all the crucial action. In 1994 Limerick were leading by five points with five minutes to go in the All-Ireland final when Offaly staged one of the most remarkable come-backs of all time. In less than five minutes Offaly scored 2–5, with Johnny Dooley hitting 1–1 and Billy knocking over 0–3. Joe had earlier scored 1–2. Between them, the Dooleys scored 2–12 of Offaly's 3–16 total.

In 1998, the Dooleys were equally influential in Offaly's All-Ireland success. Joe gave an

Kevin Fennelly: equally accomplished in goal or in attack

THE FENNELLYS (Kilkenny) ✕

Between 1981 and 1990, Ballyhale Shamrocks won the All-Ireland club hurling title three times. It was a remarkable achievement by a small club, and made all the more amazing by the make-up of the team. It featured no fewer than seven Fennelly brothers – Kevin, Seán, Michael, Ger, Brendan, Dermot and Liam – who between them won 21 All-Ireland club medals. That was only part of the huge haul amassed by the Fennelly family, whose contribution to club and county over many years ensured them a place in hurling history. Between 1972 and 1992, the Fennelly name featured on Kilkenny teams at all levels, making them one of the most instantly-recognisable clans in Irish sport.

Ger and Kevin launched the success story by winning All-Ireland minor medals in 1972 and added All-Ireland U21 titles two years later on a Kilkenny team captained by Ger. They both won a second U21 medal in 1975, playing on a team which was captained by Kevin.

And so it went. Ger was a sub on the Kilkenny senior team which won the 1975 All-Ireland final, while younger brother Liam followed his brothers' illustrious footsteps through the Kilkenny minor and U21 ranks on to the senior team. In 1979 Ger captained the Kilkenny senior team to success in the All-Ireland senior final while Kevin, who had won his underage medals as a goalkeeper, went on as a sub in attack. Three years later Liam and Ger were key members of the side which beat Cork in the All-Ireland final, a victory they repeated in 1983 with Liam as captain. In 1987 four Fennellys – Kevin (goal), Seán (left half-back), Ger (midfield) and Liam (full-forward) – were on the Kilkenny team which reached the All-Ireland final, where they lost to Galway.

Five years later Liam won his third All-Ireland medal, again as captain, leading Kilkenny to victory over Cork in the final. He won All-Star awards in 1983, '85, '87 and '92.

Liam Fennelly

Ger Fennelly

amazing exhibition against Clare in the third of their epic All-Ireland semi-final clashes, while Johnny and Billy were also ultra-effective as Offaly became the first team in history to win the All-Ireland title after losing a provincial final.

Johnny holds three All-Star awards (1994, 1995 and 2000), Billy has two (1994 and 1995) while Joe has one (1998).

Ger Henderson in the thick of a typical all-action clash between Kilkenny and Offaly

THE HENDERSONS (Kilkenny)

For 27 years between 1964 and 1991 the Henderson family name never left the Kilkenny senior hurling teamsheet. It was a remarkable achievement by brothers Pat, Ger and John who brought just about every available honour back to their native Johnstown. Pat, who was born in 1943, led the way. He won

an All-Ireland minor hurling medal in 1961 and made his senior debut three years later, reaching the All-Ireland final where Kilkenny lost heavily to Tipperary. Two years later he again experienced All-Ireland defeat when Kilkenny lost to Cork, but in 1967 his luck changed when they beat Tipperary in the final. He won four other All-Ireland titles in 1969, '72, '74 and '75 and collected National League medals in 1966 and 1976.

A strong, steady centre-back, he was a regular on the Leinster inter-provincial team for several years, winning Railway Cup medals in 1967, '71, '73, '74, '75 and '77. He won All-Star awards in 1973 and 1974, a year in which he was also chosen as Hurler of the Year.

Pat's younger brother Ger won an All-Ireland minor medal in 1972 and U21 medals in 1974 and 1975. A sub on the senior team in 1975, he eventually took over from Pat

as first-choice centre-back and went on to enjoy a hugely-successful career. He won three All-Ireland senior medals in 1979, '82 and '83 and four National League medals in 1976, '82, '83 and '86 and a Railway Cup medal with Leinster in 1979. His consistent brilliance earned him All-Star awards in 1978, '79, '82, '83 and '87 and he was chosen as Hurler of the Year in 1979.

John, the youngest of the trio, first came to prominence in 1975

son Phil, who later became known as 'Fan' to distinguish him from his cousin of the same name, inherited his father's skills and made an early impression, winning a Leinster championship minor medal in 1959.

He won his first All-Ireland senior medal in 1963 but was omitted from the Kilkenny squad after struggling against Tipperary's Donie Nealon in the 1964 All-Ireland final. It wasn't until the early 1970s that he regained his place on the Kilkenny team, but he made up for lost time, winning four All-Ireland medals in 1972, '74, '75 and '79. He captained Kilkenny to National League success in 1976 and won Railway Cup medals in 1972, '74, '75, '77 and '79. He also won All-Ireland club medals with James Stephens in 1976 and 1982. He was chosen as an All-Star in 1973, '74, '76 and '78. Although best-known as a corner-back, he was extremely effective at full-back, despite being unusually small for the position.

His son, Philip, has carried on the family tradition with considerable style. An All-Ireland minor medal winner in 1990, he collected a U21 medal as Kilkenny captain four years later and emulated his father and grandfather by winning a senior medal as a wing back in 2000.

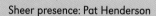

Sheer presence: Pat Henderson

when he won an All-Ireland minor medal. It was a special year for the Hendersons, as Ger won a U21 title while Pat collected a senior medal in the same season. John added an U21 title in 1977 and progressed quickly to the senior scene. He won three All-Ireland senior medals in 1979, '82 and '83 and National League honours in 1982, '83, '86 and '90. He followed in his brothers' footsteps by winning an All-Star award in 1983. He played

his last All-Ireland final in 1991, losing to Tipperary. It was the end of the Henderson brothers' era as players, during which they won 11 All-Ireland senior medals.

When their playing careers were over, all three continued to devote themselves to hurling. Pat coached Kilkenny seniors to All-Ireland titles in 1979, '82 and '83, while John managed Wicklow hurlers for a period. Ger is currently a Kilkenny selector.

THE LARKINS ✕
(Kilkenny)

The Larkin family holds the rare distinction of winning All-Ireland senior medals in three generations. Paddy Larkin won four All-Ireland senior medals in 1932, '33, '35 and '39 and also showed his defensive class at inter-provincial level, winning Railway Cup medals with Leinster in 1932, '33 and '36. His

Brian Lohan: a full-back of style and substance

THE LOWRYS (Offaly)

Seán, Mick and Brendan Lowry formed a brotherly triumvirate which contributed generously to Offaly football in the 1970s and 1980s. Seán, who was the oldest of the trio, first came to prominence in 1972 when winning an All-Ireland senior medal as a centre-back at the age of 20. It was a wonderful start to a great career by one of the most versatile players of his era. Seán played at full-forward in the 1981 All-Ireland final but was at centre-back a year later and played a big part in Offaly's famous victory over Kerry in the All-Ireland final.

His brothers Mick and Brendan were also key figures in an Offaly team which prevented Kerry from winning their fifth All-Ireland title in a row. Mick was a tenacious corner-back while Brendan, who was also a very accomplished soccer player, displayed consisted opportunism at left full-forward.

When his job took him to Mayo, Seán declared for his adopted county and won a Connacht championship medal in 1985, giving him the unusual distinction of winning provincial medals in two provinces. He is also one of only five players to win All-Star awards as a defender and a forward (1979 full-forward, 1982 centre half-back). Brendan also won an All-Star award in 1981. Seán won a Railway Cup medal with Leinster in 1974.

Seán Lowry: changed provinces

THE McCARTANS (Down)

The McCartan clan have been central to Gaelic football in Down since the 1930s. Brian McCartan played for Down in the 1930s and 1940s but they were not a major force at the time. Indeed, it was not until 1959 that Down won their first Ulster title. It was to be the start of a glory period for Down football and Brian McCartan's sons James and Dan would play a huge part in the triumphant story. Down won the All-Ireland senior title for the first time in 1960, with Dan at centre-back and James at centre-forward. They occupied the same positions a year later when Down retained the title, and Dan won a third All-Ireland medal as a full-back in 1968.

James became the first player to win the Footballer of the Year award in successive years in 1960 and 1961, which proves just how important he was to a Down team which brought a new, refreshing style to Gaelic football.

James won two Railway Cup medals with Ulster in 1964 and 1966 (as captain) while Dan won four Railway Cup medals in 1964, '65, '66 and '68.

The third generation of McCartan excellence was provided by James' son James Junior, who inherited

THE LOHANS (Clare)

When Clare won the All-Ireland senior hurling title for the first time in 81 years in 1995, Gus Lohan was one very proud father. He had watched from the stands as his sons Brian and Frank acted as vigilant sentries in front of the Clare goal. Brian was at full-back, with younger brother Frank on his left, as Clare discarded the challenges of Cork, Limerick, Galway and Offaly to win the crown. It was no accident that the young Lohans proved so efficient, as Gus himself had given great service to his native Galway and Clare. He won a National League medal with Clare in 1977.

Brian made his senior championship debut in 1993 while Frank joined him in the full-back line two years later as Clare embarked on a glory run which ultimately ended in All-Ireland triumph. They both won second All-Ireland medals in 1997. Brian was chosen as All-Star full-back in 1995, '96 and '97, while Frank was All-Star left full-back in 1999.

Brendan Lowry: All-Star in 1981

Wexford's Martin Quigley: a senior championship hurler for 19 years

John Quigley played in five All-Ireland finals in 1966, three of which were replays. He was at right full-back on the minor team which beat Cork in a replay and at left half-forward on the U21 team which lost to Cork in a second replay. He won an All-Ireland senior medal in 1968, going on as a sub in the final. A few hours earlier, younger brother Martin had won an All-Ireland minor medal when Wexford beat Cork in the final. It was to be his only All-Ireland win, despite subsequently playing in six All-Ireland finals, three U21 (1968, '69 and '70) and three senior (1970, '76 and '77). He won a National League medal in 1973 on a Wexford team captained by his brother John.

Martin won Railway Cup medals with Leinster in 1973, '74, '75 and '77, while John won inter-provincial medals in 1971 and 1975. John and Martin won five All-Star awards between them: Martin was honoured in 1973, '74, '75 and '76, while John was chosen in 1974.

Martin's senior championship career lasted from 1970 to 1979 and although he never won an All-Ireland title he –and the rest of the Quigley family – still. made a marvellous contribution to hurling.

THE RACKARDS (Wexford)

The remarkable Rackard family left an indelible mark on hurling through their exploits in the 1950s and early 1960s. Nicky, Bobby and Billy achieved every honour in the game while leaving hurling fans with precious memories of their wide range of talents.

Nicky (see The Legends of Hurling) is hailed as the best-ever full-forward, combining a dazzling array of expert skills with an intuitive hurling brain which mesmerised defenders for many years. His scoring exploits are legendary, including such incredible returns as 7–7 against Antrim in the 1954 All-Ireland semi-final, 6–4 against Dublin in the 1954 Leinster final and 5–4 against Galway in the 1956 All-

many of his father's and uncle's talents. He made an exciting impact as a minor in 1987, helping Down to win an All-Ireland medal, and four years later he was a sharp, quick left full-forward on the team which won the All-Ireland senior title for the first time since 1968. Three years later, James Jnr won a second All-Ireland medal, scoring the only goal of the game as Down beat Dublin by two points. He also collected Railway Cup medals with Ulster in 1993, '94 and '95 and was an All-Star in 1995.

THE QUIGLEYS (Wexford)

When Wexford lined up against Cork for the 1970 All-Ireland senior hurling final, it was a very special occasion for the Quigley family from Rathnure. Dan anchored the defence from centre-back while his three brothers, Martin, Pat and John, made up the half-forward line. Unfortunately for the Quigleys, Cork ruined the day by winning easily.

It was very disappointing for this outstanding hurling family, but there were lots of other days when their talents were richly rewarded. Dan blazed the trail, winning a Railway Cup medal with Leinster at full-back in 1964. He went on to win two other Railway Cup medals in 1967 and 1971 but his greatest achievements came with Wexford, with whom he won an All-Ireland medal as captain in 1968 when they staged a spirited revival to beat Tipperary in the final. He also won a National League medal in 1967.

Action man: Kerry's Pat Spillane in striking pose against Dublin's Tommy Conroy and David Synnott

Ireland semi-final.

His younger brothers Bobby and Billy were also outstanding talents. Bobby made his senior inter-county debut as a 19-year-old in 1945 and his performance over the next 12 years was a model of consistent excellence which climaxed in 1955–56 when Wexford won consecutive All-Ireland titles for the only time in their history. A defender of great style and substance, he won a National League medal in 1956, a year in which he also collected a Railway Cup medal with Leinster. He featured on four Rathnure teams which won Wexford county championship titles, and in 1999 was chosen at right full-back on the Hurling Team of the Millennium.

Billy, the youngest of the famous Rackard trio, played minor hurling and football with Wexford for two seasons in 1947 and 1948 before making his senior inter-county hurling debut in 1950. He won consecutive All-Ireland titles at centre-back in 1955 and 1956, when Wexford beat Galway and Cork respectively, and added a third in 1960 when they beat Tipperary in the final. He also won National League titles in 1956 and 1958 and played significant roles in Leinster's Railway Cup final victories in 1954, '56, '62 and '64.

THE SHEEHYS (Kerry)

Between them, John Joe Sheehy and his three sons Paudie, Niall and Seán Óg won ten All-Ireland senior football medals. A native of Tralee, John Joe won his first All-Ireland title in 1924 when Kerry beat Dublin in the final. He captained Kerry to two more All-Ireland titles in 1926 and 1930, having also won a medal in 1929, and won a Railway Cup medal with Munster in 1927.

His son Paudie made his first major breakthrough on the Kerry team which won the 1950 All-Ireland minor final, and won his first senior title at right half-forward in 1955.

By 1959, Paudie's brother Niall had taken over as Kerry full-back and the pair shared All-Ireland glory with a win over Galway in the final.

The Sheehys' proudest day came in 1962 when Paudie (left full-forward), Niall (full-back) and Seán Óg (right half-back) all played important parts in the All-Ireland final win over Roscommon. To add to their stature, Seán Óg was team captain.

Niall captained the team to the 1964 All-Ireland final but Kerry lost to Galway, a fate which also befell them in 1965.

THE SPILLANES (Kerry)

The remarkable Spillane brothers, Pat, Mick and Tom, won 19 All-Ireland senior medals in Kerry's record-breaking run between 1975 and 1986, during which they were the dominant force in Gaelic football, winning eight All-Ireland and 11 Munster titles.

Pat was one of the most amazing attacking talents of all time. Speed, acceleration, poise and intel-

Mick Spillane, winner of seven All-Ireland medals

ligence combined to make him virtually unstoppable while his finishing skills ensured that his scoring rate was invariably impressive. His high energy levels enabled him to roam far away from his left half-forward berth, and it was quite common to see him popping up in his own square before launching another surge forward.

He won his first All-Ireland senior title in 1975 and added seven others in 1978, '79, '80, '81, '84, '85 and '86. Despite sustaining a serious knee injury, he battled back to his very best and remained a serious threat to all opposition right up to his retirement.

He won four National League medals and four Railway Cup medals with Munster, was chosen as an All-Star on no fewer than nine occasions (1976, '77, '78, '79, '80, '81, '84, '85 and '86) and was Footballer of the Year in 1978 and 1986.

Mick, a resolute defender, won All-Ireland senior medals in 1978, '79, '80, '81, '84, '85 and '86 and was chosen as an All-Star in 1985.

He tended to be overshadowed by Pat's illustrious reputation but he was a fine player in his own right, bringing a disciplined authority to his defensive duties. Tom, the youngest of the trio, won the first of his four All-Ireland medals as a sub in 1981 and picked up three others as a strong, quick centre-back in 1984, '85 and '86.

Equally at home in defence or attack, he won a Munster championship medal as a centre-forward in 1982. He won three All-Star awards in 1984, '86, '87.

He switched to full-back in the latter part of his career, winning a Munster championship medal at No.3 in 1991.

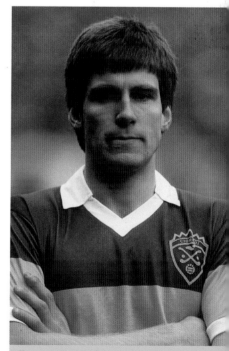

Tom, youngest of the Spillanes

7

THE GREAT MANAGERS

Alone with his thoughts: Dublin's Kevin Heffernan was one of the first high-profile managers in Gaelic football

The emergence of managers as high-profile figures in Gaelic Games can be traced almost directly to the influence of BBC's Match Of The Day *programme.*

Once BBC television became available in Ireland in the 1960s, Match Of The Day *quickly grew in popularity, particularly among younger* people who were drawn to the glamour of English soccer.

It became something of a status symbol to be sufficiently informed to discuss the various merits of the top soccer stars, including many from Ireland, who were seen on *Match Of The Day* every Saturday night. At official level, the GAA was still hostile towards soccer, not least because it was a 'foreign' game, running contrary to Irish traditions and customs. However, a younger Irish generation took a different view and enjoyed *Match Of The Day* as much for its internationalism as for its entertainment value.

Mick O'Dwyer brought record levels of success to Kerry before moving on to revitalise Kildare

Unwittingly, the programme was to play a significant role in changing the management structure of GAA teams. Before the early 1970s, teams were run by selection panels of varying numbers. They usually comprised no fewer than five but, in some instances, as many as eleven actually chose the team.

The soccer system of having an all-powerful manager, accompanied by an assistant, was seen to have very distinct merits. It was regularly alleged in Gaelic Games that large selection panels frequently resulted in self-interest overtaking sound judgement, with individual selectors showing bias towards players from their own area or club.

So it was no coincidence that Dublin, which for technical reasons had more access to the BBC and *Match Of The Day* than country areas, became the first county to appoint a GAA manager with substantial powers. It happened in 1973, at the end of a dismal run for Dublin. The man who was handed the responsibility for plotting their return to the top was Kevin Heffernan, a star player in the 1950s. Heffernan had two selectors, Donal Colfer and Lorcan Redmond, but 'Heffo', as he was affectionately known, was the main man.

In a remarkable turnaround, Dublin climbed from the darkest cavern to the sunniest peak in 1974, when they stunned the GAA world by winning the All-Ireland football title for the first time since 1963. Kevin Heffernan became a hero. The cult of the manager had been born to the GAA. A year later Dublin were beaten by Kerry, who had also embraced the manager concept. The man in charge was Mick O'Dwyer who, like Heffernan, had enjoyed an outstanding playing career which lasted until he was 38 years old. Heffernan and O'Dwyer (*see* The Legends of Gaelic Football) dominated the tactical and technical aspects of team preparation for many years and their successes with Dublin and Kerry respectively convinced other counties that a strong manager, assisted by a small selection committee, was the way forward. All counties now operate this system. Most, although not all, allow the manager to choose his own selectors.

SEAN BOYLAN
(Meath)

Boylan, best-known as a hurler during his playing career, was appointed manager of the Meath football team in 1982 at a time when the county was in depression, having failed to win an All-Ireland crown since 1967 or a Leinster title since 1970. Boylan was by no means an instant hit and, although Meath won a special competition to celebrate the GAA's centenary in 1984, it made no real impact in the championship until 1986, when it won the Leinster title.

That was the start of a sustained surge by Meath and the formal launch of a glorious managerial career. Boylan led them to All-Ireland triumphs in 1987 and 1988, and between 1986 and 1991 Meath won five Leinster titles. When that outstanding panel broke up, Boylan set about rebuilding a new force. He succeeded, and Meath won further All-Ireland titles in 1996 and 1999, as well as three National League titles under Boylan's guidance in 1988, 1990 and 1994.

EAMONN COLEMAN
(Derry)

When Eamonn Coleman was appointed as Derry football manager in 1991 his side were struggling in Division 2 of the National Football League. Two years and seven

months later, Derry had won an All-Ireland, a National League and an Ulster title. It was a remarkable transformation and Coleman, who had coached Derry to an All-Ireland minor title in 1983, was hugely influential in bringing it about.

He led Derry to their first National League title for 45 years in 1992 and, a year later, presided over the county's first All-Ireland senior football triumph, when they beat Cork by 1–14 to 2–8 in the final. His first term as Derry manager ended in 1994 but he returned four years later and, in 2000, guided his side to another National League title, beating Meath in a replayed final.

CYRIL FARRELL
(Galway)

Farrell had a deep interest in tactics and coaching from an early age and found himself training the Galway minor hurling team in 1973, when he was only 23 years old. It was to be the starting base for a magnificent career, in which he achieved the rare distinction of managing Galway to All-Ireland success at senior, Under-21 and minor level.

In 1978 he experienced All-Ireland glory for the first time with the Galway Under-21 side, and two years later led the senior team to a similar triumph. It was Galway's first All-Ireland senior title win for 57 years and was followed by their best-ever decade. Farrell led Galway to a first All-Ireland minor title in 1983 and, a year later, he resumed as senior manager. Between 1985 and 1990, Galway won two All-Ireland finals (1987 and '88), reached three other finals and picked up two National League titles, in 1987 and 1989. Farrell also guided Connacht to five inter-provincial titles in 1980, '82, '86, '87 and '89.

FATHER TOM GILHOOLY
(Offaly)

There was an air of quiet desperation in Offaly when they qualified for the 1971 All-Ireland football final against Galway. They had lost

Sean Boylan: Meath manager through three decades

two All-Ireland finals in the 1960s and, having never won the title, were desperate for success. They needed a strong guiding hand, and one was provided by Fr. Tom Gilhooly, whose role was more of a coaching than managerial nature. He succeeded in harnessing Offaly's yearning for glory into a positive force which was hugely influential in helping them to beat Galway and win their first All-Ireland title. A year later, they retained the crown, beating Kerry in a replayed final.

Fr Gilhooly's capacity to extract

the maximum from his players was central to Offaly's double success, while he also possessed an uncanny knack of correctly reading the opposition's intended game plan.

TONY HANAHOE
(Dublin)

Hanahoe, the only player ever to captain and manage a side to All-Ireland glory in the same season, was at the heart of the Dublin revival under Kevin Heffernan in 1974. If

Heffernan was the expert sideline strategist, Hanahoe was his ambassador on the pitch, ensuring that the game plan was executed in detail.

When Heffernan took a break from management after Dublin won the All-Ireland title in 1976, Hanahoe found himself in the unique position of being player/manager/captain. He took it in his stride, and 1977 turned into another remarkable season for Dublin. With Hanahoe orchestrating matters on and off the pitch, Dublin retained the All-Ireland title: their win over Kerry in the semi-final is regarded as one of the greatest football games ever played.

DERMOT HEALY
(Offaly)

Healy is a native of Kilkenny, where hurling success has always been taken for granted, but made his managerial impact away from the home environment. By the end of 1979, Offaly had never won a Leinster or All-Ireland title but Healy believed that the breakthrough was imminent.

Fired by the desire to succeed, he worked incredibly hard with Offaly in 1980 and was rewarded with an historic Leinster final win, ironically over Kilkenny. Offaly lost the All-Ireland semi-final to Galway but returned a year later to win both the Leinster and All-Ireland titles.

Four years later Healy was still in charge when Offaly won a second All-Ireland title. Their progression from ambitious outsiders to double All-Ireland winners in the space of four years was a remarkable turnaround, helped considerably by Healy's persuasive powers.

PAT HENDERSON
(Kilkenny)

Henderson, a player of immense stature, also enjoyed phenomenal success as a manager. It began in 1979 when Kilkenny, co-managed by Henderson and Eddie Keher, won the All-Ireland title. Three years later, Henderson was manager when Kilkenny took the National League

Ger Loughnane clasps the Liam McCarthy Cup after Clare's 1995 All-Ireland final win, their first for 81 years

title, and followed this up a few months later with a stunning All-Ireland win over Cork. Cork had started as the hottest of favourites but Kilkenny responded to Henderson's shrewd game plan and won easily.

Henderson's ability to keep the squad focused on every challenge was underlined in 1983 when they again won the National League and All-Ireland championship double. This was the first time since 1964–65 that a county had won the Championship-League double in successive years and no team has repeated the feat since then.

MICHAEL 'BABS' KEATING
(Tipperary)

Between 1887 and 1971 Tipperary won 22 All-Ireland senior hurling titles. Then they ran into the most

barren period in their history and, by the autumn of 1986, an air of grim desolation hung across the county. So they turned to Keating, a man with an infectious enthusiasm for hurling.

Inside ten months of his appointment, Tipperary were transformed. They won the 1987 and 1988 Munster titles and, while they were disappointed not to win the All-Ireland crown in either year, it was a treat waiting to be picked up in 1989. They beat Antrim in the All-Ireland final and added another crown in 1991, followed by a Munster title in 1993.

Keating's powers of inspiration had re-ignited Tipperary's passion and, by the time he resigned as manager in 1994, he had led the county to two All-Ireland, five Munster and two National League titles in eight seasons. He later managed both Laois and Offaly.

GER LOUGHNANE
(Clare)

He spent his playing career battling defiantly on Clare teams who never quite managed to force their way to hurling's summit. They went close on a few occasions but were always driven back by the traditional forces.

It was against that insecure background that Loughnane took over as Clare manager in late 1994. Clare had not won the All-Ireland title since 1914 or the Munster final since 1932, so expectations were not very high when Loughnane and his team set out on the championship trail in June 1995. Three months later, they had won both the Munster and All-Ireland titles.

Loughnane's contribution to changing the Clare mindset was enormous and, having experienced the joys of success, he was determined to hold on to them. Clare were eliminated from the Munster championship in 1996 but regrouped for the following season when they again won Munster and All-Ireland titles. In 1998 they won their third Munster crown in four years.

FATHER TOMMY MAHER
(Kilkenny)

He is generally acknowledged as a man who was ahead of his time when it came to training, coaching and motivating a team. Although not a manager in the accepted post-1974 sense, he was the still the main influence on several Kilkenny hurling teams in the 1957–75 period.

They won seven All-Ireland titles in that era, several having the classic Fr Maher imprint. An innovative thinker, his skills were highly-regarded inside and outside Kilkenny. Many other coaches learned from his expertise and, while he always played down his role in Kilkenny's triumphs, his name is revered as a pioneer.

BRIAN McENIFF
(Donegal)

In his playing days, he was fascinated by coaching and was always destined for managerial distinction. He was the player-coach when Donegal won their first Ulster senior football title in 1972 and when they repeated the success in 1974.

His dream of leading Donegal to their first All-Ireland title remained unfulfilled until 1992, when they embarked on a thrilling adventure which ended in ultimate triumph and McEniff's selection as Manager of the Year. Donegal had suffered major disappointments in previous years but McEniff refused to accept they would never make the breakthrough and his sheer enthusiasm, combined with a cunning tactical approach, were ultimately rewarded. McEniff led Ulster to nine inter-provincial championship successes and was manager of the Ireland International Rules team against Australia in 2000, a role he retained in 2001.

EUGENE McGEE
(Offaly)

Although an 'outsider' from Longford, McGee is guaranteed a permanent place in the affections of Offaly football fans.

When he took over in 1976, he inherited a depressed scene. The glory days of 1971–72 were distant memories and McGee knew a complete overhaul was required. He had gained valuable managerial experience with University College, Dublin, leading them to several triumphs, including two All-Ireland club titles.

The challenge in Offaly was immense but he thrived on it and, by 1979, the team was good enough to reach a Leinster final, where it lost narrowly to Dublin. Offaly absorbed the lesson and returned in 1980 to win the Leinster crown. It was to be the first of three Leinster successes but the biggest triumph of all came in 1982 when Offaly staged a dramatic comeback to beat Kerry in the All-Ireland final. Kerry was bidding for a place in history by becoming the first team to win five consecutive All-Ireland titles.

It was a personal triumph for McGee's managerial talents. He later went on to lead Ireland to victory in the International Rules series against Australia.

PETER McGRATH
(Down)

He took over as Down senior manager in 1989, having coached the minor team to All-Ireland success in 1987. The senior scene was in a depressed state when McGrath came in but he set about harnessing the county's traditional confidence.

Two years later, Down were All-Ireland champions. Their progress during the 1991 season was amazing. McGrath's patient, methodical system yielded rich dividends as Down became the first Ulster county to win the All-Ireland title since 1968. They were beaten in both the 1992 and 1993 Ulster championships but, just when critics were beginning to question whether McGrath could revive them, he delivered again. In 1994 Down dethroned reigning champions Derry and continued on to

another All-Ireland success, earning McGrath a place in the exclusive club of managers who have achieved All-Ireland glory twice.

BILLY MORGAN
(Cork)

As Kerry's greatest football rivals in Munster, Cork endured agony between 1975 and 1986 as their neighbours won eight All-Ireland and 11 Munster titles, while Cork won just one Munster title in the same period. Cork won the 1973 All-Ireland title and the Munster title a year later, but Kerry embarked on an amazing run in 1975 which continued, with a brief interruption, for 11 years. When Morgan, who had captained Cork to All-Ireland glory in 1973, took over as team manager in late 1986, his immediate priority was to unseat Kerry, which was achieved in the following year's Munster final.

However, the path to the All-Ireland peak was blocked by Meath in both 1987 and 1988, but Morgan never lost confidence and had his squad perfectly-tuned for the challenge in

Peter McGrath presided over All-Ireland football final wins by Down in 1991 and 1994

Ollie Walsh's goalkeeping pedigree served him well as Kilkenny manager

he guided Mayo into the All-Ireland senior final for the first time since 1951 and although they lost to Cork, O'Mahony's status as an emerging manager of real quality was evident.

He joined Leitrim in 1993 and, a year later, was involved in one of the great fairytales of the decade. Leitrim's previous Connacht title win was in 1927, but 67 years of misery were wiped out in July 1994 when they beat Mayo in the final. The third phase of O'Mahony's managerial career began in 1997 when he took over Galway who, despite their great tradition, had failed to win the All-Ireland title since 1966. O'Mahony took less than a year to rectify that. Galway swept through the Connacht championship before beating Derry and Kildare to land the big prize. Galway also reached the 2000 All-Ireland final but lost in a replay against Kerry.

O'Mahony's success rate with Mayo, Leitrim and Galway underlined his capacity to adapt to different styles, attitudes and expectations in an ever-changing football environment.

PÁIDÍ Ó SÉ
(Kerry)

Having won eight All-Ireland medals as a player, Páidí Ó Sé was well-equipped to handle the pressures of management when, in 1995, he fulfilled his great ambition of taking over his native Kerry. He had already led the county's Under-21 side to All-Ireland success and was a popular choice to take up the senior challenge.

Inside a year Kerry had won the Munster title and in 1997 completed a great treble, winning the Munster, All-Ireland and National League titles. The All-Ireland victory was especially welcome, because it was Kerry's first since 1986. Another Munster title followed in 1989 and, in 2000, Pàidí really stamped his authority on the managerial scene by leading Kerry to their second All-Ireland title in four seasons.

A strong, forceful defender in his

playing days, he brought the same determination and commitment to his managerial responsibilities – qualities his players embraced eagerly.

CANON BERTIE TROY
(Cork)

Winning the All-Ireland senior title for three consecutive years is a rare achievement in Gaelic Games. Cork were the last county to achieve the hurling treble, in 1976, '77 and '78, and the subtle coaching touch which underpinned their consistent excellence was provided by Canon Bertie Troy.

Cork beat Wexford in both the 1976 and 1977 All-Ireland finals and completed the treble a year later against Kilkenny. It was a glory period for Cork, and while their ability was remarkably high, Canon Troy's sideline expertise also played a major part in pulling all the strands together.

OLLIE WALSH
(Kilkenny)

Walsh took over as Kilkenny manager in 1990 after they had lost by 16 points to Offaly in the Leinster championship. It was a deeply embarrassing defeat, but Walsh felt the situation was in no way as desperate as it appeared. His vast experience as one of the best goalkeepers in hurling history gave him a deep insight into what was required at the highest level and he set about reviving Kilkenny's fortunes.

He succeeded almost immediately, guiding Kilkenny to Leinster success in 1991. A year later they beat Cork in the All-Ireland final and retained the title in 1993, beating Galway in the final. Kilkenny was the only team to win consecutive All-Ireland hurling titles in the 1990s. Much of the credit for that went to Walsh, whose sharp hurling brain brought the best out of his players. It was a special season for the Walsh family as Ollie's son Michael was the Kilkenny goalkeeper and played a major part in the double All-Ireland success of 1992–93.

1989, when they won the All-Ireland title for the first time in 16 years.

They retained the All-Ireland title in 1990 and went on to win three more Munster titles under Morgan in 1993, '94 and '95.

JOHN O'MAHONY
(Mayo, Leitrim & Galway)

His remarkable record encompassed success in three counties: his native Mayo, Leitrim and Galway. In 1989,

8

THE FAMOUS STADIUMS

Croke Park as it used to be. The Hogan Stand was demolished after the All-Ireland Football Final in 1999

When William P (Liam) Clifford first spoke of his dream of 'a field in every parish' back in the mid-1920s he began a movement that would have an extraordinary effect on the lives of Irish people and on the landscape of the country.

He created a new blueprint for the establishment and growth of the Irish village and town. Added to the list of absolute necessities for every community, along with a church, a post office and a public house, was the provision of a Gaelic Athletic Association ground. Clifford, from Limerick, and president of the GAA

from 1926 to 1928, set a pattern that would define the development of the GAA.

At that time Croke Park was already becoming the Mecca for followers of football and hurling. At the start of that decade, however, it was the only ground fully owned by the association. Other facilities were rented

Offaly fans have enjoyed some great days at Croke Park over the last 30 years

or utilised when other community events were not taking place. Clifford, among others, believed that a central part of the GAA's development was the ability to control their own fate through facilities.

The purchase and development of these facilities began in the major centres such as Cork, Limerick and Dublin. Gradually it spread throughout the country. For example, a ground was purchased in Drogheda in 1925, one in Belfast in 1927, and by the 1960s every county had at least one major ground. In tandem over the decades was the extraordinary growth of facilities in towns and villages. The GAA ground became the centre for many community activities.

In the early days the grounds were, of necessity, crude. Local officials marked the field, set up posts and organised the games. There were no extra facilities for players or spectators. Gradually, the grounds became more sophisticated. Committees, such as Bord na bPáirc (The Parks Board) in the 1960s, were given responsibility for ground development. Special grants were made available at county, provincial and national level to allow the smallest communities to develop their own grounds.

CROKE PARK
Dublin

Such was the strength of hurling and football in Dublin when the GAA was founded in 1884 that the need to find a major facility became quickly apparent. The grounds at Phoenix Park were a natural attraction, although early games were often thwarted when the authorities would close the gates on hearing of plans for a game of football or hurling.

The fields which would become famous as the home of the GAA had hosted All-Ireland finals as early as 1896. Owned at that time by the City and Suburban Racecourse and Amusements Grounds Limited, they were leased for sports meetings, including Gaelic games, and whippet-racing.

By 1906 the company was in financial difficulties and the land was put up for sale. Two years later Frank Brazil Dineen bought it for £3,250. A native of Ballylanders in Waterford, he had been a well-known athlete and had been involved in the GAA from its earliest days: eventually he would serve as sec-retary and president of the association. Because the GAA could not afford to buy the ground itself, Dineen secured a loan to do so.

In 1910 he was forced to sell four acres to the Jesuit Order for £1,090. This would become the Belvedere College grounds which, ironically, the GAA would buy back nearly 90 years later for a considerable sum to allow the multi-million pound reconstruction that is the ultra-modern Croke Park we know today.

Dineen's act can be described as one of philanthropy. He did not intend to make money out of the deal, merely to hand it over to the GAA when the time was right. That time was 18 December 1913, when he passed his interest over to the trustees of the GAA. About the same time the GAA had considered erect-

Semple Stadium, Thurles, regarded by many as the home of hurling

ing a monument to its patron, Archbishop Croke of Cashel. With its finances boosted by the successful hosting of an inter-county competition, it agreed to buy the grounds from Dineen for £1,500 and named them Croke Park.

Accommodation for spectators was primitive. Two stands existed on the Jones' Road side of the ground, one known later as the Long Stand and the other simply as the Stand. The latter was a fragile timber construction which also had an office underneath.

The first development undertaken by the GAA was the construction of the terrace now fondly known as Hill 16. This was built in 1917 from rubble, most of which came from the wreckage of O'Connell Street during the 1916 Easter Rising, including the GPO. The hill initially was known as Hill 60, the name of a hill in France which had become famous during the 1914–1918 war. It had been captured and recaptured so often that the hill was reduced to rubble. The name Hill 16 was adopted later.

The most notorious incident with which Croke Park will always be associated occurred on 21 November 1920. Ireland was in the grip of the War of Independence and on that morning 14 members of the British Secret Service in Dublin were killed by nationalist forces. In reprisal, the British military surrounded Croke Park, where Dublin and Tipperary were playing a challenge game. Volleys were fired into the ground and 13 people were killed, including

Tipperary player Michael Hogan.

Four years later, to celebrate the revival of the Tailteann Games – a festival of Gaelic sport that was not confined to the games administered by the GAA – a new stand was built along the Jones' Road side of the ground and named in honour of Michael Hogan. Along with major games of football and hurling, as well as the Tailteann Games of 1928 and 1932, Croke Park also hosted athletics and cycling until 1933 when a decision was taken to restrict the usage to hurling and football. This edict would later apply to all GAA grounds and remains in force today.

The Cusack Stand – named after the GAA's founding father Michael Cusack – was planned in 1936 but a strike by building workers delayed its completion. That meant that the 1937 All-Ireland hurling final between Tipperary and Kilkenny was played at the Fitzgerald Stadium in Killarney, which had been opened a year earlier. The Cusack Stand was completed in 1938 and officially opened on 21 August by the president of the GAA, Pádraig McNamee, during half-time of the All-Ireland football semi-final between Kerry and Laois.

The stand cost £50,000 and was regarded as one of the finest in Europe at the time, being 407 feet long and in two tiers. It seated 5,000 on the upper deck and had standing accommodation on the terraces of the lower deck, which was converted to 9,000 seats in 1966. The terracing of the Canal End was

carried out in 1949 and the Nally Stand was built in 1952.

In 1957 the GAA launched an ambitious project to replace the Hogan Stand with a new structure. The new two-tier stand was 500 feet long and had seating for 16,000. Also included for the first time were the committee rooms, which continued in use until the stand was knocked down in 1999. Because work was stopped to allow for the playing of major games, the new stand was not completed until 1959 and was officially opened on 5 June.

Croke Park now officially had seating for 23,000 and standing for 62,000, but that capacity was stretched for the football final of 1959 between Kerry and Galway, when 85,897 went through the turnstiles. A year later 87,768 watched Down and Kerry in the final, and the all-time record of 90,556 watched as Down retained their title in 1961 when defeating Offaly. The last time the 80,000 barrier was broken was in 1963 and restrictions kept attendances to around 70,000 thereafter.

Development then slowed somewhat. New dressing-rooms were built under the Hogan Stand and Hill 16 was rebuilt into a modern terrace and reopened in 1989. Four years later the grand plan for a complete reconstruction of Croke Park was launched. At a cost of over £175 million, the arena would get a complete new look and be turned into an ultra-modern stadium. The first phase involved

the construction of a new stand on the site of the old Cusack Stand and was completed in 1996. The second phase involved the continuation of the stand at the Canal End and the third phase was the demolition of the Hogan Stand in 1999 and the completion of the new stadium. The capacity will be approximately 76,000.

SEMPLE STADIUM
Thurles

To some people in the GAA this is the home of hurling; the journey to Thurles for a Munster hurling final is a sacred passage. The gathering in the market square on the day of the game is one of the traditional experiences which followers must enjoy at least once in their lives.

The land near the railway station was first used for agricultural shows when bought by a local committee in 1901. That committee retained control for nine years before selling the grounds to the local GAA committee. Known as The Sportsfield, it hosted its first Munster final in 1914 and was steadily improved over the years until singled out by Bord na bPáirc in the mid-1960s for special attention.

A new stand and terracing were built and the ground was reopened in 1968 as Semple Stadium, named in honour of Tom Semple, a native of Thurles who had been one of the committee members involved in the original purchase of the ground.

He was a famous hurler of his time with the Thurles Blues club. They won six Tipperary championships and Semple also won two All-Ireland championships. He captained a Tipperary team which toured Europe in 1910, playing exhibition games in Brussels and Fontenoy. He was also a referee (taking charge of the 1914 Munster final) and administrator. The ground as we know it today was completed in 1984, in time for the special staging of the All-Ireland hurling final between Cork and Offaly to mark the GAA's Centenary Year. It has a capacity of just under 60,000.

CASEMENT PARK
Belfast

One of the first grounds owned by the GAA outside Dublin was Corrigan Park in Belfast. Opened in 1927, it had cost £1,600 and served the city and county well, but it had a major drawback in that the surface was never of the highest quality. By the early 1940s a new ground was needed and a committee was set up to raise funds. A site in Andersonstown was chosen and the ground that became known as Casement Park was developed, costing £101,000, and opened on 1 June 1953. Such was the success of the fund-raising effort that no borrowing was needed. In recent years terracing has replaced grass embankments on one side and at both ends of the ground.

PÁIRC UI CHAOIMH
Cork

The site where the modern stadium stands beside the River Lee was used for sports events for at least 100 years before the founding of the GAA. It was under the control of the Cork Agricultural Company, which held its shows there. At the end of the 19th century the company allowed the fledgling GAA board in the county to use part of the land for football and hurling.

A new ground was constructed, and when it opened in 1904 (when the delayed 1902 All-Ireland finals were played) it was named the Athletic Grounds. Some of the great football clashes between Cork and Kerry were played thereover the decades, as well as the major hurling championship games.

Despite some upgrading, the ground was in need of a complete change at the start of the 1970s and

Munster Football Day in Páirc Uí Chaoímh, and Kerry stars Jack O'Shea and Pat Spillane take the battle to Cork

a major reconstruction was undertaken. The new stadium, named after Pádraig O'Caoimh, general secretary of the GAA from 1929 to 1964, was opened on 6 June 1976 by the president of the GAA, Corkman Con Murphy. The capacity is just under 50,000.

ST. TIERNACH'S PARK
Clones

This venue, now the home of the Ulster football final, is named after a local saint and was bought by the local club in 1944 from a merchant for £700. Major games had been played in various fields around the town from the early part of the century. The official opening took place on 6 August 1944. In the 1990s it was chosen as a special venue for redevelopment and the old grass embankment on the town side of the ground was rebuilt as seating. A new stand was erected on the other side of the field, with improved facilities for players.

DR HYDE PARK
Roscommon

As far back as 1930 Rafferty's Field, close to the hospital in Roscommon Town, had been used for major sporting fixtures with the permission of the landowner. These had included the All-Ireland football semi-final of 1930 between Kerry and Mayo. The site was never developed as a sports ground and St Coman's Park, located on the far side of the town, was the official county ground.

Because of its location, however, St Coman's Park was flooded for six months of the year and could be used only in summertime. The flooding also meant that there was little point in developing the ground to modern standards. In 1969 a local committee purchased Rafferty's Field of 14 acres for £3,000 and named it after the first president of Ireland, Douglas Hyde, who had been born in the west of the county.

The ground hosted its first major game in the Connacht championship of 1971, when Sligo played Roscommon. While facilities were regularly upgraded, the ground needed an overhaul and was chosen for special grant assistance by the Central Council in the 1990s. The embankments on the road side and at both ends were terraced and new facilities for players were built. A new stand is planned. The capacity is 30,000.

TUAM STADIUM
Galway

Tuam has always been the spiritual base of Galway football. It is also home to the famous football nursery that is St. Jarlath's College.

The town has been the venue for big games through the history of the GAA, although in the early days the games were played beside the old racecourse at Parkmore. These included All-Ireland semi-finals in the 1920s and 1930s.

In the 1930s plans were drawn up for the development of a ground on the Parkmore site and land was bought.

Nothing came of this, however, and it was not until the mid-1940s that the land at the current venue was secured and work began.

Tuam Stadium was opened in 1950. The official name of the

St Tiernach's Park, Clones, hosts most of the major Ulster Football Championship matches

Fitzgerald Stadium, Killarney, is set in one of the most picturesque locations in Europe

ground is St. Jarlath's Park but that name has not been used in modern times.

Although Pearse Stadium in Salthill was also regarded as a premier ground in Galway, Tuam Stadium was the heartland, and while the Salthill venue was being redeveloped Tuam became the prime venue in the county.

FITZGERALD STADIUM
Killarney

One of the most picturesque sporting arenas in Europe, nestling under the Magillicuddy Reeks, Fitzgerald Stadium is a popular venue with both hurling and football followers as well as the players. Now reconstructed to a very high standard, the venue on the outskirts of the tourist town has a long and distinguished history.

The ground is named after one of Kerry's greatest footballers, Dick Fitzgerald, and was developed as a monument to his memory following his death in 1930. He had won five All-Ireland championships and was Kerry's winning captain in 1913 and 1914.

The site beside the local psychiatric hospital was bought by the Kerry County Board in the early 1930s and the official opening took place on 31 May 1936, when Kerry played their great rivals of that period, Mayo.

Although primarily regarded as a football venue, located as it is in the game's heartland, Killarney also is a very popular hurling venue and has hosted many Munster championship finals. The ground had been open only a year when it hosted the 1937 All-Ireland hurling final between Tipperary and Kilkenny, at which the attendance was 43,638. It has been modernised in recent years.

GAELIC GROUNDS
Limerick

When William Clifford talked of a field in every parish, he backed up his words with action.

In October 1926 GAA president Clifford approached the Munster Council with a proposal to buy a ground in Limerick for the sole use of the GAA. His vision was of a ground that would be developed into one of the major venues for hurling and football.

The council was in a healthy state financially following a series of well-attended hurling championship games, and provided a grant of £1,000 towards the cost of the land.

It soon became a popular venue for major championship games in hurling and football.

A feature of the ground for many years was the old Hogan Stand from Croke Park, which had been transported from Dublin to Limerick when the new stand was built in Croke Park in 1957. It remained in place until a major refurbishment was carried out in Limerick in the 1990s and a new stand was built. Plans for a further £7 million development have been drawn up and work is expected to begin soon.

McHALE PARK
Castlebar

The expenditure of £650 by the Castlebar club in Mayo for purchasing land in 1930 was a sign of the growing confidence of GAA clubs in the country, and the realisation of the need to provide facilities. The ground officially opened in May 1931 and was regularly used until the late 1940s. Then it was decided that renovations were needed and the ground reopened in 1952. The stand was added in 1990, and today the ground is all-seater with a capacity of approximately 35,000, regularly hosting Connacht football finals.

9

THE GREAT MATCHES

The Tipperary squad prior to the 1968 All-Ireland hurling final which they lost to Wexford by two points

GAELIC FOOTBALL

For well over 100 years, venues all across Ireland have throbbed to the pulsating drama of hurling and Gaelic football. From humble club games to the glamour and glitz of All-Ireland finals, the passion and the excitement levels have touched the soul of the Irish nation in a manner which no other sports have achieved.

1935 ALL-IRELAND FOOTBALL FINAL, CROKE PARK

Cavan 3–6 Kildare 2–5

This marked the end of what had been a glorious era for Kildare football.

Although they were beaten in a classic final, they had made a huge contribution to a memorable game. Kildare had won two All-Ireland championships, in 1927 and 1928, and reached the finals of 1929 and 1931.

Cavan, the champions of 1933, had been unimpressive in the semi-final win over Tipperary. But in the final they gave a performance which is described in the history books as one of the most glorious of the period.

They got off to a blistering start and Paddy Boylan scored two goals before Kildare got on the scoreboard.

Cavan led by 2–5 to 1–2 at half-time and Tom O'Reilly added another goal in the second half. But Kildare, inspired by a Mick Geraghty goal, made a dramatic comeback and were unlucky not to score a third goal when a shot from Jimmy Dowling went inches over the bar.

Cavan: W Young; W Connolly, J Smith, M Denneny; T Dolan, T O'Reilly, P Phair; H O'Reilly, T O'Reilly; D Morgan P Devlin, J Smallhorn; P Boylan, L Blessing, MJ Magee.

Kildare: J Maguire, W Mangan, M Goff, J Byrne; P Watters, J Higgins, F Dowling; P Matthews, C Higgins; T Mulhall, P Byrne, P Martin; J Dowling, M Geraghty, T Keogh. Sub: J Dalton for Higgins.

Referee: S. Jordan (Galway)

1938 ALL-IRELAND FOOTBALL FINAL, CROKE PARK

Galway 3–3 Kerry 2–6 (draw)

Galway 2–4, Kerry 0–7 (replay)

Few encounters before or since produced such high drama, controversy and excitement as the drawn and replayed All-Ireland finals of 1938. And the conclusion to this epic duel between Galway and Kerry is without question one of the most bizarre in the history of the All-Ireland championships.

Kerry were the defending champions, having beaten Cavan in a replay in the 1937 All-Ireland final. The team was packed with players who would become great stars – Paddy 'Bawn' Brosnan, 'Gega' O'Connor, John Joe 'Purty' Landers, Bill Dillon and Bill Casey. Galway too had their big names: Mick Higgins had captained the team to All-Ireland success in 1934 and Dinny O'Sullivan, Mick Connaire, John Dunne and Brendan Nestor also survived from that team.

The quality of football, mostly in the catch-and-kick style of the period, was of a very high standard

and there were never more than three points between the teams at any stage. Towards the end of the drawn game Kerry staged a late rally and got on level terms. In the final minute Kerry were awarded a '50'. The shot from Séan Brosnan dropped short. Landers took possession and kicked for what would have been the winning point. As the ball sailed towards the posts the referee blew the final whistle. The ball went over the bar but did not count as a point, thereby forcing the game to a replay.

In a hugely-entertaining replay Galway were leading by four points with four minutes to go when the referee blew for a free. One Galway player jumped in celebration and the crowd took that as a signal that the game was over and swarmed on to the field. It took 15 minutes to clear the pitch, during which time the players went to the dressing-rooms. Some of the Kerry players dressed and left the ground, thinking the game was over. However, Kerry were instructed to resume and were forced to field eight substitutes. They managed to score a point but could not get back on level terms.

Galway: J McGauran; M Rafferty, M Connaire, D O'Sullivan; F Cunniffe, B Beggs, C Connolly; J Burke, J Dunne; J Flavin, M Higgins, R Griffin; E Mulholland, M Kelly, B Nestor. Subs: M Ryder for Mulholland, P McDonagh for Burke.

Kerry: D O'Keeffe; W Kinnerk, PB Brosnan, W Myers; W Dillon, B Casey, T O'Connor; J Walsh, S Brosnan, P Kennedy, A McAuliffe, C O'Sullivan, M Regan, M Doyle, T O'Leary. Sub: JJ Landers for Walsh.

Referees – Draw: T Culhane (Limerick) Replay: P Waters (Kildare)

1950 ALL-IRELAND FOOTBALL FINAL, CROKE PARK

Mayo 2–5 Louth 1–6

Forwards usually get most of the credit for victories but Mayo broke that mould when they emerged in 1950 with a defence which was regarded

All-Ireland final, 1935: Cavan's Paddy Boylan (13) in action

as one of the soundest in the history of Gaelic football. They were defiantly resolute right through the championship campaign, peaking in the All-Ireland final where they were inspired by the consistent excellence of their team captain, Séan Flanagan.

Louth led at half-time by 1–4 to 1–3 and were playing the more progressive football. However, they were unable to make lots of possession really count on the scoreboard, due mainly to the quality of the Mayo defence. Still, they were holding on to the lead as the game neared its close when Tom Langan got possession for Mayo and passed to Mick Flanagan, who set off on a solo run. The Louth players protested that he had over-carried the ball but the referee saw it differently and allowed the flying Mayo man to continue. Flanagan fisted the ball into the net and Mick Mulderrig added a point to snatch a dramatic victory.

Mayo: W Durkin; J Forde, P Prendergast, S Flanagan; P Quinn, H Dixon, J McAndrew; P Carney, E Mongey; M Flanagan, W Kenny, J Gilvarry; M Mulderrig, T Langan, P Solon. Subs: S Wynne for Durkin, M Caulfield for Kenny, S Mulderrig for Caulfield.

Louth: S Thornton; M Byrne, T Conlon, J Tuft; S Boyle, P Markey, P McArdle; J Regan, F Reid; J McDonnell, N Roe, S White; R Lynch, H Reynolds, M Reynolds. Subs: R Mooney for Roe, M McDonnell for McArdle.

Referee: S Deignan (Cavan)

1956 ALL-IRELAND FOOTBALL FINAL, CROKE PARK

Galway 2–13 Cork 3–7

Rarely, if ever, have two men dominated a major occasion in the manner achieved by Seán Purcell and Frank Stockwell in this All-Ireland final. Reports of the game focus almost solely on the contribution of the two friends, a double act that earned them the affectionate tag of 'The Terrible Twins'.

Purcell and Stockwell had grown up together in Bishop Street, Tuam, and attended the town's famous football nursery, St Jarlath's College. From their teenage days it was obvious that they had a special talent. Purcell was the play-maker, a man entirely comfortable on the ball and possessing incredible vision. His extraordinary talents combined perfectly with Stockwell's speed and intuition.

Galway had not won an All-Ireland championship since 1938 and had not appeared in the final since 1942, so the stakes were high when they lined up against Cork in 1956. Rather unusually, none of the provincial champions of the previous year had retained their titles so there was a degree of novelty about the 1956 All-Ireland series. Cork had also gone through something of a barren period and had not appeared in an All-Ireland final since they won the championship in 1945.

More than 70,000 expectant supporters packed into Croke Park for the 1956 final. Because these were new finalists, nobody was quite sure what to expect. Before long, however, the stands were buzzing with excitement as Purcell and Stockwell made an early impact. The lightly-built Stockwell scored two points in the opening minutes as the Cork backs looked on in bewildered confusion. Stockwell seemed to be playing everywhere except in his allocated position of full-forward.

In the 16th minute Purcell took a sideline kick and sent it floating over the Cork full-back line. The backs, already unnerved by Stockwell, reacted slowly and failed to sort out the situation. The ball broke to Stockwell, who scored Galway's first goal. Cork rallied, and their own full-forward Niall Fitzgerald worked hard to bring them into the game.

Five minutes before half-time Purcell and Stockwell combined again. Purcell took possession from a sideline kick and looked up to see where his friend was positioned. Stockwell had slipped behind the Cork defence. Purcell passed the ball inside and Stockwell gave Cork goalkeeper Paddy Tyres no chance. Galway led by 2–6 to 0–6 at half-time.

Early in the second half, Stockwell added two more points to give Galway an eight-points lead. Other teams might have folded but Cork showed great spirit and fought back tigerishly. Denis 'Toots' Kelleher switched to left corner forward and began to cause problems for the Galway defence. It emerged later that the Galway corner back Séan Keeley was concussed for the entire second half after taking a knock.

Kelleher took full advantage and scored two goals which revived his side's prospects. Now, it seemed that Cork might snatch victory as the momentum had clearly switched their way. But Purcell and Stockwell reinforced their influence on the game. Stockwell finished with a remarkable tally of 2–5, all from play, on a day when his understanding with Purcell broke Cork hearts.

Galway: J Mangan; S Keeley, G Daly, T Dillon; J Kissane, J Mahon, M Greally; F Evers, M McDonagh; J Coyle, S Purcell, B O'Neill; J Young, F Stockwell, G Kirwan. Sub: A Swords for Young.

Cork: P Tyres; P O'Driscoll, D O'Sullivan, D Murray; P Harrington, D Bernard, M Gould; S Moore, E Ryan; D Kelleher, C Duggan, P Murphy; T Furlong, N Fitzgerald, J Creedon. Sub: E Goulding for Murphy.

Referee: P McDermott (Meath).

1968 MUNSTER FOOTBALL FINAL, FITZGERALD STADIUM, KILLARNEY

Kerry 1-21 Cork 3-8

In the long and illustrious history of the Munster football championship, the domination of Kerry and Cork has produced dozens of wonderful games. Indeed, there are many Gaelic Games followers who argue that a Munster final between the two superpowers in Killarney or Páirc Uí Chaoímh is the most consistently-exciting occasion on the calendar.

More often than not, Kerry have held the upper hand. But when the two great rivals met in the 1968 Munster final, Cork were enjoying a rare period of superiority. They had won the two previous meetings with Kerry and had only narrowly lost the All-Ireland finals of 1966 and 1967 to Galway and Meath respectively. And with some new exciting talent coming through in a steady flow, Cork's optimism levels were rising all the time.

Kerry, meanwhile, were in a state of disarray in the months preceding the game. Mick O'Dwyer had retired prematurely and it was also thought that Mick O'Connell would not be available. Another great star, Séamus Murphy, was also taking a break. But in the build-up to the championship O'Dwyer, by then a selector with the team, organised a game between Kerry Past and Kerry Present. O'Dwyer played, as did O'Connell, and they made a huge

impression. Séamus Murphy was also persuaded to return and the trio were back in action when the big day arrived in July.

Kerry followers were not entirely convinced of their team's merits and after a mere eight minutes they were almost in despair. Cork, inspired by 19-year-old Ray Cummins, had an explosive start. He and Donal Hunt scored a goal each in the opening period to help Cork to a 2–3 to 0–2 lead.

It was at this stage that O'Connell put his unique stamp on the game. The man many would argue was the greatest footballer of all time had not always produced his brilliant best in Munster finals. It was

different this time. He was majestic in his fielding and led a Kerry revival that took them right back into the contest by half-time when they trailed by just one point, 0–10 to 2–5. Kerry also had played against the wind, so the advantage was now very definitely with them.

O'Connell and O'Dwyer were outstanding in the second half and but for the brilliance of Cork goalkeeper Billy Morgan Kerry might have won with greater comfort. O'Connell's dominance in the middle of the field had starved the Cork forwards of possession for much of the game, although Cork's 3-8 return suggested that, had they got a decent supply of possession, they had the

The Cork team which lost to Galway in the classic All-Ireland football final of 1956

capacity to cause problems for Kerry. However, scoring some majestic points, Kerry cruised to a seven-point win. They beat Longford by two points (2–13 to 2–11) in the All-Ireland semi-final but lost the final to Down 2–12 to 1–13.

Kerry: T Bowler; S Murphy, P O'Donoghue, S Burrows; D O'Sullivan, T Sheehan, D O'Sullivan; M O'Connell, M Fleming; B Lynch, P Griffin, E O'Donoghue; T Prendergast, DJ Crowley, M O'Dwyer. Sub: D Crowley for O'Connell.

Cork: B Morgan; B Murphy, F Kehilly, J O'Mahoney; P O'Sullivan, D Coughlan, K Dillon; M Burke, M O'Loughlin; JJ Murphy, C O'Sullivan, B O'Neill; D Hunt, R Cummins, J Carroll. Subs:

E Ryan for JJ Murphy, J Crowley for P O'Sullivan, P Harte for B Murphy.

Referee: J Dowling (Offaly)

1970 LEINSTER FOOTBALL FINAL, CROKE PARK

Meath 2-22 Offaly 5-12

Some months before the start of the 1970 championships, the GAA re-examined its match regulations and after much deliberation decided to increase the duration of championship games from 60 to 80 minutes. The extra 20 minutes would prove a huge test for amateur players and many felt it was unfair to impose such a demanding schedule on them.

In their very first season, the 80-minute championship games would play a major part in producing a truly amazing contest. The Leinster final between Meath and Offaly has gone down in history as one of the most spectacular, bewildering and unbelievable games ever played. A total of seven goals and 34 points were scored, with only one point separating the teams at full-time.

Offaly had turned a five-point deficit during the first half into an 11-point lead shortly after half-time

149

Eugene Mulligan: the first Offaly man to win Footballer of the Year in 1971

and still lost the game. They scored a remarkable 4–6 in a 25-minute period of the first half. It was as close to perfection as they could ever have hoped for, but ultimately it wasn't enough to win the day.

Meath, who had won the All-Ireland title three years earlier, started in confident mood and were leading by 0–6 to 0–1 after 15 minutes. Suddenly Offaly, beaten All-Ireland finalists in 1969, came alive. Kieran Claffey took control in midfield and his high fielding and strong running caused huge problems for a perplexed Meath defence. Johnny Cooney scored Offaly's first goal and then Claffey himself burst through the Meath defence to get another. Sean Evans added two more goals and the game had been completely transformed. The Meath

players were visibly distressed by what had happened and looked well-beaten when they trailed by 4–7 to 0–9 at half-time.

To Meath's great credit, they refused to yield. Tony McTague had been one of their chief tormentors and they switched Ollie Shanley from attack to defence to try and curb the Offaly sharpshooter. The move worked well. Still, with 25 minutes remaining, Meath were trailing by seven points, 0–16 to 4–11. Meath sub Mickey Fay then made a major contribution to yet another amazing sequence. As the Offaly defence hesitated when dealing with a cross from Tony Brennan, Fay reacted quickly and fisted the ball into the net. A minute later Fay added another goal before Mick Mellett levelled the game with a point.

Meath then went into a three-point lead but the drama still wasn't over. Offaly midfielder Willie Bryan punched a goal in the 78th minute to bring the teams level, Offaly 5–12, Meath 2–21. Just when it seemed an incredible game would end in a draw, Meath right half forward Tony Brennan won possession about 50 yards from the Offaly goal and sent the ball high over the bar for the winning point.

Meath: S McCormack; B Cunningham, J Quinn, P Black; M White, T Kearns, P Reynolds; V Foley, V Lynch; T Brennan, M Kerrigan, M Mellett; K Rennicks, J Murphy, O Shanley. Subs: M Fay for Black, P Moore for Foley.

Offaly: M Furlong; E Mulligan, J Smith, J Egan; N Clavin, L Coughlan, P Monaghan; W Bryan, K Claffey; P Fenning, J Cooney, T McTague; P Keenan, M Connor, J Gunning. Subs: J Hanlon for Monaghan, S Kilroy for Gunning, W Molloy for Claffey.

Referee: B Hayden (Carlow).

1977 ALL-IRELAND FOOTBALL SEMI-FINAL, CROKE PARK

Dublin 3–12 Kerry 1–13

It is widely-accepted that the emergence of Dublin and Kerry in the mid-1970s changed attitudes to Gaelic football. They brought a whole new approach to coaching and training and, with the hand pass very much in vogue, physical fitness became as crucial to success as the traditional skills.

The rivalry that developed between Dublin and Kerry added a certain aura to their encounters, although there were some occasions when the reality didn't quite match up to everyone's hopes. However, the 1977 All-Ireland semi-final lived up to the highest expectations, producing a game which is still regarded as one of the greatest of all time.

Dublin had beaten Kerry in the 1976 All-Ireland final and were fancied to retain their title. Their inspiration and chief motivator Kevin Heffernan had stepped down after

the 1976 triumph and his place as manager was taken over by team captain Tony Hanahoe. The transition was smooth and Hanahoe made few changes either on or off the field, opting to retain what had been a winning formula. His counterpart Mick O'Dwyer had introduced some new talent into the Kerry team in the form of Jack O'Shea, Séan Walsh and Barry Walsh.

Almost 60,000 spectators packed into Croke Park and got an early indication of the pace and quality which would take the game to unprecedented heights.

Barely a minute into the game, Dublin's full-forward Jimmy Keaveney was presented with a goal

chance when he found himself one-on-one with Kerry goalkeeper Paud O'Mahony. Untypically, Keaveney hesitated and drove the ball just wide. Still, the pattern for a day of high drama had been set.

Kerry led at half-time by 1–6 to 0–6, the goal coming from their new full-forward Séan Walsh.

The Dublin management team opted to make changes which would prove crucial. Bernard Brogan was brought in to partner Brian Mullins at midfield and gradually the Dublin pair began to break the stranglehold of Jack O'Shea and Páidí Ó Sé.

Immediately after the restart Dublin got back on level terms when John McCarthy scored a goal after taking a pass from Hanahoe.

The game was now being played at a breathtaking pace and the teams exchanged point after point. Walsh had a chance of a second goal for Kerry but was denied by a goal-line clearance from Kevin Moran.

Kerry led by 1–13 to 1–11 when Hanahoe set up David Hickey for a second Dublin goal. That gave them a one-point lead with five minutes remaining.

Kerry counter-attacked but Dublin full-back Séan Doherty cleared the danger. The ball was moved swiftly upfield where Hanahoe was waiting. He held up the ball while Brogan sprinted forward. Once Hanahoe released the ball to Brogan, the result was inevitable. Brogan held his nerve and rifled in Dublin's third goal to

Bobby Doyle kicks a point for Dublin in the memorable 1977 All-Ireland semi-final against Kerry

ensure a magnificent victory.

Hanahoe, who had been the chief architect of this victory in a variety of ways – manager, coach, captain and play-maker – scored the final point of the game. It was his finest afternoon in the Dublin colours and the following month he led Dublin to All-Ireland glory when they easily overcame the challenge of Armagh in the final to win by 5–12 to 3–6.

Dublin: P Cullen; G O'Driscoll, S Doherty, R Kelleher; T Drumm, K Moran, P O'Neill; B Mullins, F Ryder; A O'Toole, T Hanahoe, D Hickey; B Doyle, J Keaveney, J McCarthy. Subs: B Brogan for Ryder, P Gogarty for McCarthy.

Kerry: P O'Mahony; J Deenihan, J O'Keeffe, G O'Keeffe; D Moran, T Kennelly, G Power; J O'Shea, P Ó Sé; J Egan, P Lynch, P Spillane; B Walsh, S Walsh, M Sheehy. Subs: T Doyle for B Walsh, P McCarthy for O'Shea.

Referee: S Murray (Monaghan).

1991 LEINSTER FOOTBALL CHAMPIONSHIP FIRST ROUND, CROKE PARK

Meath 1–12 Dublin 1–12 (draw).

Meath 1–11 Dublin 1–11 (first replay, after extra time).

Meath 2–11 Dublin 1–14 (second replay, after extra time).

Meath 2–10 Dublin 0–15 (third replay)

When Meath and Dublin lined out for the first round of the Leinster championship on 2 June 1991, they could not have imagined the drama that would unfold. Five weeks later, after five hours and 40 minutes of football over four games, including two periods of extra time, just one point separated the teams, with Meath advancing to the quarter-final.

Here we go again: watched by referee Tommy Howard and team-mate

Almost 240,000 spectators attended the four games, generating gate receipts of £1.1 million. The whole country became gripped by the extraordinary drama taking place at Croke Park and TV viewing figures were among the highest ever recorded for Gaelic football. It was drama of a heart-stopping nature, an event that catapulted the sport on to a new level in terms of public interest.

Meath had been the dominant team in Leinster over the previous five years and had lost to Dublin only once during that period. Meath

had beaten their great rivals in the Leinster finals of 1986, '87, '88 and '90, while Dublin's sole win had come in 1989. Dublin entered the 1991 campaign with a new management team led by former goalkeeper Paddy Cullen. Prior to 1991, Dublin and Meath would not have met in the first round because of a seeding system used by the Leinster Council, which was designed to keep the stronger teams apart in the earlier stages of the competition. However, that was dispensed with for the 1991 championship.

Dublin were the dominant force

in the opening half of the first game but failed to hold their interval lead of 1–7 to 1–2. The quality of football was not good and the game would be remembered more for the excitement of the final minutes as the teams traded scores while also missing chances. Dublin were ahead by one point in the final moment when Meath's PJ Gillic attempted a kicked pass to Tommy Dowd. Gillic mis-hit the ball but it fortuitously bounced in front of goal and hopped over the bar. The final whistle sounded immediately afterwards. In the first replay Dublin again

Brian Stafford, Meath's David Beggy takes the challenge to Dublin during the epic four-match saga in 1991

missed many good chances, kicking 13 wides in normal time. The teams finished level at 0–10 each. In the first six minutes of extra time they each added 1–1 but in the final 24 minutes failed to add another score. Two weeks later a crowd of 63,730 watched Dublin build a 0–10 to 0–5 lead with 15 minutes to go, but a goal from Bernard Flynn and two pointed frees from Brian Stafford brought the teams level again. In extra time Meath's Colm Coyle and Dublin's Paul Clarke traded goals as the quality of football continued to rise. Despite the best efforts of both sides it was all square at the end, sending the tie into a third replay.

The fourth game took place on 6 July. Again, Dublin dominated for most of the game and were three points ahead entering the final quarter. Finally, it looked as if an amazing duel would end in a Dublin victory. But, once again, they faltered and Meath rose to the challenge, this time decisively. Dublin were on the attack in the final minute but Meath defender Martin O'Connell intercepted an intended pass. Nine Meath passes later, the ball was directed into the eager hands of advancing defender Kevin Foley, who had run to within ten yards of the Dublin goal. He had the simplest task in scoring a goal which brought the game level. Dublin were stunned. Mattie McCabe won the kick out for Meath and transferred the ball to Liam Hayes, who delivered an inch-perfect pass to PJ Gillic. He spotted David Beggy running free to the right of the Dublin goal and made a quick transfer which sent Beggy sprinting through before kicking a priceless point. Dublin's Jack Sheedy had a late chance to equalise from a long-range free but it drifted just wide. The extraordinary drama had ended.

Meath later beat Wicklow (after a replay), Offaly, Laois and Roscommon to reach the All-Ireland final, where they lost to Down by two points, 1–16 to 1–14.

Teams for the fourth game:

Meath: M McQuillan; B O'Malley, M Lyons, P Lyons; K Foley, L Harnan, M O'Connell; L Hayes, PJ Gillic; D Beggy, C O'Rourke, T Dowd; C Coyle, B Stafford, B Flynn. Subs: F Murtagh for P Lyons, G McEntee for Murtagh, M McCabe for Flynn. Other players used during the series: T Ferguson, S Kelly, J McDermott, B Reilly, T Connor, A Browne,.

Dublin: J O'Leary; M Deegan, G Hargan, M Kennedy; T Carr, K Barr, E Heery; J Sheedy, P Bealin; C Redmond, P Curran, N Guiden; D Sheehan, P Clarke, M Galvin. Subs: R Holland for Carr, J McNally for Clarke, V Murphy for Redmond. Other players used in the series: C Walsh, D Foran, P Doherty, C Duff, B Rock, D McCarthy.

Referee: T Howard (Kildare)
(All 4 games).

1994 ULSTER CHAMPIONSHIP FIRST ROUND, CELTIC PARK, DERRY.

Down 1–14 Derry 1–12

The early 1990s was unquestionably the golden age for Ulster football, with the province completely dominating the All-Ireland championship.

Having failed to win an All-Ireland title since 1968, serious questions were being raised as to the overall standard in Ulster.

However, everything changed utterly when Down emerged in 1991 to win the championship in dramatic circumstances.

One year later, Donegal continued the Ulster surge under the captaincy of Anthony Molloy and the shrewd management of Brian McEniff to win their first All-Ireland title.

Derry, the National League champions of 1992, got in on the act in 1993, winning their first All-Ireland senior championship. Having been dismissive of Ulster football a few years earlier, the rest of the country could only sit back and admire the new sense of style and flair emanating from the north.

So when the draw for the 1994 championship was made, the biggest interest centred on the Ulster campaign. When Derry were drawn at home to play Down in the opening round of the Ulster campaign the sense of anticipation soared. This had all the ingredients of a classic.

The date was 29 May and the venue Celtic Park, in Derry's Bogside. The ground had only just been refurbished, creating the perfect amphitheatre for a splendid sporting occasion.

When a capacity crowd of 30,000 fills Celtic Park it has a unique atmosphere. The day itself brought brilliant sunshine, intense heat and a game that has gone down in history as one of the best ever seen in the province of Ulster or beyond. The Down manager, Peter McGrath, had planned well for the occasion. Having studied videos of all Derry's championship games in 1993 he knew that he would have to break the domination of their exceptionally-talented midfielders, Anthony Tohill and Brian McGilligan. When Down won the All-Ireland title in 1991 they had a midfield pairing of Eamon Burns and Barry Breen. The management decided that they would be assigned defensive roles in 1994.

McGrath moved Conor Deegan, who had been at full-back in 1991, to midfield and paired him with Gregory McCartan. Supporters questioned the wisdom of McGrath's actions, believing that he was taking huge risks. The forward line featured just one change from 1991, with Gerard Deegan replacing the injured Gary Mason.

Derry also had changes from their

Down, 1994: their second All-Ireland football win in three years

1993 team. Karl Diamond replaced Johnny McGurk in defence, while in attack Séamus Downey's injury problems prevented him starting the game.

From the earliest minutes the pace was frantic, the exchanges torrid but fair.

Tohill started well for Derry but it quickly became evident that the Down manager had planned well. The Deegan-McCartan pairing gradually asserted themselves and were soon competing on level terms with the highly-rated Derry midfield. This ensured Derry could never gain the sort of control which had marked their march to glory in 1993.

Down had another ace in the pack. Mickey Linden was in spectacular form at right corner forward and scored six points from play. He was also involved in the crucial move of the day, a few minutes from the end, when Down substitute Ciaran McCabe was put through and sent the ball crashing to the roof of the Derry net for the winning goal. Down had dethroned the reigning All-Ireland champions and built on that achievement to go on and win their second All-Ireland title in four seasons.

1998 ALL-IRELAND FOOTBALL FINAL, CROKE PARK

Galway 1–14 Kildare 1–10

When Enda Colleran captained Galway to their third All-Ireland football championship in a row in 1966, nobody could have envisaged how bleak the next 30 years would be for Connacht football. From the 1920s onwards, Connacht teams had always played a leading role in deciding the destination of the Sam Maguire Cup and the famous trophy crossed the Shannon in every decade. But through the 1970s, 1980s and most of the 1990s Connacht counties could only look on enviously as the big prizes were shared by the other provinces.

When Mayo lost both the 1996 and 1997 finals, despair became entwined with hopelessness. No Connacht team appeared capable of breaking the losing sequence. Then, in October 1997, Galway appointed John O'Mahony as their team manager and a transformation took place that would bring them the All-Ireland championship of 1998 after a spectacular final win against Kildare.

O'Mahony had enjoyed success with his native Mayo and with Leitrim, and applied the same strict discipline and meticulous planning to the Galway squad. He knew he had inherited players of high potential and was determined to make that talent shine on the biggest stage.

The build-up to the final was quite remarkable. Galway's participation was completely overshadowed by Kildare's fanatical supporters, who were convinced that the 70-year wait for an All-

Ireland crown was about to end. In terms of style there was a massive difference between Galway and Kildare. Galway used a more traditional approach, mixing catch-and-kick with the modern running game, while Kildare relied essentially on hand-passing at speed, combined with good ball retention skills.

That contrast helped produce one of the most entertaining and free-flowing finals of the modern era. Neither team indulged in the physical tactics that had marred some other major championship games in previous seasons. The second half, in particular, produced some wonderful passing moves and scoring flourishes.

In an electric atmosphere, Kildare got the bonus of an early goal from Dermot Earley when he fisted the ball past Galway goalkeeper Martin McNamara. It gave Kildare the edge but also brought a response from McNamara which would have a huge bearing on the game. Thereafter the goalkeeper was inspired, denying Earley a second goal before half-time and using tactical kick-outs to great advantage.

Kildare led by 1–5 to 0–5 at half-time but were overwhelmed in the third quarter when Galway turned on the style. Jarlath Fallon began to dictate the pace of the game; Michael Donnellan forged deep into his own defence to get possession and then sprinted past helpless Kildare defenders to set up some great scores.

Four minutes into the second half John Divilly delivered a long ball out of the Galway defence. Donnellan collected and laid off to Pádraig Joyce who rounded the Kildare goalkeeper, Christy Byrne, and placed the ball into an empty net. Galway went from strength to strength and were 1–13 to 1–7 ahead with 13 minutes remaining. Kildare, however, keep the contest alive with a brave fightback and reduced the margin to three points. Earley saw another shot for goal tipped over the bar. It was the last real chance for Kildare. Séan Og

1998 All-Ireland final: Galway's Shay Walsh makes a high catch

de Paor added a point for Galway and a 32-year wait for an All-Ireland had ended for Galway and Connacht.

Galway: M McNamara; T Meehan, G Fahy, T Mannion; R Silke, J Divilly, S de Paor; K Walsh, S O'Domhnaill; M Donnellan, S Walsh, J Fallon; D Savage, P Joyce, N Finnegan. Subs: P Clancy for S Walsh.

Kildare: C Byrne; B Lacey, J Finn, K Doyle; S Dowling, G Ryan, A Rainbow; N Buckley, W McCreery; E McCormack, D Kerrigan, D Earley; M Lynch, K O'Dwyer, P Gravin. Subs: P Brennan for Gravin, B Murphy for Lynch.

Referee: J Bannon (Longford).

HURLING

1947 ALL-IRELAND HURLING FINAL, CROKE PARK

Kilkenny 0-14 Cork 2-7

This was classed as the original clash of the hurling titans. Cork's fabulous Forties, the decade in which they won five out of six All-Ireland championships in the 1941-46 period, was about to come to an end. Kilkenny, with a supremely talented team, had lost the finals of 1940, '45 and '46. The ingredients were right for a classic in 1947.

One statistic alone paints a clear picture of how the game was played. The referee, Phil Purcell of Tipperary, awarded just 25 frees during the hour, underlining the marvellous sense of sportsmanship which prevailed. More than 61,000 spectators were enthralled by the action in a final still rated as one of the greatest ever.

The day did not start well for Kilkenny. Bill Walsh was forced to cry off before the start and they had to reshape their team completely, with Jimmy Heffernan called up to play at midfield. In addition, Paddy Grace was unable to take part in the pre-game parade because of a knee injury and took up his position only after the playing of the national anthem.

However, with Terry Leahy in

superb form – he would end the game with a total of six points – Kilkenny led at half-time by 0–7 to 0–5. They were also fortunate that goalkeeper Jim Donegan was playing extremely well and had foiled Cork on a number of occasions in the half.

Leahy would be a central figure in one of the most talked-about moments in the game. Cork had gone into a one-point lead entering the final minutes when Kilkenny were awarded a free. Leahy lined up to take it but decided to change the position of the ball with his hurley. The referee moved the ball back into the original position despite protests that the free should have been awarded to Cork because Leahy had re-sited the ball. Despite the confusion, Leahy kept his composure and scored the equalising point.

Leahy also scored the winning point, driving the ball over the bar from 65 yards.

Kilkenny: J Donegan; P Grace, P Hayden, M Marnell; J Kelly, P Prendergast, J Mulcahy; D Kennedy, J Heffernan; T Walton, T Leahy, J Langton; S Downey, W Cahill, L Reidy. Sub: E Kavanagh for Prendergast.

Cork: T Mulcahy; W Murphy, C Murphy, DJ Buckley; P Donovan, A Lotty, J Young; J Lynch, C Cottrell; S Condon, C Ring, C Murphy; M O'Riordan, G O'Riordan, J Kelly.

Referee: P Purcell (Tipperary).

1956 ALL-IRELAND HURLING FINAL, CROKE PARK

Wexford 2-14 Cork 2-8

Two of hurling's legends bade farewell to the game's biggest stage in the All-Ireland final of 1956, but not before another great instalment in their respective sporting careers had been penned. Nicky Rackard of Wexford ended his career by winning a second All-Ireland medal. In the process, he and Wexford denied the great Christy Ring a

record ninth medal.

Wexford and Cork had met in the final of 1954 when a goal by Johnny Clifford had snatched the title away from Wexford. The following year Wexford returned to Croke Park and beat Limerick and Galway to win the championship, so when Cork and Wexford qualified for the 1956 final it was such an attractive prospect that more than 80,000 supporters packed into Croke Park. They would not be disappointed: the teams served up a feast of hurling.

Wexford dominated the early stages and a goal from Padge Kehoe helped them to a 1-5 to 0-2 lead. Ring began to make an impact with some astute passing and accurate free-taking. By half-time Wexford led by 1–6 to 0–5.

They increased that lead to six points early in the second half but goals by Ring (from a 21-yard free) and Paddy Barry brought Cork level with 15 minutes remaining. Nicky Rackard scored two points to restore Wexford's lead with four minutes left.

Then came the deciding moment. Ring got possession near the right sideline, ran towards the Wexford goal and, from 25 yards, sent a fierce shot towards the roof of the net. Wexford goalkeeper Art Foley produced a wonderful save, plucking the ball out of the air with his left hand and clearing the danger. It was a breathtaking save and even drew the admiration of Ring, who continued his run to congratulate the goalkeeper.

At the other end of the field the ball fell to the unmarked Nicky Rackard, who scored the goal that sealed the contest for Wexford.

Wexford: A Foley; Bobby Rackard, N O'Donnell, M Morrissey; J English, Billy Rackard, J Morrissey; S Hearne, E Wheeler; P Kehoe, M Codd, T Flood; T Ryan, N Rackard, T Dixon.

Cork: M Cashman; J Brohan, J Lyons, A O'Shaughnessy; M Fuohy, WJ Daly, P Philpott; E Goulding, P Dowling; M Regan, J Hartnett, P Barry; C O'Shea, T Kelly, C Ring. Subs: V Twomey for O'Shaughnessy, G Murphy for Hartnett.

Referee: T O'Sullivan (Limerick).

Dan Quigley leads Wexford in the pre-match parade for the 1968 All-Ireland hurling final where they beat Tipperary by 5-8 to 3-12

1968 ALL-IRELAND HURLING FINAL, CROKE PARK

Wexford 5-8 Tipperary 3-12

As the Tipperary players walked towards the dressing-room at half-time in the 1968 All-Ireland final, two players had a brief exchange of words. 'All-Ireland titles can't be won as easily as this', Donie Nealon commented to his friend Michael 'Babs' Keating. Tipperary led by

1–11 to 1–3 and had enjoyed almost total dominance in the opening half-hour.

Nealon's words would prove prophetic. The second half produced a most dramatic turnaround in fortunes. Wexford, who had looked forlorn and helpless in the early stages, suddenly found their form. Inspired by Tony Doran, scorer of two goals in the second half, they stunned Tipperary.

Tipperary were warm favourites going into the game and were in command early on. Mick Roche

was dominating the game from centre half-back and forwards of the quality of Keating, Liam Devaney and Jimmy Doyle were tormenting the Wexford defence. It was almost totally one-sided and Doyle's goal, flicked in from a sideline ball from Nealon, gave Tipperary a 1–9 to 0–3 lead. Pat Nolan, the Wexford goalkeeper, had made a number of excellent saves as Tipperary mounted wave after wave of attacks.

The despondent Wexford supporters had their hopes raised when Jack Berry scored a goal before half-time. But such had been Tipperary's authority that nobody could have forecast a Wexford win at half-time.

Some Tipperary players later felt they were too complacent in the second half and were punished. They also suffered the loss of Jimmy Doyle, who had injured an ankle when scoring the goal in the first half. He played on but was not as effective as he might have been, missing a number of chances early in the second half. Keating was also hampered by a foot injury and could not maintain the early momentum.

Wexford found inspiration from a number of sources. Pat Nolan continued to make outstanding saves, especially one from a fierce drive by Liam Devaney. Had that shot reached the net it would have consolidated Tipperary's position. Instead, the Wexford players began to believe that victory was possible. Dan Quigley and Phil Wilson gradually took control and the tempo increased enormously.

Doran scored his first goal eight minutes into the second half. It was typical of his style, taking the ball in his left hand, turning and beating off two tackles before driving the ball to the net. Two points from Jack Berry meant that ten minutes into the half Wexford were just three points behind. Although Devaney added a point for Tipperary, Wexford were now in full flow. A point from Jimmy O'Brien and a goal from a free by Paul Lynch brought Wexford level, 3–6 to 1–12. Doran scored his second goal to give Wexford the lead. Another goal from Berry and points from O'Brien and Doran gave Wexford an eight-point lead as the game entered its final minutes. But the drama was still not over.

In the final minute Sean McLoughlin scored a goal for Tipperary, finally beating the outstanding goalkeeper, Nolan. From the puck out Tipperary won the ball and another attack was set up. Francis Loughnane, who had replaced the injured Doyle, ran at the Wexford defence. He was pulled down and a 21-yard free was awarded. Keating drove the ball to the net, leaving

just two points between the teams. However, time had run out for Tipperary, as referee John Dowling sounded the final whistle shortly afterwards to bring an amazing contest to an end.

Wexford: P Nolan; T Neville, E Kelly, E Colfer; V Staples, D Quigley, W Murphy; P Wilson, D Bernie; P Lynch, T Doran, C Jacob; J O'Brien, S Whelan, J Berry. Sub: J Quigley for Whelan.

Tipperary: J O'Donoghue; J Costigan, N O'Gorman, J Gleeson; M Burns, M Roche, L Gaynor; PJ Ryan, D Nealon; M Keating, J Ryan, J Doyle; L Devanney, J McKenna, S McLoughlin. Sub: F Loughnane for Doyle.

Referee: J Dowling (Offaly).

Tipperary's Tadhg O'Connor

1971 MUNSTER HURLING FINAL, FITZGERALD STADIUM, KILLARNEY

Tipperary 4–16 Limerick 3–18

Nine weeks before this memorable game, Limerick and Tipperary contested the National League final. Limerick won a close and exciting game by just one point (3–12 to 3–11) and were marginal favourites when the two teams came together again in a Munster championship final which has gone down in history as one of the most dramatic ever played.

Rain fell in Killarney from early morning of the day of the game

and the tens of thousands of supporters who arrived in the town were concerned the conditions would destroy the spectacle. Their fears were not realised, however, because the quality of hurling played by both teams was of an exceptionally high standard.

'Babs' Keating later described the game as 'the greatest I ever played in.' Along with Mick Roche, Len Gaynor and Jimmy Doyle, he was one of the more experienced Tipperary players in a relatively young team. They were coached by former player Donie Nealon, who would play a big part in one of the controversial incidents in the second half.

Limerick, with players of the quality of Tony O'Brien, Pat Hartigan, Richie and Phil Bennis, Eamonn Cregan and Eamon Grimes aboard, were fiercely ambitious. Their game plan involved moving the ball at speed along the ground in an effort to stretch the Tipperary defence. In the early stages it worked perfectly and the Tipperary backline struggled to keep tabs on Cregan and Donal Flynn.

In the opening ten minutes Limerick scored two goals, courtesy of Cregan and Flynn. PJ Ryan responded with a goal for Tipperary but it was Limerick who were dictating the pace and tempo of the game. The quality of hurling in the conditions was exceptional. Tipperary gradually settled into the game and began to ask some serious questions of Limerick. At half-time, however, Limerick led by 2–10 to 1–7 and their supporters were optimistic that the long wait for their first Munster title since 1955 was almost over.

The opening period of the second half changed the entire game. After four minutes Mick Roche won possession in the centre of the field and spotted Keating slipping inside the defence. The pass from Roche was perfect and Keating struck the ball to the net. A few minutes later, John Flanagan was heading for the Limerick goal when he was fouled. As he fell to the ground he struck the ball and sent it in among the spectators.

As there was a delay in the ball being returned, Tipperary trainer Nealon went on to the field with a towel for free-taker Keating to dry his hurley. Keating asked him for a dry ball, knowing it would be easier to strike than the wet ball which had been in use up to then. Eventually the wet ball did come back but Keating kept the dry ball. He struck it with venom and the ball hit the net.

The sides were level and Limerick had clearly lost their concentration. Tipperary built up a four-point lead before the Limerick players regained their composure. Pat Hartigan roused them with some great catches and clearances. It was from one of his bursts out of defence and a long clearance that Eamon Grimes got possession and scored Limerick's third goal to cut the deficit to one point: Tipperary 4–14, Limerick 3–16.

Another moment of controversy followed. Limerick substitute Willie Moore scored a goal but the referee, Frank Murphy, did not allow it to stand because he had blown his whistle for a foul on Moore seconds before the ball was struck. Richie Bennis scored a point from the free to level the scores. Len Gaynor and Bennis then exchanged points. As the game entered the final minute John Flanagan broke free to score the winning point. Tipperary went on to win the All-Ireland championship. However Limerick gained their revenge in the 1973 Munster final, winning an equally dramatic game by a point, 6–7 to 2–18.

Tipperary: P O'Sullivan; N Lane, J Kelly, J Gleeson; T O'Connor, M Roche, L Gaynor; S Hogan, PJ Ryan; F Loughnane, N O'Dwyer, J Flanagan; J Doyle, M Keating, D Ryan. Subs: R Ryan for Doyle, L King for Lane, P Byrne for O'Dwyer.

Limerick: J Hogan; T O'Brien, P Hartigan, J O'Brien; C Campbell, J O'Donnell, P Bennis; B Hartigan, S Foley; R Bennis, M Graham, E Grimes; D Flynn, M Cregan, E Cregan. Sub: W Moore for Flynn.

Referee: F Murphy (Cork)

1972 ALL-IRELAND HURLING FINAL, CROKE PARK

Kilkenny 3–24 Cork 5–11

The statistics reveal the amazing story of this game. With 20 minutes to go in this 80-minute All-Ireland final Cork led by eight points, 5–11 to 1–15, and their supporters in the attendance of more than 66,000 were already celebrating. Two Cork goals, scored in rapid succession by Ray Cummins and Seanie O'Leary, looked to have conclusively settled the argument. There seemed no way back for Kilkenny.

A great All-Ireland final up to then had seen the two best teams in the game serve up quite a treat. Kilkenny were led by Noel Skehan, the long-time goalkeeping understudy to Ollie Walsh.

Cork had a team of high-class stars, from Paddy Barry in goal to Pat McDonnell at full-back, Con Roche at left half-back, Justin McCarthy and Denis Coughlan at midfield, Gerald McCarthy, Ray Cummins and Charlie McCarthy in attack.

Cork led by 2–8 to 0–12 at half-time. Eddie Keher and Liam 'Chunky' O'Brien scored two points for Kilkenny early in the second half to level the game. And it was then that the incredible story began to unfold.

Gerald McCarthy drove the ball hard at Skehan, who parried it. Phil 'Fan' Larkin went to clear the ball but was injured in doing so.

Cork forward Mick Malone swung his hurley and nudged the ball to the net. O'Leary and Cummins added two more points to swing the initiative Cork's way.

Kilkenny then made the decisive move. Eddie Keher had been confined to a corner forward role up to then but Fr. Tommy Maher, the Kilkenny trainer, decided to allow him to roam.

The effect was immediate. Keher enjoyed the extra space and his presence further out in the field unnerved the Cork defence. Cork seemed unsure how to respond and Keher was unmarked when he scored his first point from play from near the sideline.

He then added a spectacular goal, taking possession from O'Brien and cleverly side-stepping Cork defender Tony Maher before driving the ball towards goal from 40 yards.

Goalkeeper Barry seemed to have it covered but the ball spun off his chest and into the net.

Cork responded in style. Cummins and O'Leary snatched two goals in 30 seconds and when Con Roche drove the ball over the bar from 80 yards to give Cork an eight-point lead, it looked all over for Kilkenny.

But Cork did not score again and, in a pulsating finish, Kilkenny scored 2–9, Keher giving a wonderful exhibition and ending up with a record personal tally of 2–9.

It was Keher who started the incredible comeback when he stood over a 21-yard free.

Knowing a goal was needed, he went for it and beat the Cork defence. He added a point from another free and then the scores came in rapid succession. Pat Delaney scored a point. Then, with just 11 minutes to go, Frank Cummins burst through from midfield and fired an unstoppable shot to the net. Kilkenny 3–17 (26 points), Cork 5–11 (26 points).

Noel Skehan of Kilkenny

In the final ten minutes Keher scored three further points, Delaney scored two and Mossie Murphy and Kieran Purcell added one each to turn an eight-point deficit into a seven-point victory.

Kilkenny: N Skehan; P Larkin, P Dillon, J Treacy; P Lawlor, P Henderson, E Morrissey; F Cummins, L O'Brien; M Crotty, P Delaney, J Kinsella; E Byrne, K Purcell, E Keher. Subs: M Murphy for Byrne, M Coogan for Larkin, P Moran for Kinsella.

Cork: P Barry; T Maher, P McDonnell, B Murphy; F Norberg, S Looney, C Roche; J McCarthy, D Coughlan; G McCarthy, M Malone, P Hegarty; C McCarthy, R Cummins, S O'Leary. Subs: T O'Brien for Norberg, D Collins for Hegarty.

Referee: M Spain (Offaly).

1975 ALL-IRELAND HURLING SEMI-FINAL, CROKE PARK

Galway 4–15 Cork 2–19

In his playing days with Galway, MJ 'Inky' Flaherty had experienced many disappointments. Regarded nationally as a player of great talent, Flaherty was forced to spend his career in a vacuum. Although there was great passion for hurling in Galway, the county team was never quite able to make the breakthrough.

When he became team trainer in the mid-1970s, Flaherty vowed he would change attitudes. He had watched a group of players emerge in the county who he believed were good enough to take on the traditional powers and win. The task was to get them to believe. In the folklore of Galway hurling Sunday, 17 August 1975 is very special because it was the day the players did believe, and changed history.

The year had begun well for Galway when the team won the National League for the first time in 24 years, beating Cork, Kilkenny and Tipperary on their way to the title. While the success sparked off wild celebrations in Galway, there were still many around the country who wondered if Galway could match any of the superpowers in the heat of championship.

Galway qualified for the All-Ireland semi-final of 1975, easily disposing of the challenge of Westmeath in the quarter-final. They met a Cork team many observers regarded as one of the best of the period, with forwards of the outstanding ability of Charlie McCarthy, Jimmy Barry-Murphy, Dinny Allen, Ray Cummins and Seanie O'Leary.

Galway had great strength throughout in many departments but there was a suspicion that they lacked the necessary guile in attack to beat Cork. They had their stars, though, especially John Connolly in midfield, and he would play a major role in this game.

In the Galway dressing-room before the game Flaherty repeated his message time after time. 'You are good enough', he kept telling the players, and created an atmosphere of real intent. By throw-in time, the players were tuned to perfection and they exploded into action in a manner that not only stunned Cork but also surprised the Galway supporters.

The experienced PJ Qualter opened the scoring for Galway in the early minutes. Cork attacked from the puck out but Galway corner back Niall McInerney gave an early indication of how difficult it would be for the Cork forwards when he burst clear and drove the ball downfield. Pádraig Fahy took possession and laid off to Frank Burke, who sent the ball to the net with a great drive.

P J Molloy scored another point and then Galway added a second goal. John Connolly took possession on the right wing and sprinted towards goal. The Cork defenders anticipated that Connolly would pass the ball or go for a point. Instead, Connolly turned away from two defenders and drove the ball low and hard into the net. It was 2–2 to 0–0 after eight minutes.

Barry-Murphy scored Cork's first point but Galway's power surge was far from over. A minute later Fahy dispossessed Cork full-back Pat McDonnell and passed to Qualter, who scored Galway's third goal.

Cork, unexpectedly, found themselves chasing the game. They got a lifeline when Barry-Murphy scored a goal after Galway goalkeeper Michael Conneely had saved a penalty. He would save another before half-time. Despite soaring temperatures, the game was played

Nicky English: a scoring ace who later became Tipperary manager

at a frantic pace. Galway led at the break by 3–7 to 1–6.

Cork reorganised at half-time and began a fightback early in the second half. O'Leary reduced the arrears by a point and Gerald McCarthy added another. Galway substitute Michael Connolly replied with two points as Galway built on their lead. After Con Roche added another point for Cork the game took another unexpected twist.

Qualter was awarded a free 25 yards from the Cork goal. Gerry Coone intended to go for a point but mis-hit the ball. It flew towards the goal and was deflected into the net. Galway now led by 4–9 to 1–9. They continued to trade points in a non-stop game and when Galway led by 4–13 to 2–12 the chance of a Cork recovery seemed remote, but a Con Roche free started off another Cork scoring spree. Eamon O'Donoghue, O'Leary and Roche added points and Cork trailed by just three points. O'Leary won possession on the edge of the Galway square. Referee Mick Spain awarded a penalty for a foul by Galway full-back Joe Clarke. It was a great chance for O'Leary to level the scores. Instead he opted for a

point. Four minutes remained and Cork were two points behind. Gerald McCarthy cut the margin to one. Then Coone scored for Galway, with Con Roche replying for Cork.

In the final minute Galway, still holding on by one point, won a '70'. John Connolly kept his composure and drove the ball over the bar to secure a famous victory.

Although Galway lost the All-Ireland final to Kilkenny, the semi-final victory was the platform from which future success was launched. Cork went on to win the next three All-Ireland championships (1976, '77, '78) but Galway finally broke the All-Ireland hoodoo in 1980, winning the title for the first time since 1923.

Galway: M Conneely; N McInerney, J Clarke, P Lally; J McDonagh, S Silke, I Clarke; J Connolly, S Murphy; G Coone, F Burke, P J Molloy; M Barrett, P J Qualter, P Fahy. Sub: M Connolly for Barrett.

Cork: M Coleman; T Maher, P McDonnell, B Murphy; T O'Brien, M O'Doherty, C Roche; G McCarthy, P Hegarty; J Barry-Murphy, W Walsh, D Allen; C McCarthy, R Cummins, S O'Leary. Subs: D Burns for T O'Brien, J Horgan for O'Doherty, E O'Donoghue for Walsh.

Referee: M Spain (Offaly).

1984 MUNSTER HURLING FINAL, THURLES

Cork 4–15 Tipperary 3–14

To celebrate the centenary of its founding, the GAA decided to hold the All-Ireland Hurling final of 1984 in its birthplace, Thurles. From the moment the decision was made, a major effort began in Tipperary to put together a team good enough to contest, and possibly win, the All-Ireland title on home territory. It had been 13 years since Tipperary had won either a Munster or All-Ireland championship and it felt like an eternity in a county which, up to then, had enjoyed consistent success.

Although the ultimate aim of All-Ireland glory would not be achieved, Tipperary did make rapid progress in the build-up to the 1984 championship and played an enormous role in one of the most memorable Munster finals of the modern era. Their opponents were their traditional rivals Cork, the beaten All-Ireland finalists in the two previous years.

While hurling followers nationally recognised veteran Noel

O'Dwyer and the new young star Nicky English on the Tipperary team, the names of virtually the Cork players fairly tripped off the tongue. From Ger Cunningham in goal to Seanie O'Leary at left corner forward, they were household names. So strong was the team that a player of the outstanding quality of Tony O'Sullivan was on the bench.

The pressure on a relatively young Tipperary team was immense but, roused by the home support in Semple Stadium, they began the game powerfully. John McIntyre at centre back, along with Ralph Callaghan and Philip Kennedy at midfield, provided a physical presence which allowed Tipperary to compete comfortably with their more illustrious opponents. An early goal by full-forward Séamus Power also helped them to settle into the game, which was full of incident. Jimmy Barry-Murphy replied with a Cork goal before Tipperary were forced to replace injured corner back Dinny Cahill. The selectors decided Bobby Ryan, recognised essentially as a wing-back, should switch to the corner with John Doyle coming in at left half-back.

Cork's stylish midfielder and free-taker John Fenton was in good form from placed balls. Then, in the 16th minute, Barry-Murphy scored his second goal to give Cork a 2–4 to 1–2 lead. Cork had won the two previous Munster finals with ease. This time, however, Tipperary would prove to be much tougher opponents. Before half-time Donie O'Connell and English scored a goal each and, at the break, Cork led by just two points, 2–10 to 3–5.

Séamus Power had been a major influence at full-forward for Tipperary and he was unlucky on the restart to see his shot for goal hit the side netting. Minutes later, supporters were amazed when Power was moved from the attack into defence. Bobby Ryan had suffered an injury and had to be replaced. Shortly afterwards, the Cork selectors made a significant move when they brought in Tony O'Sullivan in place of Tim Crowley. O'Sullivan would make a big contribution.

Tipperary drew level, 3–9 to 2–12, in the 13th minute of the second half and then went a point ahead when Liam Maher scored. Pat Hartnett equalised for Cork. Then Tipperary were awarded a penalty. Power ran from the full-back line to take it. He chose to go for a point. Noel O'Dwyer from a free, and Philip Kennedy from a '65', increased Tipperary's lead to three points. When Noel O'Dwyer widened the margin to four with another point, Tipperary supporters began to believe that victory was possible. Just six minutes remained in the game.

Fenton pointed a '65' for Cork with four minutes left. Then O'Sullivan slipped inside the defence and was waiting when Tipperary goalkeeper John Sheedy saved a shot from Hartnett. The rebound fell to O'Sullivan and he flashed the ball to the net. Level again.

Tipperary attacked. Michael Doyle raced at the Cork defence and gave a pass intended for English. Denis Mulcahy intercepted and drove the ball downfield. O'Sullivan got possession and shot for a point. Goalkeeper Sheedy jumped and stretched his hurley high in the air to block the ball. He made contact but the ball fell to the feet of Seanie O'Leary, who struck it to the net. From the puck-out Cork were awarded a free. Fenton pointed. The final whistle blew and Cork had snatched victory from the jaws of defeat.

Cork went on to beat Offaly in the All-Ireland final.

Cork: G Cunningham; D Mulcahy, D O'Grady, J Hodgins; T Cashman, J Crowley, D MacCurtain; J Fenton, P Hartnett; P Horgan, T Crowley, K Hennessy; T Mulcahy, J Barry-Murphy, S O'Leary. Subs: J Blake for O'Grady, T O'Sullivan for Crowley, D Walsh for Horgan.

Tipperary: J Sheedy; J Bergin, J Keogh, D Cahill; P Fitzelle, J McIntyre, B Ryan; R Callaghan, P Kennedy; N English, D O'Connell, L Maher; M Doyle, S Power, N O'Dwyer. Subs: J Doyle for Cahill, B Heffernan for Fitzelle, P Dooley for Ryan.

Referee: J Moore (Waterford)

1987 ALL-IRELAND HURLING SEMI-FINAL, CROKE PARK

Galway 3-20 Tipperary 2-17

Galway entered the 1987 championship as a team on a serious mission, having been beaten in the All-Ireland finals of 1985 and '86. The exciting squad assembled by Cyril Farrell on his return to the senior team management in 1984 was regarded as one of the best in the game but they had failed to deliver on the biggest occasions.

Their participation in the 1987 championship series was overshadowed by the return of Tipperary to Croke Park after a 16-year absence. They had won the Munster final in dramatic circumstances, beating Cork after extra time in a replay, and arrived in Croke Park on a wave of emotion. Tipperary provided the majority of the near-50,000 attendance at a game that would begin a keen rivalry which has lasted until the present day.

The more experienced Galway team took an early advantage. Brendan Lynskey, their strong centre forward, laid off a good pass to Martin Naughton who scored Galway's first goal. Galway went into a 1–4 to 0–1 lead in seven minutes. However, once Tipperary settled into a routine the game would develop into an absorbing contest, full of fascinating clashes. Conor Hayes and Nicholas English fought a great duel in front of the Galway goal. It was a foul on English which won Tipperary a penalty before half-time which Pat Fox converted. At half time Galway led by 1–13 to 1–9.

Tipperary took the battle to Galway in the second half and, in the 21st minute, they edged in front for the first time. Steve Mahon had given Galway a two-point lead at 1–16 to 1–14 when Pat Fox scored an excellent individual goal to give Tipperary a one-point advantage. Galway brought on the experienced Noel Lane and moved Joe Cooney to full-forward.

Then came a moment of controversy. Galway goalkeeper John

Conor O'Donovan (right) was a solid defensive presence for Tipperary in some epic clashes with Galway in the 1980s

1990: Galway's Noel Lane takes on Cork's David Quirke and Jim Cashman

Commins had a clearance blocked down and English scored a point. The referee, Gerry Kirwan, disallowed the score because he deemed that John McGrath had fouled Commins. Conor Hayes took the free, Lynskey won possession and passed to Ryan, who handpassed the ball to the net. Instead of trailing by a point, Galway led by three. Tipperary kept battling on but when Lane added Galway's third goal, it ensured a memorable victory.

Galway went on to beat Kilkenny in the All-Ireland final.

Galway: J Commins; S Linnane, C Hayes, O Kilkenny; P Finnerty, T Keady, G McInerney; S Mahon, T Kilkenny; M McGrath, J Cooney, M Naughton; E Ryan, B Lynskey, A Cunningham. Subs: P Malone for T Kilkenny, N Lane for McGrath, PJ Molloy for Naughton.

Tipperary: K Hogan; J Heffernan, C O'Donovan, S Gibson; R Stakelum, J Kennedy, P Delaney; C Bonnar, J Hayes; M McGrath, D O'Connell, A Ryan; P Fox, N English, B Ryan. Subs: J McGrath for Gibson, M Doyle for M McGrath.

Referee: G Kirwan (Offaly)

1990 ALL-IRELAND HURLING FINAL, CROKE PARK

Cork 5–15 Galway 2–21

When Kevin Hennessy scored a Cork goal in the first minute of the 1990 All-Ireland final it was a signal for 70 minutes of breathtaking action to begin. Rarely have fortunes swayed so dramatically, with Galway recovering from the early setback to dominate the first half and then Cork taking over in the second half.

Though Cork were deserving winners in the end, this game will forever be remembered for the first-half performance of the Galway centre-forward, Joe Cooney. Some pundits suggest that it was one of the greatest individual displays ever, as Cooney turned in an amazing display.

He was at the heart of Galway's

recovery from a shaky start, scoring 1–6 and setting up several other points to help Galway into an interval lead of 1–13 to 1–8. Galway increased their lead to seven points early in the second half thanks to Michael McGrath and Anthony Cunningham. Cork were still struggling to get a grip but the switch of the team captain, Tomás Mulcahy, to centre half forward was to make a big difference. Tony Keady had been dominant for Galway at centre back but found Mulcahy a far more difficult opponent.

Mulcahy scored an excellent goal to reduce the deficit to three points. Then, at the other end, Cork goalkeeper Ger Cunningham made a brave point-blank save from Martin Naughton. The ball cannoned off Cunningham's face-out for a '65' but, inexplicably, the umpire waved a wide, which was a real blow to Galway and the start of a run of bad luck for them. A few minutes later Tony O'Sullivan scored a point for Cork, after Galway claims that Keady had been fouled were ignored.

With Jim Cashman becoming dominant at centre back for Cork, they gradually assumed control. With eight minutes to go John Fitzgibbon scored a goal and quickly followed up with another. Although Brendan Lynskey scored a late goal for Galway, they had lost the initiative. Joe Cooney got a late point for Galway, but Cork held on for a three-point victory in the highest-scoring final since 1972, when Kilkenny beat Cork by 3–24 to 5–11 in a game played over 80 minutes.

Cork: G Cunningham; J Considine, D Walsh, S O'Gorman; S McCarthy, J Cashman, K McGuckian; B O'Sullivan, T McCarthy; G Fitzgerald, M Foley, T O'Sullivan; T Mulcahy, K Hennessy, J Fitzgibbon. Subs: D Quirke for McGuckian, C Casey for B O'Sullivan.

Galway: J Commins; D Fahy, S Treacy, O Kilkenny; P Finnerty, T Keady, G McInerney; M Coleman, P Malone; A Cunningham, J Cooney, M Naughton; M McGrath, N Lane, E Ryan. Subs: T Monaghan for Malone, B Lynskey for Cunningham.

Referee: J Moore (Waterford)

Joe Dooley, the only Offaly man to win three All-Ireland

senior hurling titles

1998 ALL-IRELAND HURLING SEMI-FINAL, CROKE PARK AND THURLES

Clare 1–13 (draw)

Clare 1–16, Offaly 2–10 (unfinished)

Offaly 0–16, Clare 0–13.

When James O'Connor scored the equalising point for Clare in Croke Park on 9 August 1998 he sparked off one of the most extraordinary dramas in the modern history of Irish sport.

Clare, the reigning All-Ireland champions, had been given the fright of their lives by an Offaly team who had been written off a month earlier. The Offaly manager Michael 'Babs' Keating had resigned in controversial circumstances after the Leinster final defeat by Kilkenny and was replaced by a Galway man, Michael Bond.

Under the new 'back door' system introduced for the hurling championship a year earlier, Offaly were able to re-enter the title race as beaten provincial finalists and had qualified for the All-Ireland semi-final by beating Antrim. However, they were given little chance, either by bookmakers or neutral observers, of upsetting Clare.

They raised their game substantially in the opening joust with Clare, who were without influential midfielder Colin Lynch. He had been suspended rather controversially after the Munster final replay win over Waterford, a decision which enraged Clare and, in particular, their manager Ger Loughnane.

The Clare-Offaly replay proved to be a quite extraordinary occasion. Played on a Saturday, it attracted a crowd of 38,000 who saw an absorbing game end bizarrely.

Clare led by 1–16 to 2–10, with Alan Markham scoring an impressive 1–3, when referee Jimmy Cooney from Galway blew the full-time whistle.

However, Cooney had made an error. There were still two minutes remaining. The referee later accepted his error, and the following day the Games Administration Committee of the GAA ordered a re-fixture.

The third and decisive game was played in Semple Stadium on 29 August.

A contest of exceptional quality saw the veteran Joe Dooley perform majestically for Offaly while their young goalkeeper Stephen Byrne produced an outstanding performance with a series of excellent saves. Thirteen players scored in the first half, at the end of which Offaly led by 0–9 to 0–6.

They still held a three-point lead 19 minutes into the second half when goalkeeper Byrne made an excellent save from Markham. Byrne followed it up with another sensational block from substitute Danny Scanlon. Offaly were six points ahead with five minutes left. Clare, who had won All-Ireland titles in 1995 and 1997, refused to yield, however. Inspirational captain Anthony Daly scored a fine point and then O'Connor added two from frees to reduce the margin to three, but Offaly held out for victory.

Offaly beat Kilkenny in the All-Ireland final by 2–16 to 1–13 to become the first team to win the All-Ireland final having earlier been beaten in the provincial championships.

Teams in third game:

Offaly: S Byrne; S Whelahan, K Kinahan, M Hanamy; B Whelahan, H Rigney, K Martin; Johnny Dooley, J Pilkington; M Duignan, J Errity, P Mulhare; B Dooley, J Troy, Joe Dooley. Subs: G Hanniffy for Mulhare, J Ryan for Troy, K Farrell for B Dooley. Other players used in series: D Hanniffy, G Oakley.

Clare: D Fitzgerald; F Lohan, B Lohan, B Quinn; L Doyle, S McMahon, A Daly; J Reddan, O Baker; J O'Connor, F Tuohy, A Markham; N Gilligan, G O'Loughlin, D Forde. Subs: F Hegarty for Tuohy, D Scanlan for O'Loughlin, C Clancy for Scanlan. Other players used in series: R Woods, PJ O'Connell, E Taaffe, C Chaplin, B Murphy.

Referees: Jimmy Cooney (Galway): Drawn and unfinished games. Dickie Murphy (Wexford): Third game.

10

CONTROVERSIES AND SCANDALS

Paddy Doherty, Down's All-Ireland-winning captain in 1961, was suspended by the GAA in 1957 for playing soccer

A s the largest sports organisation in Ireland, it is inevitable that the GAA would have had its share of controversies and scandals, although the former outflank the latter by a considerable distance.

Interestingly, most of the major controversies relate to issues not directly con-nected to the playing of hurling and football but rather to matters of a quasi-political nature.

Rule 27 (The Ban) was a particularly controversial subject for many years. It prevented GAA members from playing, or having any involvement with 'foreign' games, especially soccer and rugby. The view was that they were English games and the GAA felt duty-bound to oppose them. Even attending a social function organised by a soccer or rugby club was enough to cause a GAA member to be suspended from the Association. Rule 27 remained in force until 1971.

Rule 21, which prevents members of the Royal Ulster Constabulary and the British armed forces from becoming members of the GAA, is still in operation, although there is a commitment to abolish it when the policing situation in Northern Ireland has the support of the majority of the Nationalist population.

RULE 27   The Ban

For 67 years, Rule 27 spread a highly-charged and emotive blanket right across the GAA landscape. Introduced in 1902, it prohibited GAA members from playing, attending or promoting rugby, soccer, hockey and cricket. Infringement was punishable by suspension.

The rule, which became known as 'The Ban', a title it retained until its abolition in 1971, was introduced at a time of surging nationalism in Ireland. It was felt that English sports and culture were becoming far too influential, so the GAA decided to make a very clear statement of its commitment to all things Irish.

From an early stage, it was a divisive issue. The more moderate elements within the GAA felt that 'The Ban' went altogether too far and that it would become a source of ongoing acrimony. They were proved correct.

After the Anglo-Irish Treaty was ratified in 1922, there were moves to have 'The Ban' removed. It was discussed at the GAA's Annual Congress for three consecutive years, 1923, 1924 and 1925, but despite strong arguments by the pro-abolition lobby they could never muster sufficient support to have the rule deleted.

Those who wanted it retained claimed that it was an important symbol of the GAA's unique identity, and they were sufficiently persuasive to sway others their way. In 1926, it was decided that an annual discussion on the removal of 'The Ban' was divisive, repetitive and counter-productive and, from there on, it could be debated only every three years.

While discussion of 'The Ban' was restricted to every third year, it continued to be a hugely-controversial rule. In December 1938 it shot to the forefront of the GAA agenda when the Central Council took the highly-provocative step of removing Dr Douglas Hyde, President of Ireland, from his position as patron of the GAA. He had

attended an international soccer match in his role as President of Ireland but the GAA adopted an intransigent line and removed him as patron.

The decision attracted huge publicity but the GAA refused to relent. Despite the fact that Dr Hyde was a man who was deeply committed to Irish culture, language and ideals, in the GAA's eyes he had broken Rule 27 and, consequently, could not continue as patron. His removal led to a cooling in relations between the GAA and the Irish Government. It also highlighted in a very public way the lengths to which the GAA were prepared to go to ensure that Rule 27 was implemented.

Dr Hyde was never reinstated. However, his memory has been perpetuated in Roscommon where the GAA's county ground is called Dr Hyde Park. While his case is one of the more high-profile examples of the dramatic impact Rule 27 had on the ordinary lives of GAA members, others arose too from time to time. While there were frequent violations of Rule 27, not all County Boards took action against those who infringed it, believing that it was unnecessarily restrictive. However, a young Limerick hurler, Sean Herbert, lost his chance to win an All-Ireland minor hurling medal in 1940 after being suspended for breaking Rule 27, while three years earlier Dave Creedon of Cork had missed his chance to play in an All-Ireland minor hurling final after being caught playing soccer.

The strict application of Rule 27 was to cost one of Waterford's most renowned players a National League medal in 1963. Tom Cheasty, who had been a central figure in most of Waterford's more exciting days in the late 1950s and early 1960s, gave possibly his best-ever performance in the National League 'home' final against Tipperary, which Waterford won by 2–15 to 4–7. However, he was suspended before Waterford travelled to New York for the League final proper because he had attended a dance run by a soccer club. It was a very harsh interpretation of Rule 27, but it indi-

Pat Fanning was GAA president when 'The Ban' was removed in 1971

cates just how seriously it was taken in some parts of the country.

Paddy Doherty, who captained Down to All-Ireland football glory in 1961, also felt the wrath of Rule 27. Early in his career, he was a soccer player of considerable substance and signed for an English club, Lincoln City. However, he returned home after only eight weeks and joined Ballyclare Comrades. His involvement with soccer resulted in a 12-month GAA suspension but he was reinstated after six months and went on to make a huge contribution to Down football in the late 1950s and right through the 1960s.

In 1962, yet another attempt to have Rule 27 abolished was defeated at the GAA Congress, and while Cheasty's high-profile suspension a year later appeared initially to strengthen the case for the removal of 'The Ban' it was again retained after a debate in 1965. Three years later a proposal for removal was again defeated but, significantly, it was decided to set up a special committee to examine all aspects of 'The Ban', including its relevance in a rapidly-changing society.

The committee was given three years to draft a report. Completed in 1970, it was sent to all GAA clubs, who studied its findings in great detail. The mood for change was gathering momentum rapidly and, in the run-up to the 1971 Congress in Belfast, 28 of the 32 counties

supported the deletion of Rule 27.

Although it was evident that the controversial rule had run its course, there were fears that a small but vocal number of Rule 27 supporters would make an emotive plea for its retention and reignite the whole debate at the GAA's most public forum. That didn't happen.

Con Shortt (Armagh) proposed that Rule 27 be abolished. The motion was seconded by Dublin's Tom Woulfe, a man who had crusaded for its removal for years. There were no dissenting voices and, after a short pause, GAA president Pat Fanning declared that Rule 27 no longer existed. Antrim chairman Jack Rooney registered his county's support for the rule but did not propose that it be retained.

A rule which had caused so much division and bitterness for 69 years was wiped out without debate. Even its most passionate supporters recognised that it no longer had any validity and decided against launching an argument for a case that was already lost.

RULE 21

The ban on British soldiers and RUC officers

Rule 21 precludes members of the British Army and the Royal Ulster Constabulary from becoming

Emotions ran high prior to the debate on Rule 21 at a special GAA congress in Dublin in 1998

members of the GAA. Its roots are to be found deep in the tradition of the GAA which has, as its basic aim, 'the strengthening of the national identity in a 32-county Ireland, through the preservation and promotion of Gaelic Games pastimes'.

Rule 21 reads: 'Members of the British armed forces and police shall not be eligible for membership of the association.' To those who see the GAA purely as a games organisation, Rule 21 may appear quite extraordinary, even unnecessary. Why have a rule which, in the case of members of the RUC, prevents Irish people from joining an Irish organisation?

The GAA was founded on a Nationalist tradition and retains that ethos to the present day. The presence of the British Army in Ireland has always been seen as a stumbling-block to the avowed aim of the GAA to have a united, 32-county Ireland. The RUC, although comprised of Irish men and women, has always had a credibility problem

with the Roman Catholic population in Northern Ireland, and the RUC has been perceived as being 'a Protestant police force for a Protestant people'.

It is in that context that the GAA, which has always drawn the vast bulk of its membership from the Roman Catholic population, saw – and continues to see – fit to retain Rule 21.

However, opinion is sharply-divided within the GAA on the Rule 21 question. Those who want to see it removed argue that it introduces politics into sport and that it serves no purpose in a rapidly-changing Ireland. Others contend that until such time as Northern Ireland has a police force which has the allegiance of all the people, the GAA is correct to retain Rule 21 as a symbol of its support for the need for policing reform.

The debate rages on every year. Essentially, counties from Southern Ireland tend to allow the six Northern Ireland counties to set the

agenda. Armagh, Antrim, Derry, Down, Fermanagh and Tyrone are the counties which come under the security jurisdiction of the RUC and the British Army.

Stories of harassment of GAA members by the RUC and the British Army are well-documented. Over the years, there have been numerous reports of GAA players being stopped on their way to games and training for no apparent reason other than to delay and annoy them. The GAA feels that the British Army and, more specifically, the RUC have been singularly hostile to them because of their Nationalist traditions.

One of the highest-profile controversies involved the occupation by the British Army of part of the grounds owned by the Crossmaglen Rangers GAA club in South Armagh. The Army commandeered some of the club's property in the early 1970s for use as a base but in 1999 gave a commitment to return it to the GAA club. For almost three decades

it was a hugely-controversial issue. Crossmaglen Rangers insisted that the Army behaved disgracefully, not only by commandeering part of their property but by also engaging in deeply-provocative activities, including flying helicopters low over the pitch to disrupt matches. Several high-profile political figures took up Crossmaglen Rangers' complaints but while it was raised at British-Irish governmental meetings, little progress was made until 1999. While the controversy was not directly involved with the Rule 21 issue, it continued to sour the climate and reduced the prospects of having the rule removed.

When the IRA ceasefire came into effect in August 1994, it was inevitable that the Rule 21 issue would return to the top of the GAA's debating agenda. In a new spirit of peace and reconciliation, the GAA came under pressure to make a gesture on Rule 21. Dublin, Sligo, Carlow and Down put forward motions for the 1995 Congress proposing the deletion of Rule 21. Down's call for its removal was seen as especially significant as, unlike Dublin, Sligo and Carlow, they were directly impacted upon by the British Army and the RUC.

Despite Down's support for change, senior GAA figures feared that the debate at Congress could prove hugely-divisive. On the morning of Congress, a meeting of the GAA's Central Council came up with a plan to defer discussion on Rule 21. They drafted a motion, proposing that extra powers be given to Central Council to call a special Congress to discuss Rule 21, 'should the circumstances in the Six Counties call for such action'.

It required the suspension of Standing Orders to have the Central Council motion put to Congress and, while Dublin objected to such a move, it was clear that the majority of delegates were happy to defer discussion of Rule 21 until another time.

Three years passed before the debate materialised but when then-GAA president Joe McDonagh announced in April 1998 that the Special Congress to discuss Rule 21 would take place a month later, it was felt that the GAA was prepared for the dramatic deletion of one of its most controversial rules. The climate looked right because the Good Friday agreement, involving the British and Irish Governments and most of the political parties in Northern Ireland, had created a new atmosphere. McDonagh supported the removal of Rule 21, and for a time it looked certain to go.

However, as the Special Congress approached it became clear that the deletion of Rule 21 was still a bridge too far for many GAA members, especially those from Ulster. The four-hour debate, which was held in private in a Dublin hotel, ended with a declaration that while the GAA was committed to the abolition of Rule 21 it would not happen until the time was right.

Several delegates spoke of the intimidation and harassment GAA members had suffered at the hands of the Northern Ireland security forces and argued that it would be wrong to delete Rule 21 without getting any guarantees in return. As the discussion progressed, it became evident that any proposal to remove Rule 21 would not get the necessary two-thirds majority. Senior GAA figures were keen to avoid a divisive vote, so a compromise was reached. While the GAA 'pledged its intent' to remove Rule 21 at a future, unspecified date, it was decided to leave it in place for the present, pending a review of the RUC which was ordered under the Good Friday agreement.

In effect, the GAA decided to defer any further decision on Rule 21 until such time as the RUC had been reformed. That still remains the official position. Meanwhile, Rule 21 stays in force.

THE RDS AFFAIR 1994

When the Clanna Gael-Fontenoys GAA club in south Dublin came up with a novel fund-raising plan late in 1994, they could never have envisaged that it would turn out to be one of the decade's major sporting controversies. Not only did it cause a massive problem for the GAA authorities and the Dublin and Down football teams, but it also involved two soccer clubs.

The issue took on a life of its own, filling the news and sports pages for days in the run-up to Christmas 1994, as chaos reigned over what started out as a relatively minor matter. The Clanna Gael-Fontenoys GAA club, based in the Ballsbridge-Ringsend area of Dublin, had decided that as part of their centenary celebrations, they would stage a unique Gaelic football-soccer double header at the RDS (Royal Dublin Society) grounds in Ballsbridge.

The RDS is best-known as a venue for major show-jumping events, but in 1994 it was also being used as Shamrock Rovers soccer club's home ground. The Clanna Gael-Fontenoys planned to stage a Gaelic football game between Dublin and Down and a soccer match between big Dublin rivals Shamrock Rovers and Bohemians at the RDS on Sunday, 15 December 1994.

It would be a unique occasion, with Gaelic football and soccer played on the one pitch on the same day. Clanna Gael-Fontenoys saw it as a fun occasion for the Christmas season, one which hopefully would also help in their fund-raising activities. The GAA authorities were not all that enthusiastic about the idea but eventually gave their permission for the Dublin v Down clash, which would have been a repeat of the 1994 All-Ireland final. However, the GAA imposed certain conditions regarding how the proceeds from the game should be divided.

On 4 December advertisements were placed in the national newspapers urging fans to buy tickets at £8, £6 or £4. Three days later the GAA's Central Council met and, following a routine meeting which was open to the press, went into private session and subsequently issued a statement, explaining the surprise decision to withdraw permission for the RDS game. The GAA claimed that conditions relating to the disbursement of monies from the RDS games had not been observed.

The GAA's statement was confusing and raised more questions that it answered. It read: 'At a meeting of the Central Council today, it was decided that the game planned for the RDS on 15 December between Dublin and Down could not go ahead. This decision was taken on the basis that conditions set out by the Games Administration Committee, with regard to the fixture, had been violated.

'Last Thursday, it emerged that the game, and its arrangements, were being billed as a joint venture involving Shamrock Rovers and that conditions relating to the collection and disbursement of monies appeared not to be adhered to. The Dublin and Down County Boards, the Games Administration Committee and the Management Committee were not informed or consulted in relation to these arrangements. At a meeting of the executive committee of the Down County Board on Thursday night, they decided that they could not play the game on 15 December as they considered that they could be in breach of GAA policy, unless Central Council were able to confirm that no breach of policy was involved.

'If an application is received to play a game on an alternative date, it will receive every consideration. The Association wishes to affirm that it has no objection to a game being played at the RDS under the control of a GAA unit and provided it conforms to GAA policy.'

If the GAA hoped that their statement would satisfy a bewildered public, they were mistaken. It was alleged by critics that behind the GAA's vague wording lay a deep-rooted dislike of soccer and that, basically, they didn't want anything to do with a promotion involving a soccer club. Senior GAA officials denied that. In an attempt to clarify the position, the then GAA president Peter Quinn and the director-general Liam Mulvihill both gave major newspaper interviews on the following Sunday.

Mulvihill insisted that money, not soccer, lay behind the GAA decision to withdraw permission for the RDS games. Basically, the GAA felt that unrealistic financial targets had been set. 'Our decision to withdraw backing for the game was taken on practical, rather than idealistic, grounds. There were certain aspects of the whole deal we found disturbing and these had nothing to do with an anti-soccer crusade,' he said.

While the GAA's PR machine swung into action in an effort to convince the public that their withdrawal of support for the RDS venture was based purely on practical considerations, it was a difficult task.

Their statements had been at best ambiguous, and while there were practical considerations behind their decision, there was also a suspicion that they were deeply unhappy at the prospects of having the two best football teams in the country involved

The British Army's presence on the property of Crossmaglen Rangers GAA club was a source of deep resentment for almost 30 years

in a promotion which involved soccer.

The whole affair was a public relations disaster for the GAA. Their misgivings regarding the financial aspects of the RDS promotion may have been well-founded but their failure to sell their message in a clear, concise way provided critics with an endless supply of ammunition to fire at the GAA's decision-making process.

THE KEADY AFFAIR 1989

In May 1989, Tony Keady stood proudly on the peak of the hurling world.

As Galway's towering centre half-back, the 25-year-old Killimordaly clubman had already won two All-Ireland senior medals and two

National League titles. He had also been chosen as Hurler of the Year in 1988.

Galway had won the 1987 and 1988 All-Ireland finals and were setting out on another great adventure as they pursued the three-in-a-row dream in 1989.

After winning the National League title in April, Galway travelled to New York in May and, as Galway's championship campaign wasn't due to start until August, Keady stayed on for a few weeks after his colleagues returned.

While in New York, he played with Laois against Tipperary. Under local New York bye-laws, a player can line out for any county, so despite being a Galwayman Keady was allowed to play for Laois, provid-ed the transfer formalities had been completed. Keady was told by offi-cials in New York that he was cleared

to play for Laois on a temporary basis but it subsequently transpired that not all the necessary paper-work was in order.

Playing in New York had long been a minefield in terms of eligi-bility. For years, Irish-based play-ers travelled to New York in the summer months to play hurling and football and sample the sights and experiences of the Big Apple. Some stayed for months while others flew out for weekends only, leaving on Friday, playing on Sunday and returning on Monday.

The GAA authorities were uneasy about the trans-Atlantic traffic, fear-ing that players were being paid for their weekend trips.

In order to minimise the traf-ficking, the GAA imposed a rule whereby players could join New York clubs only if they lived there for a period of time. That, effec-

tively, ruled out the weekend jun-kets.

Shortly after Keady played for Laois in May 1989, an investiga-tion was launched into his eligibil-ity by the New York GAA authorities. He was found to be illegal and was suspended for two games, but it really didn't matter to him because he had no intention of remaining in New York for the summer and the two-match ban was not applic-able in Ireland. However, the GAA's Games Administration Committee decided to initiate their own inves-tigation back home. Keady and two other Galway panellists, Michael Helebert and Aidan Staunton, who also had played in New York, were suspended for a year.

Galway were stunned. The prospect of trying to defend their All-Ireland crown without Keady alarmed them greatly and they immediately set about attempting to have the ban overturned. Public sympathy came down heavily behind Keady. Technically he may have been guilty of a minor eligibility transgression in the US, but a 12-month ban looked totally out of proportion to the offence.

While Galway were deciding whether to appeal to the GAA's Management Committee or Central Council, a newspaper report emerged claiming that Galway were considering withdrawing from the All-Ireland semi-final against Tipperary in protest at the Keady ban. Such a

dramatic move would have brought hurling into chaos, but the Galway team management felt so strongly about the affair that withdrawal figured very highly in their considerations. In the end, however, they decided against it.

Five days before Galway were

due to play Tipperary, a Central Council meeting was held to consider Keady's appeal. It was one of the most high-profile appeals of all time. Galway prepared a very strong case, arguing that Keady's original suspension was illegal because the objection against his playing for

Hurler of the Year in 1988, Tony Keady (Galway) was suspended in controversial circumstances a year later

Laois had not been lodged inside the stipulated seven days. However, after a long debate, a proposal that Keady's ban be lifted was defeated by 20 votes to 18.

Galway were outraged. They felt that they – and Keady – had been the victims of an appalling injustice and their mood was not improved the following Sunday when they lost to Tipperary by 1–17 to 2–11 in an ill-tempered game, with two Galway players, Sylvie Linnane and Michael McGrath, sent off.

The Keady affair took another twist shortly after the All-Ireland semi-final when it was alleged that Tipperary corner-back Paul Delaney had played in London without getting the proper clearance. Fearing that they might be disqualified if they played him in the All-Ireland

final, Tipperary left him off the team.

The fall-out from the Keady affair lasted for months and prompted the GAA to take a very unusual step early in 1990. They decided to grant an amnesty to any player who came forward and admitted having played illegally in New York. Quite a few took the opportunity and were suspended and reinstated on the same night.

That further angered Galway, who felt that they were the only county who had really suffered from the unfortunate saga. They were also annoyed that no action had been taken against the officials in New York who told Keady initially that he was eligible to play there.

It was altogether a sad story, with Keady himself being the biggest loser, robbed of a season at the height of his playing powers.

DUBLIN v GALWAY
1983 All-Ireland football final

Sunday, 18 September 1983 dawned to an unseasonal mixture of strong winds, heavy showers and below-average temperatures. As the Galway and Dublin players pulled back their curtains to assess the conditions for that afternoon's All-Ireland football final, they were not pleased.

The high winds would make ball control very difficult, while the intermittent, squally showers would leave the Croke Park surface slippy and unpredictable. However, as they packed their gear a few hours later, they could have no idea that they would be involved in one of the most controversial All-Ireland finals in GAA history.

First to go: Dublin's Brian Mullins is ordered off by referee John Gough in the 1983 All-Ireland final against Galway

Prior to 1983, there had been no history of antagonism between Dublin and Galway. Galway had a small residue of resentment after the 1974 All-Ireland final when they claimed that Dublin's defensive tactics bordered on intimidation. However, nine years later, the 1974 final was no longer relevant. Besides, Dublin and Galway had clashed in the 1976 All-Ireland semi-final and it had passed off without incident.

Dublin had a great championship record against Galway, who hadn't beaten them in the championship since the 1934 All-Ireland final.

Dublin lined up for the 1983 All-Ireland final with the elements behind them as they played into the Railway goal. They made good use of the strong wind and a goal by Barney Rock steadied them as they set about

building up a commanding half-time lead, which they would almost certainly require once Galway came back at them in the second half.

The tackling was fierce and there were some niggly exchanges before Dublin midfielder Brian Mullins was sent off by referee John Gough, in the 23rd minute for a retaliatory foul on Galway's Brian Talty.

Mullins, one of the best midfielders in the history of the game, was a huge loss and his absence handed Galway a definite psychological edge.

The dismissal heightened the tension and, as the tackles flew in, two more players, Ray Hazley (Dublin) and Tomás Tierney (Galway), were sent off just before half-time after wrestling each other to the ground near the sideline. In normal circumstances, the referee might have adopted a more lenient approach but in the sulphurous atmosphere which prevailed, Gough stuck to the letter of the law.

As tempers raced out of control, players from both sides became involved in an ugly altercation as they headed down the tunnel towards the dressing-rooms for the half-time break. Brian Talty received a blow to the head and was unable to play in the second half.

The nasty undercurrent continued into the second half and Gough again showed his willingness to dismiss anybody who misbehaved by sending off a third Dublin player. Ciaran Duff swung a boot dangerously close to defender Pat O'Neill's head and was immediately sent to the dug-out.

The crowd of 71,988 could scarcely believe what was happening. What if the sendings-off continued? Would the game finish? Thankfully common sense made a welcome, if belated, intervention and there were no further dismissals, although the tackling remained fierce to the finish.

Although Dublin held an eight-point lead of 1–7 to 0–2 after Duff's dismissal, the odds appeared stacked against them. Galway had a two-man advantage and were playing with an ever-increasing gale. However, in one of the most defiant efforts ever seen in an All-Ireland final, Dublin hung on grimly. Galway

cut the lead to three points with 20 minutes remaining but Dublin refused to yield to the mounting odds. Their four-man forward line improvised brilliantly and kicked some crucial points which enabled them to remain in front. They eventually won by 1–10 to 1–8.

With the All-Ireland title secured, Dublin headed on to the celebration trail while Galway returned home, embarrassed by their failure to exploit a two-man advantage for most of the second half. The GAA authorities immediately set about taking disciplinary action but several weeks passed before the many cases were finally closed.

Duff was suspended for a year; Mullins got a five-month ban, and Hazley and Tierney were each banned for a month. Galway centre-back Peter Lee, who had not been sent off, was suspended for a month because it was felt that he had committed a serious foul which had not been detected during the match. Dublin manager Kevin Heffernan was suspended for three months for unauthorised incursions on the pitch during the match.

Dublin were aggrieved by the eventual outcome of the GAA's deliberations, believing that they had been made to shoulder too much of the responsibility for the disciplinary breakdown. However, they had the All-Ireland title while Galway had nothing to console them.

The whole affair was very embarrassing for the GAA. The showpiece game of the season had disintegrated into a bad-tempered shambles which went into the record books for the most unfortunate of reasons.

CHAMPIONS WITHOUT A FINAL

In the early years of the GAA championships, it was quite usual for All-Ireland finals to be played behind schedule. The first All-Ireland final, scheduled for 1887, didn't take place until 1 August 1888. It was a pattern that would be quite

common for the next 24 years.

The 1911 hurling final between Limerick and Kilkenny was fixed for 18 February 1912 in Cork. A crowd of 12,000 turned up on a wet, miserable afternoon but, following a pitch inspection by the referee and other officials, it was deemed unplayable.

Limerick refused to accept the decision and insisted that the ground was playable. They were convinced that, for some reason, Kilkenny were not prepared to play. Limerick went through the ritual of togging out and taking the pitch, prior to claiming the game. However, it made little impression on the GAA authorities, who ordered that the game be re-fixed for Thurles on 21 April.

Limerick were incensed. They wanted the game to be played in Cork and refused to accept Thurles as a venue. Limerick brought a motion to the GAA Congress seeking to have the game played in Cork but it was heavily defeated.

Limerick were now entrenched in their attitude and were not prepared to compromise. They were given one final chance to play the game in Thurles on 18 May but, once again, they refused, and on 2 June Central Council awarded the All-Ireland title to Kilkenny.

A highly unsatisfactory situation had developed and a furious Central Council suspended the Limerick County Board. The lack of an All-Ireland final presented the GAA with a financial problem, because they were relying on gate receipts to fund much of their activity. They decided to improvise by ordering Kilkenny to play the beaten Munster finalists, Tipperary, in a substitute final at Dungarvan on 28 July 1912. Kilkenny won by 3–3 to 2–1.

Effectively, Limerick had robbed themselves of a glorious opportunity to win an All-Ireland title by their intransigent attitude towards the venue, while Kilkenny could not believe their luck as they won their fifth All-Ireland title without having to play the final.

It was the only time in the GAA's history that an All-Ireland senior hurling final was won on a walkover.

11

THE HISTORY OF THE RULES OF GAELIC GAMES

Under the first rules of hurling the number of players per team varied from 14 to 21

The first official playing rules of Gaelic football and hurling were adopted by the GAA at its convention in January 1885 and published in United Ireland a month later. They formed no more than a rough guide as to how the games should be played and even failed to specify how many players comprised a team.

The minimum number of players allowed was 14 while the maximum was 21. Such variation created endless opportunities for controversy and confusion. It was alleged that in some parts of Ireland, rugby clubs had changed their allegiance to the fledgling GAA but had not altered the rules. The rules which were in use in parts of Cork city were described as 'undisguised rugby' at

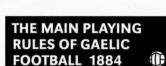

a GAA meeting in late 1885.

While the outfield action resembled rugby, the goalposts suggested a different influence, looking much like modern soccer posts. A goal was scored when the ball was driven inside the posts and under the crossbar. The point, which is now such an important feature of Gaelic games, did not figure on the original scoring system. It was introduced a year later, following the addition of point posts. These were situated seven yards outside each goal post. A point was scored when the ball passed inside them but outside the goalposts. In 1910, the point posts were dispensed with. Instead, the height of the goalposts was increased to 16 feet and a point was awarded when the ball passed through them over the crossbar.

Up until 1892, a goal in both Gaelic football and hurling outweighed any number of points. In 1891 Dublin beat Cork in the All-Ireland football final by 2–1 to 1–9 which, in the modern game, would have made Cork winners by five points. However Dublin won in 1891, having outscored Cork 2–1 in goals. The value of the goal was set at five points between 1892 and 1895, when it was reduced to three points. It has remained so ever since.

The maximum number of players per team was cut from 21 to 17 in 1892 and remained so until 1913 when it was further reduced to 15. It has remained at 15 ever since.

Gaelic football games were set at one hour's duration in 1884 while hurling games lasted 80 minutes. Hurling, however, quickly reverted to one hour and this remained in force in both codes until 1970, when it was decided to extend senior championship matches to 80 minutes. In 1975, they were reduced to 70 minutes, which remains their current duration.

Although Gaelic football and hurling were very different games, the original rule structure had a common theme. That has remained the case to the present day, although there are some variations. Among the more significant rule modifications in both codes was the elimination of the 'third man tackle'. This allowed a player to challenge an opponent who was not in possession of the ball but was moving towards the action. It led to some very unseemly skirmishes and, in the modern game, a player can be tackled only when in possession of the ball.

One aspect of the rules of Gaelic football which has continued to cause confusion over the years relates to the handpass, which allows players to transfer the ball by using the open hand. Its use was abolished in 1945 but reintroduced a year later following a proposal from Antrim, whose players were regarded as experts in the art of hand-passing. The handpass was banned again in 1950, forcing players to use the fisted pass only, which remained in vogue for 25 years.

The handpass was re-admitted in 1975 but came under pressure a few years later, amid claims that Gaelic football was becoming like basketball. Moves to have it banned failed in 1981 but it was redefined, with a stipulation that there must be a 'clear striking action' to render it legal. The handpass is still a source of controversy in Gaelic football, with critics claiming that it should not be allowed in a game where kicking the ball should be a core value.

THE MAIN PLAYING RULES OF GAELIC FOOTBALL 1884

1. *There shall be not less than 14 or more than 21 players a side.*

2. *There shall be two umpires and a referee. When the umpires disagree, the referee's decision shall be final.*

3. *The ground shall be at least 120 yards long by 80 in breadth and properly marked by boundary lines which must be at least 5 yards from fences.*

4. *The goalposts shall stand at each end in the centre of the goal line. They shall be 15 feet apart with the cross-bar 8 feet from the ground.*

5. *The captains of each team shall toss for choice of sides before starting play and the players shall stand in two ranks opposite each other until the ball is thrown up, each man holding a hand of one on the other side.*

6. *Pushing or tripping from behind, holding from behind or butting with the head shall all be deemed foul, and the player so offending shall be ordered to stand aside, and may not afterwards take part in the match, nor can his side substitute another man for him.*

7. *The time of actual play shall be one hour. Sides to be changed only at half-time.*

8. *The match shall be decided by the greater number of goals. If no goal is kicked, the match shall be deemed a draw. A goal is when the ball is kicked through the goalposts under the crossbar.*

9. *When the ball is kicked over the side line, it shall be thrown back by a player of the opposite side to he who kicked it over. If kicked over the goal line by a player whose goal line it is, it shall be thrown back in any direction by a player of the other side. If kicked over the goal line by a player of the other side, the goalkeeper whose line it crosses shall have a free kick. No player of the other side to approach nearer than 25 yards of him until the ball is kicked.*

10. *The umpires and the referee shall have, during the match, full power to disqualify any player, or order him to stand aside and discontinue play, for any act which they may consider unfair as set out in Rule 6.*

THE MAIN PLAYING RULES OF GAELIC FOOTBALL 1934

(50 years after the foundation of the GAA)

1. The field of play shall not be less than 140 yards or more than 170 yards long and not less than 84 yards or more than 100 yards wide.

2. In the centre of the goal-line shall stand the goal posts, 16 feet high and 21 feet apart. There shall be a crossbar 8 feet from the ground.

3. Lines, five yards long, and at right angles to the goal-line, shall be marked four yards from each goalpost. The ends of these lines shall be joined so as to form a parallelogram, 15 by 5 yards, in front of each scoring space.

4. The players shall be 15 a side in all matches but a team may start with 13 players. The second half-hour, however, cannot be started unless there are 15 players on each side. The team failing to field the full number of players shall forfeit the match.

5. The time of actual play is one hour, sides to be changed at half-time. The referee shall be empowered to allow time for delays.

6. A goal is scored when the ball is driven or played by either side over the crossbar and between the goalposts, except when thrown by the attacking side. A point is scored when the ball is driven or played by either side over the crossbar and between the goal posts, except when thrown by the attacking side. A goal shall be equal to three points. Should the ball be played through the goal space by one of the defending side, it shall count a goal. If played through a point space, it shall count a point to the opposing team.

7. When the ball is driven over the goal-line by the opposing team, it shall be kicked out from off the ground, within the small parallelogram. No team from the opposing side shall approach nearer than the 21-yard line until the ball has been kicked.

8. The ball, when off the ground, may be struck with the hand. It may be caught when off the ground. It may be kicked in any direction but not carried. Carrying shall be taking more than four steps while holding the ball, which must not be held longer than is necessary to hop it, kick it or fist it away. Tipping it on the hand is considered carrying. The ball must not be thrown. When caught, the ball may be kicked or struck with the hand or hopped once with either one or both hands, except in the case of a player knocked to the ground while in possession of the ball who may fist it away, even though it is on the ground. The goalkeeper, within the parallelogram, may touch the ball with his hands while on the ground. A player of the opposing team must not enter the parallelogram until the ball enters it in play.

9. Pushing, tripping, kicking, catching, holding or jumping at a player or butting with the head shall be deemed foul. No player shall be charged from behind and no player shall be charged, or in any way interfered with, unless he is moving to play the ball. In the case of rough play, the referee shall caution the player and, should the offence be repeated, or without any caution in the event of dangerous play, violent conduct or improper language, the referee shall order the offender out of play.

10. The weight of the ball shall be from 13 to 15 ounces; 27 to 29 inches in circumference.

THE MAIN PLAYING RULES OF GAELIC FOOTBALL 2000

1. The field of play shall be rectangular and its dimensions shall be as follows: Length 130 metres minimum and 145 metres maximum. Width: 80 metres minimum and 90 metres maximum. The dimensions may be reduced by local bye-laws for under-15 or younger grades.

2. The scoring space shall be at the centre of each endline. Each shall be formed by two goalposts, circular in cross-section, which shall have a height of not less than seven metres above ground level and be 6.5 metres apart. Goal nets shall be securely fixed to the back of the crossbar and the back of each goalpost.

3. A team shall consist of 15 players but a county committee may reduce the number for non-championship games. A team may start with 13 players but shall have fielded 15, inclusive of players ordered off or retired injured, by the start of the second half.

4. The football shall weigh not less than 370g and not more than 425g and have a circumference of not less than 69 cms and not more than 74 cms.

5. A goal shall be awarded when the ball is played over the goal-line and between the posts and under the crossbar by either team. A point is awarded when the ball is played over the crossbar between the posts by either team. A goal is equivalent to three points.

6. When a player is in possession of the ball, it may be (a) carried a maximum of four consecutive steps or held in the hand(s) for no longer than the time needed to take four steps; (b) played from the foot to the hand(s) – toe-tapped; (c) bounced once after each toe-tap; (d) struck with the open hand(s) or fist, provided there is a definite striking action; (e) tossed for a kick, a toe-tap or a pass with the hand(s). The ball may be knocked from an opponent's hand(s) by flicking it with the open hand.

7. Players may tackle an opponent for the ball. Provided he has at least one foot on the ground, a player may make a side-to-side charge on an opponent. When within the small rectangle, the goalkeeper may not be charged but may be challenged for possession of the ball and the kick or pass away may be blocked. Incidental contact with the goalkeeper while playing the ball is allowed.

8. A penalty kick is awarded for an aggressive foul within the opponent's large rectangle or for any foul within the small rectangle. The penalty kick is taken from the centre of the 13-metre line. A goalkeeper may move along his goal-line when a penalty kick is being taken.

9. A player who is fouled has the option of (a) taking the free kick from the hand(s); (b) taking the free kick from the ground (c) allowing another player to take the free kick from the ground.

10. A score shall be allowed if, in the opinion of the referee, the ball was prevented from crossing the goal-line by anyone other than a player or the referee.

Opposite: Cork's Teddy McCarthy demonstrates the high fielding which makes Gaelic Football so thrilling.
Overleaf: Goalkeeper Davy Fitzgerald was hugely influential in Clare's hurling revival in the 1990s.

THE MAIN PLAYING RULES OF HURLING 1884 ✕

1. The ground shall, when convenient, be at least 200 yards long by 150 yards broad, or as near to that size as can be got.

2. There shall be boundary lines all around the ground, at a distance of at least five yards from the fence.

3. The goal shall be two upright posts, 20 feet apart, with a crossbar 10 feet from the ground. A goal is won when the ball is driven between the posts and under the bar.

4. The ball shall not be lifted off the ground with the hand when in play.

5. There shall not be less than 14 or more than 21 players aside in regular matches.

6. There shall be an umpire for each side and a referee who will decide in cases where the umpires disagree. The referee keeps the time and throws up the ball at the commencement of each half.

7. The time of play shall be one hour and 20 minutes. Sides to be changed at half-time.

8. Before commencing play, hurlers shall draw up in two lines in the centre of the field, opposite to each other, and catch hands or hurleys across, then separate. The referee then throws the ball along the ground between the players or up high over their heads.

9. No player to catch, trip or push from behind. Penalty: disqualification of the offender and free puck to the opposite side.

10. No player to bring his hurley intentionally in contact with the person of another player. Penalty as in Rule 9.

11. If the ball is driven over the side-lines, it shall be thrown in towards the middle of the ground by the referee or one of his umpires.

12. If the ball is driven over the end-line and not through the goal, the player who is defending the goal shall have a free puck from the goal. No player of the opposite side to approach nearer than 20 yards until the ball is struck. The other players to stand on the goal-line. But if the ball is driven over the goal-line by a player whose goal it is, the opposite side shall have a free puck on the ground, 20 yards out from the goalposts. Players whose goal it is to stand on the goal-line until the ball is struck.
N.B. Hitting both right and left is allowable.

THE MAIN PLAYING RULES OF HURLING 1934 ✕

(50 years after the foundation of the GAA)

1. The ground shall not be less than 140 yards or more than 170 yards long, and not less than 84 yards or more than 100 yards wide.

2. In the centre of the goal shall stand the goalposts, 16 feet high and 21 feet apart. There shall be a crossbar, 8 feet from the ground.

3. The ball shall weigh from three and a half to four and a half ounces and be 9–10 inches in circumference.

4. The players shall be 15 a side in all matches but a team may start with 13 players. The second half cannot be started unless there are 15 players on each side. The team failing to field the full number of players shall forfeit the match.

5. The actual time for play is one hour, sides to be changed only at half-time.

6. A goal is scored when the ball is driven or played by either team between the goal posts and under the crossbar. A point is scored when the ball is driven or played by either side over the crossbar and between the goal-posts. A goal shall count for three points.

7. When the ball is driven over the goal-line by the opposing team, it shall be pucked out from within the small paral-lelogram. The player taking the puck-out may take the ball into his hands to puck out. Should he miss the first stroke, the ball must be pucked off the ground.

8. The penalty for all breaches of the rules shall be a free puck. The ball shall not be pucked until the referee has whistled.

9. The ball must not be lifted off the ground with the hand when in play. It may be struck with the hand when off the ground. It may also be kicked. It may be caught when off the ground and the player so catching it may puck it any way he pleases but must not carry it (except on the hurley) or throw it. Tipping on the hand is considered carrying. Should a player hold the ball longer than is necessary to puck it away, or take more than three steps while holding it, the opposing side shall have a free puck from where the foul occurred.

10. Pushing, tripping, kicking, catching, holding or jumping at a player, or butting with the head, shall be deemed foul. No player shall be charged from behind and no player shall be charged, or in any way interfered with, except when in the act of moving to play the ball or playing it. No player shall intentionally bring his hurley in contact with the person of another player. A player must not throw his hurley in any circumstances. The penalty for each breach of this rule shall be a free puck.

THE MAIN PLAYING RULES OF HURLING 2000 ✕

1. The field of play shall be rectangular and its dimensions shall be as follows: Length: 130 metres minimum and 145 metres maximum: Width: 80 metres minimum and 90 metres maximum. The dimensions may be reduced by local bye-laws for Under-15 or younger grades.

2. The ball may be struck with the hurley when it is on the ground, in the air, tossed from the hand or lifted with the hurley.

3. A player may run with the ball balanced on, or hopping on his hurley. A player may catch the ball, play it on his hurley and bring it back on to his hand once. A player who has not caught the ball may play it from the hurley into his hand twice. The ball may be struck with the hand, kicked, or lifted off the ground with the feet.

4. The ball may not be touched on the ground with the hand(s) except when a player is knocked down or falls and the ball in his hand touches the ground. The ball may be carried in the hand for a maximum of four consecutive steps or held in the hand for no longer than the time needed to take four steps.

5. Players may tackle an opponent for the ball. Provided that at least one foot remains on the ground, a player may make a side-to-side charge on an opponent who is (a) in possession of the ball or (b) who is playing the ball or (c) when both players are moving in the direction of the ball to play it.

6. For a run-up to a free kick, side-line puck or puck-out, a player may go outside the boundary lines, but otherwise players shall remain within the field of play.

7. A goal is scored when the ball is played over the goal-line between the posts and under the crossbar by either team. A point is scored when the ball is played over the crossbar between the posts by either team. A goal is equivalent to three points.

8. For all free pucks, including penalties, the ball may be struck with the hurley in either of two ways: (a) lift the ball with the hurley at the first attempt and strike it with the hurley or (b) strike the ball off the ground.

9. A penalty puck shall be awarded for an aggressive foul within the large rectangle. The penalty puck shall be taken from the centre point of the 20-metre line. A free puck from the centre of the 20-metre line shall be awarded for a technical foul within the large rectangle. Only three defenders may remain on the goal-line to defend against a penalty by the opposition.

10. When the ball is played over the end line and outside the goalposts by the team defending that end, a free puck shall be awarded to the opposing team on the 65-metre line, opposite where the ball crossed the end line.

FOOTBALL

All-Ireland Senior Football Final Results

Teams: 21-a-side

1887: Limerick 1-4 Louth 0-3
1888: Championship unfinished
1889: Tipperary 3-6 Laois 0-0
1890: Cork 2-4 Wexford 0-1
1891: Dublin 2-1 Cork 1-9
(A goal outweighed any number of points)

Teams were reduced to 17-a-side from 1892 onwards. A goal was revalued to 5 points.

1892: Dublin 1-4 Kerry 0-3
1893: Wexford 1-1 Cork 0-1
1894: Dublin 0-6 Cork 1-1 (draw)
Dublin 0-5 Cork 1-2 (replay):
Match unfinished:
Title awarded to Dublin.
1895: Tipperary 0-4 Meath 0-3

A goal was revalued to 3 points from 1896 onwards.

1896: Limerick 1-5 Dublin 0-7
1897: Dublin 2-6 Cork 0-2
1898: Dublin 2-8 Waterford 0-4
1899: Dublin 1-10 Cork 0-6
1900: Tipperary 3-7 London 0-2
Home final: Tipperary 2-17 Galway 0-1
1901: Dublin 0-14 London 0-2
Home final: Dublin 1-2 Cork 0-4
1902: Dublin 2-8 London 0-4
Home final: Dublin 0-6 Tipperary 0-5
1903: Kerry 0-11 London 0-3
Home final: Kerry 1-4 Kildare 1-3 (disputed)
Kerry 0-7 Kildare 1-4 (re-fixture)
Kerry 0-8 Kildare 0-2 (replay)
1904: Kerry 0-5 Dublin 0-2
1905: Kildare 1-7 Kerry 0-5
1906: Dublin 0-5 Cork 0-4
1907: Dublin 0-6 Cork 0-2
1908: Dublin 1-10 London 0-4
Home final: Dublin 0-10 Kerry 0-3
1909: Kerry 1-9 Louth 0-6
1910: Louth walkover Kerry, who refused to travel to Dublin due to a dispute with Great Southern and Western Railway Company

1911: Cork 6-6 Antrim 1-2
1912: Louth 1-7 Antrim 1-2

Teams reduced to 15-a-side in 1913

1913: Kerry 2-2 Wexford 0-3
1914: Kerry 1-3 Wexford 2-0 (draw)
Kerry 2-3 Wexford 0-6
1915: Wexford 2-4 Kerry 2-1
1916: Wexford 3-4 Mayo 1-2
1917: Wexford 0-9 Clare 0-5
1918: Wexford 0-5 Tipperary 0-4
1919: Kildare 2-5 Galway 0-1
1920: Tipperary 1-6 Dublin 1-2
1921: Dublin 1-9 Mayo 0-2
1922: Dublin 0-6 Galway 0-4
1923: Dublin 1-5 Kerry 1-3
1924: Kerry 0-4 Dublin 0-3
1925: Galway declared champions.*
1926: Kerry 1-3 Kildare 0-6 (draw)
Kerry 1-4 Kildare 0-4 (replay)
1927: Kildare 0-5 Kerry 0-3
1928: Kildare 2-6 Cavan 2-5
1929: Kerry 1-8 Kildare 1-5
1930: Kerry 3-11 Monaghan 0-2
1931: Kerry 1-11 Kildare 0-8
1932: Kerry 2-7 Mayo 2-4
1933: Cavan 2-5 Galway 1-4
1934: Galway 3-5 Dublin 1-9
1935: Cavan 3-6 Kildare 2-5
1936: Mayo 4-11 Laois 0-5
1937: Kerry 2-5 Cavan 1-8 (draw)
Kerry 4-4 Cavan 1-7 (replay)
1938: Galway 3-3 Kerry 2-6 (draw)
Galway 2-4 Kerry 0-7 (replay)
1939: Kerry 2-5 Meath 2-3
1940: Kerry 0-7 Galway 1-3
1941: Kerry 1-8 Galway 0-7
1942: Dublin 1-10 Galway 1-8
1943: Roscommon 1-6 Cavan 1-6 (draw) Roscommon 2-7 Cavan 2-2 (replay)
1944: Roscommon 1-9 Kerry 2-4
1945: Cork 2-5 Cavan 0-7
1946: Kerry 2-4 Roscommon 1-7 (draw) Kerry 2-8 Roscommon 0-10 (replay)
1947: Cavan 2-11 Kerry 2-7
1948: Cavan 4-5 Mayo 4-4
1949: Meath 1-10 Cavan 1-6
1950: Mayo 2-5 Louth 1-6
1951: Mayo 2-8 Meath 0-9
1952: Cavan 2-4 Meath 1-7 (draw) Cavan 0-9 Meath 0-5 (replay)
1953: Kerry 0-13 Armagh 1-6
1954: Meath 1-13 Kerry 1-7
1955: Kerry 0-12 Dublin 1-6
1956: Galway 2-13 Cork 3-7
1957: Louth 1-9 Cork 1-7
1958: Dublin 2-12 Derry 1-9
1959: Kerry 3-7 Galway 1-4

1960: Down 2-10 Kerry 0-8
1961: Down 3-6 Offaly 2-8
1962: Kerry 1-12 Roscommon 1-6
1963: Dublin 1-9 Galway 0-10
1964: Galway 0-15 Kerry 0-10
1965: Galway 0-12 Kerry 0-9
1966: Galway 1-10 Meath 0-7
1967: Meath 1-9 Cork 0-9
1968: Down 2-12 Kerry 1-13
1969: Kerry 0-10 Offaly 0-7

Games were extended from 60 to 80 minutes between 1970 and 1974

1970: Kerry 2-19 Meath 0-18
1971: Offaly 1-14 Galway 2-8
1972: Offaly 1-13 Kerry 1-13 (draw)
Offaly 1-19 Kerry 0-13 (replay)
1973: Cork 3-17 Galway 2-13
1974: Dublin 0-14 Galway 1-6

Games were reduced from 80 to 70 minutes from 1975 onwards.

1975: Kerry 2-12 Dublin 0-11
1976: Dublin 3-8 Kerry 0-10
1977: Dublin 5-12 Armagh 3-6
1978: Kerry 5-11 Dublin 0-9
1979: Kerry 3-13 Dublin 1-8
1980: Kerry 1-9 Roscommon 1-6
1981: Kerry 1-12 Offaly 0-8
1982: Offaly 1-15 Kerry 0-17
1983: Dublin 1-10 Galway 1-8
1984: Kerry 0-14 Dublin 1-6
1985: Kerry 2-12 Dublin 2-8
1986: Kerry 2-15 Tyrone 1-10
1987: Meath 1-14 Cork 0-11
1988: Meath 0-12 Cork 1-9 (draw)
Meath 0-13 Cork 0-12 (replay)
1989: Cork 0-17 Mayo 1-11
1990: Cork 0-11 Meath 0-9
1991: Down 1-16 Meath 1-14
1992: Donegal 0-18 Dublin 0-14
1993: Derry 1-14 Cork 2-8
1994: Down 1-12 Dublin 0-13
1995: Dublin 1-10 Tyrone 0-12
1996: Meath 0-12 Mayo 1-9 (draw)
Meath 2-9 Mayo 1-11 (replay)
1997: Kerry 0-13 Mayo 1-7
1998: Galway 1-14 Kildare 1-10
1999: Meath 1-11 Cork 1-8
2000: Kerry 0-14 Galway 0-14 (draw)
Kerry 0-17 Galway 1-10 (replay)

*1925: Both Cavan and Kerry were ruled out of the championship in a row over the eligibility of some players. Mayo beat Wexford in the All-Ireland semi-final but were later beaten by Galway in the Connacht final. Galway were declared All-Ireland champions by the GAA's

Central Council. Galway later defeated Cavan by 3-2 to 1-2 in a special competition played in lieu of the All-Ireland series.

All-Ireland U21 Football Final Results

1964: Kerry 1-10 Laois 1-3
1965: Kildare 2-11 Cork 1-7
1966: Roscommon 2-10 Kildare 1-12
1967: Mayo 2-10 Kerry 2-10 (draw)
Mayo 4-9 Kerry 1-7 (replay)
1968: Derry 3-9 Offaly 1-9
1969: Antrim 1-8 Roscommon 0-10
1970: Cork 2-11 Fermanagh 0-9
1971: Cork 3-10 Fermanagh 0-3
1972: Galway 2-6 Kerry 0-7
1973: Kerry 2-13 Mayo 0-13
1974: Mayo 0-9 Antrim 0-9 (draw)
Mayo 2-10 Antrim 2-8 (replay)
1975: Kerry 1-15 Dublin 0-10
1976: Kerry 0-14 Kildare 1-3
1977: Kerry 1-11 Down 1-5
1978: Roscommon 1-9 Kerry 1-8
1979: Down 1-9 Cork 0-7
1980: Cork 2-8 Dublin 1-5
1981: Cork 0-14 Galway 2-8 (draw)
Cork 2-9 Galway 1-6 (replay)
1982: Donegal 0-8 Roscommon 0-5
1983: Mayo 2-5 Derry 1-8 (draw)
Mayo 1-8 Derry 1-5 (replay)
1984: Cork 0-9 Mayo 0-6
1985: Cork 0-14 Derry 1-8
1986: Cork 3-16 Offaly 0-12
1987: Donegal 1-7 Kerry 0-10 (draw)
Donegal 1-12 Kerry 2-4 (replay)
1988: Offaly 0-11 Cavan 0-9
1989: Cork 2-8 Galway 1-10
1990: Kerry 5-12 Tyrone 2-11
1991: Tyrone 4-16 Kerry 1-5
1992: Tyrone 1-10 Galway 1-7
1993: Meath 1-8 Kerry 0-10
1994: Cork 1-12 Mayo 1-5
1995: Kerry 2-12 Mayo 3-9 (draw)
Kerry 3-10 Mayo 1-12 (replay)
1996: Kerry 1-17 Cavan 2-10
1997: Derry 1-12 Meath 0-5
1998: Kerry 2-8 Laois 0-11
1999: Westmeath 0-12 Kerry 0-9
2000: Tyrone 3-12 Limerick 0-13

All-Ireland Minor Football Final Results

1929: Clare 5-3 Longford 3-5
1930: Dublin 1-3 Mayo 0-5
1931: Kerry 3-4 Louth 0-4
1932: Kerry 3-8 Laois 1-3

Offaly captain Willie Bryan raises the Sam Maguire Cup in 1971

1933: Kerry 4-1 Mayo 0-9
1934: Semi-finalists Tipperary and
  Tyrone were disqualified.
  Tipperary awarded title
1935: Mayo 1-6 Tipperary 1-1
1936: Louth 5-1 Kerry 1-8
1937: Cavan 1-11 Wexford 1-5
1938: Cavan 3-3 Kerry 0-8
1939: Roscommon 1-9
  Monaghan 1-7
1940: Louth 5-5 Mayo 2-7
1941: Roscommon 3-6 Louth 0-7
1942: No minor Championship
  played
1943: No minor Championship
  played
1944: No minor Championship
  played
1945: Dublin 4-7 Leitrim 0-4
1946: Kerry 3-7 Dublin 2-3
1947: Tyrone 4-4 Mayo 4-3
1948: Tyrone 0-11 Dublin 1-5
1949: Armagh 1-7 Kerry 1-5
1950: Kerry 3-6 Wexford 1-4
1951: Roscommon 2-7 Armagh 1-5
1952: Galway 2-9 Cavan 1-6
1953: Mayo 2-11 Clare 1-6
1954: Dublin 3-3 Kerry 1-8
1955: Dublin 5-4 Tipperary 2-7
1956: Dublin 5-14 Leitrim 2-2
1957: Meath 3-9 Armagh 0-4
1958: Dublin 2-10 Mayo 0-8
1959: Dublin 0-11 Cavan 1-4
1960: Galway 4-9 Cork 1-5
1961: Cork 3-7 Mayo 0-5
1962: Kerry 6-5 Mayo 0-7
1963: Kerry 1-10 Westmeath 0-2
1964: Offaly 0-15 Cork 1-11
1965: Derry 2-8 Kerry 2-4
1966: Mayo 1-12 Down 1-8

1967: Cork 5-14 Laois 2-3
1968: Cork 3-5 Sligo 1-10
1969: Cork 2-7 Derry 0-11
1970: Galway 1-8 Kerry 2-5 (draw)
  Galway 1-11 Kerry 1-10 (replay)
1971: Mayo 2-15 Cork 2-7
1972: Cork 3-11 Tyrone 2-11
1973: Tyrone 2-11 Kildare 1-6
1974: Cork 1-10 Mayo 1-6
1975: Kerry 1-10 Tyrone 0-4
1976: Galway 1-10 Cork 0-6
1977: Down 2-6 Meath 0-4
1978: Mayo 4-9 Dublin 3-8
1979: Dublin 0-10 Kerry 1-6
1980: Kerry 3-12 Derry 0-11
1981: Cork 4-9 Derry 2-7
1982: Dublin 1-11 Kerry 1-5
1983: Derry 0-8 Cork 1-3
1984: Dublin 1-9 Tipperary 0-4
1985: Mayo 3-3 Cork 0-9
1986: Galway 3-8 Cork 2-7
1987: Down 1-12 Cork 1-5
1988: Kerry 2-5 Dublin 0-5
1989: Derry 3-9 Offaly 1-6
1990: Meath 2-11 Kerry 2-9
1991: Cork 1-9 Mayo 1-7
1992: Meath 2-5 Armagh 0-10
1993: Cork 2-7 Meath 0-9
1994: Kerry 0-16 Galway 1-7
1995: Westmeath 1-10 Derry 0-11
1996: Laois 2-11 Kerry 1-11
1997: Laois 3-11 Tyrone 1-14
1998: Tyrone 2-11 Laois 0-11
1999: Down 1-14 Mayo 0-14
2000: Cork 2-12 Mayo 0-13

National Football League Final Results

1926: Laois 2-1 Dublin 1-0
1927: No Competition
1928: Kerry 2-4 Kildare 1-6
1929: Kerry 1-7 Kildare 2-3
1930: Kerry 1-3 Cavan 1-2
1931: Kerry 5-2 Cork 3-3
1932: No Competition
1933: Meath 0-10 Cavan 1-6
1934: Mayo 2-4 Dublin 1-5
1935: Mayo 6-8 Tipperary 2-5
1936: No final. Mayo won
  League outright
1937: Mayo 5-4 Meath 1-8
1938: Mayo 3-9 Wexford 1-3
1939: Meath 5-9 Mayo 0-6
1940: Galway 2-5 Meath 1-5
1941: Mayo 3-7 Dublin 0-7
1942-45: National League
  suspended
1946: Meath 2-2 Wexford 0-6
1947: Derry 2-9 Clare 2-5
1948: Cavan 2-11 Cork 3-8 (draw)
  Cavan 5-9 Cork 2-8 (replay)
1949: Mayo 1-8 Louth 1-6
1950: New York 2-8 Cavan 0-12
1951: Meath 1-10 New York 0-10
1952: Cork 1-12 New York 0-3
1953: Dublin 4-6 Cavan 0-9
1954: Mayo 2-10 Carlow 0-3
1955: Dublin 2-12 Meath 1-3
1956: Cork 0-8 Meath 0-7
1957: Galway 1-8 Kerry 0-6
1958: Dublin 3-13 Kildare 3-8
1959: Kerry 2-8 Derry 1-8
1960: Down 0-12 Cavan 0-9
1961: Kerry 4-16 Derry 1-5
1962: Down 2-5 Dublin 1-7
1963: Kerry 1-18 New York 0-10
1964: New York 2-12 Dublin 1-13
1965: New York 0-8 Galway 1-4
  (first leg)
  Galway 3-8 New York 0-9
  (second leg)
  Galway 4-12 New York 0-17
1966: Longford 1-9 New York 0-7
  (first leg)
  New York 0-10 Longford 0-9
  (second leg)
  Longford 1-18 Longford 0-17
  (aggregate)
1967: New York 3-5 Galway 1-6
  (first leg)
  New York 4-3 Galway 0-10
  (second leg)
  New York 7-8 Galway 1-16
  (aggregate)
1968: Down 2-14 Kildare 2-11
1969: Kerry 0-12 New York 0-12
  (first leg)
  Kerry 2-21 New York 2-12
  (second leg)
  Kerry 2-33 New York 2-24
  (aggregate)
1970: Mayo 4-7 Down 0-10

1971: Kerry 0-11 Mayo 0-8
1972: Kerry 2-11 Mayo 1-9
1973: Kerry 2-12 Offaly 0-14
1974: Kerry 1-6 Roscommon 0-9
  (draw)
  Kerry 0-14 Roscommon 0-8 (replay)
1975: Meath 0-16 Dublin 1-9
1976: Dublin 2-10 Derry 0-15
1977: Kerry 1-8 Dublin 1-6
1978: Dublin 2-18 Mayo 2-13
1979: Roscommon 0-15 Cork 1-3
1980: Cork 0-11 Kerry 0-10
1981: Galway 1-11 Roscommon 1-2
1982: Kerry 1-9 Cork 0-5
1983: Down 1-8 Armagh 0-8
1984: Kerry 1-11 Galway 0-11
1985: Monaghan 1-11 Armagh 0-9
1986: Laois 2-6 Monaghan 2-5
1987: Dublin 1-11 Kerry 0-11
1988: Meath 0-11 Dublin 1-8 (draw)
  Meath 2-13 Dublin 0-11 (replay)
1989: Cork 1-12 New York 1-5
  (first leg)
  Cork 2-9 New York 1-9 (second leg)
  Cork 3-21 New York 2-14
  (aggregate)
1990: Meath 2-7 Down 0-11
1991: Dublin 1-9 Kildare 0-10
1992: Derry 1-10 Tyrone 1-8
1993: Dublin 0-9 Donegal 0-9 (draw)
  Dublin 0-10 Donegal 0-6 (replay)
1994: Meath 2-11 Armagh 0-8
1995: Derry 0-12 Donegal 0-8
1996: Derry 1-16 Donegal 1-9
1997: Kerry 3-7 Cork 1-8
1998: Offaly 0-9 Derry 0-7
1999: Cork 0-12 Dublin 1-7
2000: Derry 1-12 Meath 1-12 (draw)
  Derry 1-8 Meath 0-9 (replay)
2001: Mayo 0-13 Galway 0-12

Railway Cup Interprovincial Football Final Results

1927: Munster 2-3 Connacht 0-5
1928: Leinster 1-8 Ulster 2-4
1929: Leinster 1-7 Munster 1-3
1930: Leinster 2-3 Munster 0-6
1931: Munster 2-2 Leinster 0-6
1932: Leinster 2-10 Munster 3-5
1933: Leinster 0-12 Connacht 2-5
1934: Connacht 2-9 Leinster 2-8
1935: Leinster 2-9 Munster 0-7
1936: Connacht 3-11 Ulster 2-3
1937: Connacht 2-4 Munster 0-5
1938: Connacht 2-6 Munster 1-5
1939: Leinster 3-8 Ulster 3-3
1940: Leinster 3-7 Munster 0-2
1941: Munster 1-8 Ulster 1-8 (draw)
  Munster 2-6 Ulster 1-6 (replay)
1942: Ulster 1-10 Munster 1-5
1943: Ulster 3-7 Leinster 2-9
1944: Leinster 1-10 Ulster 1-3
1945: Leinster 2-5 Connacht 0-6
1946: Munster 3-5 Leinster 1-9
1947: Ulster 1-6 Leinster 0-3

1948: Munster 4-5 Ulster 2-6
1949: Munster 2-7 Leinster 2-7 (draw)
 Munster 4-9 Leinster 1-4 (replay)
1950: Ulster 4-11 Leinster 1-7
1951: Connacht 1-9 Munster 1-8
1952: Leinster 0-5 Munster 0-3
1953: Leinster 2-9 Munster 0-6
1954: Leinster 1-7 Connacht 1-5
1955: Leinster 1-14 Connacht 1-10
1956: Ulster 0-12 Munster 0-4
1957: Connacht 2-9 Munster 1-6
1958: Connacht 2-7 Munster 0-8
1959: Leinster 2-7 Munster 0-7
1960: Ulster 2-12 Munster 3-8
1961: Leinster 4-5 Munster 0-4
1962: Leinster 1-11 Ulster 0-11
1963: Ulster 2-8 Leinster 1-9
1964: Ulster 0-12 Leinster 1-6
1965: Ulster 0-19 Connacht 0-15
1966: Ulster 2-5 Munster 1-5
1967: Connacht 1-9 Ulster 0-11
1968: Ulster 1-10 Leinster 0-8
1969: Connacht 1-12 Munster 0-6
1970: Ulster 2-11 Connacht 0-10
1971: Ulster 3-11 Connacht 2-11
1972: Munster 2-14 Leinster 0-10
1973: Combined Universities 2-12
 Connacht 0-18 (draw)
 Combined Universities 4-9
 Connacht 1-1 (replay)
1974: Leinster 2-10 Connacht 1-7
1975: Munster 6-7 Ulster 0-15
1976: Munster 2-15 Leinster 2-8
1977: Munster 1-14 Connacht 1-9
1978: Munster 2-7 Ulster 2-7 (draw)
 Munster 4-12 Ulster 0-19 (replay)
1979: Ulster 1-7 Munster 0-6
1980: Ulster 2-10 Munster 1-9
1981: Munster 3-10 Connacht 1-9
1982: Munster 1-8 Connacht 0-10
1983: Ulster 0-24 Leinster 2-10
1984: Ulster 1-12 Connacht 1-7
1985: Leinster 0-9 Munster 0-5
1986: Leinster 2-8 Connacht 2-5
1987: Leinster 1-13 Munster 0-9
1988: Leinster 2-9 Ulster 0-12
1989: Ulster 1-11 Munster 1-8
1990: No competition played
1991: Ulster 1-11 Munster 1-8
1992: Ulster 2-7 Munster 0-8
1993: Ulster 1-12 Leinster 0-12
1994: Ulster 1-6 Munster 1-4
1995: Ulster 1-9 Leinster 0-8
1996: Leinster 1-13 Munster 0-9
1997: Leinster 2-14 Connacht 0-12
1998: Ulster 0-20 Leinster 0-17
1999: Munster 0-10 Connacht 0-6
2000: Ulster 1-9 Connacht 0-3

All-Ireland Senior Football Titles

32: Kerry – 1903, 1904, 1909, 1913, 1914, 1924, 1926, 1929, 1930, 1931, 1932, 1937, 1939, 1940, 1941, 1946, 1953, 1955, 1959, 1962, 1969, 1970, 1975, 1978, 1979, 1980, 1981, 1984, 1985, 1986, 1997, 2000.
22: Dublin – 1891, 1892, 1894, 1897, 1898, 1899, 1901, 1902, 1906, 1907, 1908, 1921, 1922, 1923, 1942, 1958, 1963, 1974, 1976, 1977, 1983, 1995.
8: Galway – 1925, 1934, 1938, 1956, 1964, 1965, 1966, 1998.
7: Meath – 1949, 1954, 1967, 1987, 1988, 1996, 1999.
6: Cork – 1890, 1911, 1945, 1973, 1989, 1990.
5: Wexford – 1893, 1915, 1916, 1917, 1918.
5: Cavan – 1933, 1935, 1947, 1948, 1952.
5: Down – 1960, 1961, 1968, 1991, 1994.
4: Kildare – 1905, 1919, 1927, 1928.
4: Tipperary – 1889, 1895, 1900, 1920.
3: Louth – 1910, 1912, 1957.
3: Mayo – 1936, 1950, 1951.
3: Offaly – 1971, 1972, 1982.
2: Limerick – 1887, 1896.
2: Roscommon – 1943, 1944.
1: Donegal – 1992.
1: Derry – 1993.

All-Ireland U21 Football Titles

9: Cork – 1970, 1971, 1980, 1981, 1984, 1985, 1986, 1989, 1994.
9: Kerry – 1964, 1973, 1975, 1977, 1990, 1995, 1996, 1998.
3: Mayo – 1967, 1974, 1983.
3: Tyrone – 1991, 1992, 2000.
2: Derry- 1968, 1997.
2: Donegal – 1982, 1987.
2: Roscommon – 1966, 1978.
1: Antrim – 1969.
1: Down – 1979.
1: Galway – 1972.
1: Kildare – 1965.
1: Meath – 1993.
1: Offaly – 1988.
1: Westmeath – 1999.

All-Ireland Minor Football Titles

11: Kerry – 1931, 1932, 1933, 1946, 1950, 1962, 1963, 1975, 1980, 1988, 1994.
10: Cork – 1961, 1967, 1968, 1969, 1972, 1974, 1981, 1991, 1993, 2000.
10: Dublin – 1930, 1945, 1954, 1955, 1956, 1958, 1959, 1979, 1982, 1984.
6: Mayo – 1935, 1953, 1966, 1971, 1978, 1985.
5: Galway – 1952, 1960, 1970, 1976, 1986.
4: Tyrone – 1947, 1948, 1973, 1998.
3: Derry – 1965, 1983, 1989.
3: Down – 1977, 1987, 1999.
3: Meath – 1957, 1990, 1992.
3: Roscommon – 1939, 1941, 1951.
2: Cavan – 1937, 1938.
2: Laois – 1996, 1997.
2: Louth – 1936, 1940.
1: Armagh – 1949.
1: Clare – 1929.
1: Offaly – 1964.
1: Tipperary – 1935.
1: Westmeath – 1995.

National Football League Titles

16: Kerry – 1928, 1929, 1931, 1932, 1959, 1961, 1963, 1969, 1971, 1972, 1973, 1974, 1977, 1982, 1984, 1997.
11: Mayo – 1934, 1935, 1936, 1937, 1938, 1939, 1941, 1949, 1954, 1970, 2001.
8: Dublin – 1953, 1955, 1958, 1976, 1978, 1987, 1991, 1993.
7: Meath – 1933, 1946, 1951, 1975, 1988, 1990, 1994.
5: Derry – 1947, 1992, 1995, 1996, 2000.
4: Cork – 1952, 1956, 1980, 1989.
4: Down – 1960, 1962, 1968, 1983.
4: Galway – 1940, 1957, 1965, 1981.
3: New York – 1950, 1964, 1967.
2: Laois – 1927, 1986.
1: Cavan – 1948.
1: Longford – 1966.
1: Monaghan – 1985
1: Offaly – 1998
1: Roscommon – 1979

Railway Cup Interprovincial Football Titles

25: Ulster – 1942, 1943, 1947, 1950, 1956, 1960, 1963, 1964, 1965, 1966, 1968, 1970, 1971, 1979, 1980, 1983, 1984, 1989, 1991, 1992, 1993, 1994, 1995, 1998, 2000.
24: Leinster -1928, 1929, 1930, 1932, 1933, 1935, 1939, 1940, 1944, 1945, 1952, 1953, 1954, 1955, 1959, 1961, 1962, 1974, 1985, 1986, 1987, 1988, 1996, 1997.
14: Munster – 1927, 1931, 1941, 1946, 1948, 1949, 1972, 1975, 1976, 1977, 1978, 1981, 1982, 1999.
9: Connacht – 1934, 1936, 1937, 1938, 1951, 1957, 1958, 1967, 1969.
1: Combined Universities – 1973.
(No competition in 1990).

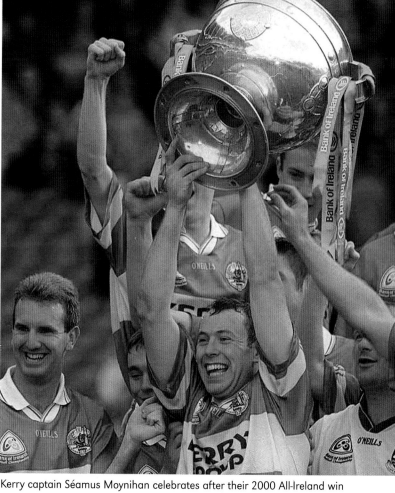

Kerry captain Séamus Moynihan celebrates after their 2000 All-Ireland win

All-Ireland Senior Hurling Final Results

Teams 21-a-side: Goal worth more than any number of points

1887: Tipperary 1-1 Galway 0-0
1888: Championship unfinished
1889: Dublin 5-1 Clare 1-6
1890: Cork 1-6 Wexford 2-2*
1891: Kerry 2-3 Wexford 1-5
1892: Cork 2-4 Dublin 1-1

Teams reduced from 21 to 17-a-side and goal valued at 5 points from 1892 onwards

1893: Cork 6-8 Kilkenny 0-2
1894: Cork 5-20 Dublin 2-0
1895: Tipperary 6-8 Kilkenny 1-0
1896: Tipperary 8-14 Dublin 0-4

Goal re-valued at 3 points from 1896

1897: Limerick 3-4 Kilkenny 2-4
1898: Tipperary 7-13 Kilkenny 3-10
1899: Tipperary 3-12 Wexford 1-4
1900: Tipperary 2-5 London 0-6
1901: Cork 2-8 Wexford 0-6
1901: London 1-5 Cork 0-4
1902: Cork 2-13 London 0-0
1903: Cork 3-16 London 1-1
1904: Kilkenny 1-9 Cork 1-8
1905: Cork 5-10 Kilkenny 3-13
   (replay ordered due to objections)
   Kilkenny 7-7 Cork 2-9 (replay)
1906: Tipperary 3-16 Dublin 3-8
1907: Kilkenny 3-12 Cork 4-8
1908: Tipperary 2-5 Dublin 1-8
   (draw)
   Tipperary 3-15 Dublin 1-5 (replay)
1909: Kilkenny 4-6 Tipperary 0-12
1910: Wexford 7-0 Limerick 6-2
1911: Kilkenny 3-3 Tipperary 2-1
1912: Kilkenny 2-1 Cork 1-3
1913: Kilkenny 2-4 Tipperary 1-2

Teams reduced to 15-a-side from 1913 onwards

1914: Clare 5-1 Laois 1-0
1915: Laois 6-2 Cork 4-1
1916: Tipperary 5-4 Kilkenny 3-2
1917: Dublin 5-4 Tipperary 4-2
1918: Limerick 9-5 Wexford 1-3
1919: Cork 6-4 Dublin 2-4
1920: Dublin 4-9 Cork 4-3
1921: Limerick 8-5 Dublin 3-2
1922: Kilkenny 4-2 Tipperary 2-6
1923: Galway 7-3 Limerick 4-5
1924: Dublin 5-3 Galway 2-6

1925: Tipperary 5-6 Galway 1-5
1926: Cork 4-6 Kilkenny 2-0
1927: Dublin 4-8 Cork 1-3
1928: Cork 6-12 Galway 1-0
1929: Cork 4-9 Galway 1-3
1930: Tipperary 2-7 Dublin 1-3
1931: Cork 1-6 Kilkenny 1-6 (draw)
   Cork 5-8 Kilkenny 3-4 (replay)
1932: Kilkenny 3-3 Clare 2-3
1933: Kilkenny 1-7 Limerick 0-6
1934: Limerick 2-7 Dublin 3-4 (draw)
   Limerick 5-2 Dublin 2-6 (replay)
1935: Kilkenny 2-5 Limerick 2-4
1936: Limerick 5-6 Kilkenny 1-5
1937: Tipperary 3-11 Kilkenny 0-3
1938: Dublin 2-5 Waterford 1-6
1939: Kilkenny 2-7 Cork 3-3
1940: Limerick 3-7 Kilkenny 1-7
1941: Cork 5-11 Dublin 0-6
1942: Cork 2-14 Dublin 3-4
1943: Cork 5-16 Antrim 0-4
1944: Cork 2-13 Dublin 1-2
1945: Tipperary 5-6 Kilkenny 3-6
1946: Cork 7-5 Kilkenny 3-8
1947: Kilkenny 0-14 Cork 2-7
1948: Waterford 6-7 Dublin 4-2
1949: Tipperary 3-11 Laois 0-3
1950: Tipperary 1-9 Kilkenny 1-8
1951: Tipperary 7-7 Wexford 3-9
1952: Cork 2-14 Dublin 0-7
1953: Cork 3-3 Galway 0-8
1954: Cork 1-9 Wexford 1-6
1955: Wexford 3-13 Galway 2-8
1956: Wexford 2-14 Cork 2-8
1957: Kilkenny 4-10 Waterford 3-12
1958: Tipperary 4-9 Galway 2-5
1959: Waterford 1-17 Kilkenny 5-5
   (draw)
   Waterford 3-12 Kilkenny 1-10
   (replay)
1960: Wexford 2-15 Tipperary 0-11
1961: Tipperary 0-16 Dublin 1-12
1962: Tipperary 3-10 Wexford 2-11
1963: Kilkenny 4-17 Waterford 6-8
1964: Tipperary 5-13 Kilkenny 2-8
1965: Tipperary 2-16 Wexford 0-10
1966: Cork 3-9 Kilkenny 1-10
1967: Kilkenny 3-8 Tipperary 2-7
1968: Wexford 5-8 Tipperary 3-12
1969: Kilkenny 2-15 Cork 2-9

Games extended from 60 to 80 minutes between 1970 and 1974

1970: Cork 6-21 Wexford 5-10
1971: Tipperary 5-17 Kilkenny 5-14
1972: Kilkenny 3-24 Cork 5-11
1973: Limerick 1-21 Kilkenny 1-14
1974: Kilkenny 3-19 Limerick 1-13

Games reduced to 70 minutes from 1975 onwards

1975: Kilkenny 2-22 Galway 2-10
1976: Cork 2-21 Wexford 4-11
1977: Cork 1-17 Wexford 3-8
1978: Cork 1-15 Kilkenny 2-8
1979: Kilkenny 2-12 Galway 1-8
1980: Galway 2-15 Limerick 3-9
1981: Offaly 2-12 Galway 0-15
1982: Kilkenny 3-18 Cork 1-13
1983: Kilkenny 2-14 Cork 2-12
1984: Cork 3-16 Offaly 1-12
1985: Offaly 2-11 Galway 1-12
1986: Cork 4-13 Galway 2-15
1987: Galway 1-12 Kilkenny 0-9
1988: Galway 1-15 Tipperary 0-14
1989: Tipperary 4-24 Antrim 3-9
1990: Cork 5-15 Galway 2-21
1991: Tipperary 1-16 Kilkenny 0-15
1992: Kilkenny 3-10 Cork 1-12
1993: Kilkenny 2-17 Galway 1-15
1994: Offaly 3-16 Limerick 2-13
1995: Clare 1-13 Offaly 2-8
1996: Wexford 1-13 Limerick 0-14
1997: Clare 0-20 Tipperary 2-13
1998: Offaly 2-16 Kilkenny 1-13
1999: Cork 0-13 Kilkenny 0-12
2000: Kilkenny 5-15 Offaly 1-14

*1890: Unfinished. Cork left the pitch, complaining that Wexford were over-aggressive. Cork were awarded the title.

All-Ireland Minor Hurling Final Results

1928: Cork 1-8 Dublin 3-2 (draw)
   Cork 7-6 Dublin 4-0 (replay)
1929: Waterford 5-0 Meath 1-1
1930: Tipperary 4-1 Kilkenny 2-1
1931: Kilkenny 4-7 Galway 2-3
1932: Tipperary 8-6 Kilkenny 5-1
1933: Tipperary 4-6 Galway 2-3
1934: Tipperary 4-3 Laois 3-5
1935: Kilkenny 4-2 Tipperary 3-3
1936: Kilkenny 2-4 Cork 2-3
1937: Cork 8-5 Kilkenny 2-7
1938: Cork 7-2 Dublin 5-4
1939: Cork 5-2 Kilkenny 2-2
1940: Limerick 6-4 Antrim 2-4
1941: Cork 3-11 Galway 1-1
1942: Suspended
1943 Suspended
1944: Suspended
1945: Dublin 3-14 Tipperary 4-6
1946: Dublin 1-6 Tipperary 0-7
1947: Tipperary 9-5 Galway 1-5
1948: Waterford 3-8 Kilkenny 4-2
1949: Tipperary 6-5 Kilkenny 2-4
1950: Kilkenny 3-4 Tipperary 1-5
1951: Cork 4-5 Galway 1-8
1952: Tipperary 9-9 Dublin 2-3
1953: Tipperary 8-6 Dublin 3-6
1954: Dublin 2-7 Tipperary 2-3

1991: a jubilant Nicky English

1955: Tipperary 5-15 Galway 2-5
1956: Tipperary 4-16 Kilkenny 1-5
1957: Tipperary 4-7 Kilkenny 3-7
1958: Limerick 5-8 Galway 3-10
1959: Tipperary 2-8 Kilkenny 2-7
1960: Kilkenny 7-12 Tipperary 1-11
1961: Kilkenny 3-13 Tipperary 0-15
1962: Kilkenny 3-6 Tipperary 0-9
1963: Wexford 6-12 Limerick 5-9
1964: Cork 10-7 Laois 1-4
1965: Dublin 4-10 Limerick 2-7
1966: Wexford 6-7 Cork 6-7 (draw)
   Wexford 4-1 Cork 1-8 (Replay)
1967: Cork 2-15 Wexford 5-3
1968: Wexford 2-13 Cork 3-7
1969: Cork 2-15 Kilkenny 3-6
1970: Cork 5-19 Galway 2-9
1971: Cork 2-11 Kilkenny 1-11
1972: Kilkenny 8-7 Cork 3-9
1973: Kilkenny 4-5 Galway 3-7
1974: Cork 1-10 Kilkenny 1-8
1975: Kilkenny 3-19 Cork 1-14
1976: Tipperary 2-20 Kilkenny 1-7
1977: Kilkenny 4-8 Cork 3-11 (draw)
   Kilkenny 1-8 Cork 0-9 (replay)
1978: Cork 1-15 Kilkenny 1-8
1979: Cork 2-11 Kilkenny 1-9
1980: Tipperary 2-15 Wexford 1-10
1981: Kilkenny 1-20 Galway 3-9
1982: Tipperary 2-7 Galway 0-4
1983: Galway 0-10 Dublin 0-7
1984: Limerick 1-14 Kilkenny 3-8
   (draw)

Limerick 2-5 Kilkenny 2-4 (replay)
1985: Cork 3-10 Wexford 0-12
1986: Offaly 3-12 Cork 3-9
1987: Offaly 2-8 Tipperary 0-12
1988: Kilkenny 3-13 Cork 0-12
1989: Offaly 2-16 Clare 1-12
1990: Kilkenny 3-14 Cork 3-14 (draw)
Kilkenny 3-16 Cork 0-11 (replay)
1991: Kilkenny 0-15 Tipperary 1-10
1992: Galway 1-13 Waterford 2-4
1993: Kilkenny 1-17 Galway 1-12
1994: Galway 2-10 Cork 1-11
1995: Cork 2-10 Kilkenny 1-2
1996: Tipperary 0-20 Galway 3-11
(draw)
Tipperary 2-14 Galway 2-12 (replay)
1997: Clare 1-11 Galway 1-9
1998: Cork 2-15 Kilkenny 1-9
1999: Galway 0-13 Tipperary 0-10
2000: Galway 2-19 Cork 4-10

All Ireland Under-21 Hurling Final Results

1964: Tipperary 8-9 Wexford 3-1
1965: Wexford 3-7 Tipperary 1-4
1966: Cork 3-12 Wexford 5-6 (draw)
Cork 4-9 Wexford 4-9 (replay)
Cork 9-9 Wexford 5-9 (second replay)
1967: Tipperary 1-8 Dublin 1-7
1968: Cork 2-18 Kilkenny 3-9
1969: Cork 5-13 Wexford 4-7
1970: Cork 3-8 Wexford 2-11 (draw)
Cork 5-17 Wexford 0-8 (replay)
1971: Cork 7-8 Wexford 1-11
1972: Galway 2-9 Dublin 1-10
1973: Cork 2-10 Wexford 4-2
1974: Kilkenny 3-8 Waterford 3-7
1975: Kilkenny 5-13 Cork 2-19
1976: Cork 2-17 Kilkenny 1-8
1977: Kilkenny 2-9 Cork 1-9
1978: Galway 3-5 Tipperary 2-8 (draw)
Galway 3-15 Tipperary 2-8 (replay)
1979: Tipperary 2-12 Galway 1-9
1980: Tipperary 2-9 Kilkenny 0-14
1981: Tipperary 2-16 Kilkenny 1-10
1982: Cork 0-12 Galway 0-11
1983: Galway 0-12 Tipperary 1-6
1984: Kilkenny 1-12 Tipperary 0-11
1985: Tipperary 1-10 Kilkenny 2-6
1986: Galway 1-14 Wexford 2-5
1987: Limerick 2-15 Galway 3-6
1988: Cork 4-11 Kilkenny 1-5
1989: Tipperary 4-10 Offaly 3-11
1990: Kilkenny 2-11 Tipperary 1-11
1991: Galway 2-17 Offaly 1-9
1992: Waterford 4-4 Offaly 0-16 (draw)
Waterford 0-12 Offaly 2-3 (replay)
1993: Galway 2-14 Kilkenny 3-11 (draw)
Galway 2-9 Kilkenny 3-3 (replay)
1994: Kilkenny 3-10 Galway 0-11
1995: Tipperary 1-14 Kilkenny 1-10

1996: Galway 1-14 Wexford 0-7
1997: Cork 3-11 Galway 0-13
1998: Cork 2-15 Galway 2-10
1999: Kilkenny 1-13 Galway 0-14
2000: Limerick 1-13 Galway 0-13

National Hurling League Final Results

1926: Cork 3-7 Dublin 1-5
1927: No competition
1928: Tipperary
(Winners on points system)
1929: Dublin 7-4 Cork 5-5
1930: Cork 3-5 Dublin 3-0
1931: No competition
1932: Galway 4-5 Tipperary 4-4
1933: Kilkenny 3-8 Limerick 1-3
1934: Limerick 3-6 Dublin 3-3
1935: Limerick
(Winners on points system)
1936: Limerick
(Winners on points system)
1937: Limerick
(Winners on points system)
1938: Limerick 5-2 Tipperary 1-1
1939: Dublin 1-8 Waterford 1-4
1940: Cork 8-9 Tipperary 6-4
1941: Cork 4-11 Dublin 2-7
1942: No competition
1943: No competition
1944: No competition
1945: No competition
1946: Clare 1-6 Dublin 1-6 (draw)
Clare 2-10 Dublin 2-5 (replay)
1947: Limerick 4-5 Kilkenny 2-11 (draw)
Limerick 3-8 Kilkenny 1-7 (replay)
1948: Cork 3-3 Tipperary 1-2
1949: Tipperary 3-5 Cork 3-3
1950: Tipperary 1-12 New York 3-4
1951: Galway 2-11 New York 2-8
1952: Tipperary 6-14 New York 2-5
1953: Cork 2-10 Tipperary 2-7
1954: Tipperary 3-10 Kilkenny 1-4
1955: Tipperary 3-5 Wexford 1-5
1956: Wexford 5-9 Tipperary 2-14
1957: Tipperary 3-11 Kilkenny 2-7
1958: Wexford 5-8 Limerick 4-8
1959: Tipperary 0-15 Waterford 0-7
1960: Tipperary 2-15 Cork 3-8
1961: Tipperary 6-6 Waterford 4-9
1962: Kilkenny 1-16 Cork 1-8
1963: Waterford 3-6 New York 3-6 (draw)
Waterford 3-10 New York 1-10
1964: Tipperary 4-16 New York 6-6
1965: Tipperary 4-10 New York 2-11 (first leg)
New York 3-9 Tipperary 2-9 (second leg)
Tipperary 6-19 New York 5-20
1966: Kilkenny 3-10 New York 2-7 (first leg)
Kilkenny 7-5 New York 0-8 (second leg)
Kilkenny 10-15 New York 2-15

(aggregate)
1967: New York 2-14 Tipperary 2-13 (first leg)
Tipperary 4-14 New York 2-8 (second leg)
Tipperary 6-27 New York 4-22
1969: Cork 3-12 Wexford 1-14
1970: Cork 4-11 New York 4-8 (first leg)
New York 2-8 Cork 1-10 (second leg)
Cork 5-21 New York 6-16 (aggregate)
1971: Limerick 3-12 Tipperary 3-11
1972: Cork 3-14 Limerick 2-14
1973: Wexford 4-13 Limerick 3-7
1974: Cork 6-15 Limerick 1-12
1975: Galway 4-9 Tipperary 4-6
1976: Kilkenny 0-16 Clare 2-10 (draw)
Kilkenny 6-14 Clare 1-14 (replay)
1977: Clare 2-8 Kilkenny 0-9
1978: Clare 3-10 Kilkenny 1-10
1979: Tipperary 3-15 Galway 0-8
1980: Cork 2-10 Limerick 2-10 (draw)
Cork 4-15 Limerick 4-6 (replay)
1981: Cork 3-11 Offaly 2-8
1982: Kilkenny 2-14 Wexford 1-11
1983: Kilkenny 2-14 Limerick 2-12
1984: Limerick 3-16 Wexford 1-9
1985: Limerick 3-12 Clare 1-7
1986: Kilkenny 2-10 Galway 2-6
1987: Galway 3-12 Clare 3-10
1988: Tipperary 3-15 Offaly 2-9
1989: Galway 2-16 Tipperary 4-8
1990: Kilkenny 0-18 New York 0-9
1991: Offaly 2-6 Wexford 0-10
1992: Limerick 0-14 Tipperary 0-13
1993: Cork 2-11 Wexford (draw)
Cork 0-18 Wexford 3-9 (replay)
Cork 3-11 Wexford 1-12 (second replay)
1994: Tipperary 2-14 Galway 0-12
1995: Kilkenny 2-12 Clare 0-9
1996: Galway 2-10 Tipperary 2-8
1997: Limerick 1-12 Galway 1-9
1998: Cork 2-14 Waterford 0-13
1999: Tipperary 1-14 Galway 1-10
2000: Galway 2-18 Tipperary 2-13
2001: Tipperary 1-19 Clare 0-17

Railway Cup Interprovincial Hurling Final Results

1927: Leinster 1-11 Munster 2-6
1928: Munster 2-2 Leinster 1-2
1929: Munster 5-3 Leinster 3-1
1930: Munster 4-6 Leinster 2-7
1931: Munster 1-12 Leinster 2-6
1932: Leinster 6-8 Munster 4-4
1933: Leinster 4-6 Munster 3-6
1934: Munster 6-3 Leinster 3-2
1935: Munster 3-4 Leinster 3-0
1936: Leinster 2-8 Munster 3-4
1937: Munster 1-9 Leinster 3-1

1938: Munster 6-2 Leinster 4-3
1939: Munster 4-4 Leinster 1-6
1940: Munster 4-9 Leinster 5-4
1941: Leinster 2-5 Munster 2-4
1942: Munster 4-9 Leinster 4-5
1943: Munster 4-3 Leinster 3-5
1944: Munster 4-10 Connacht 4-4
1945: Munster 6-8 Ulster 2-0
1946: Munster 3-12 Connacht 4-8
1947: Connacht 2-5 Munster 1-1
1948: Munster 3-5 Leinster 2-5
1949: Munster 5-3 Connacht 2-9
1950: Munster 0-9 Leinster 1-3
1951: Munster 4-9 Leinster 3-6
1952: Munster 5-11 Connacht 4-2
1953: Munster 5-7 Leinster 5-5
1954: Leinster 0-9 Munster 0-5
1955: Munster 6-8 Connacht 3-4
1956: Leinster 5-11 Munster 1-7
1957: Munster 5-7 Leinster 2-5
1958: Munster 3-7 Leinster 3-5
1959: Munster 7-11 Connacht 2-6
1960: Munster 6-6 Leinster 2-7
1961: Munster 4-12 Leinster 3-9
1962: Leinster 1-11 Munster 1-9
1963: Munster 5-5 Leinster 5-5 (draw)
Munster 2-8 Leinster 2-7 (replay)
1964: Leinster 3-7 Munster 2-9
1965: Leinster 3-11 Munster 0-9
1966: Munster 3-13 Leinster 3-11
1967: Leinster 2-14 Munster 3-5
1968: Munster 0-14 Leinster 0-10
1969: Munster 2-9 Connacht 2-9 (draw)
Munster 3-13 Connacht 4-4 (replay)
1970: Munster 2-15 Leinster 0-9
1971: Leinster 2-17 Munster 2-12
1972: Leinster 3-12 Munster 1-10
1973: Leinster 1-13 Munster 2-8
1974: Leinster 2-15 Munster 1-11
1975: Leinster 2-9 Munster 1-11
1976: Munster 4-9 Leinster 4-8
1977: Leinster 2-17 Munster 1-13
1978: Munster 2-13 Leinster 1-11
1979: Leinster 1-13 Connacht 1-9
1980: Connacht 1-5 Munster 0-7
1981: Munster 2-16 Leinster 2-6
1982: Connacht 3-8 Leinster 2-9
1983: Connacht 0-10 Leinster 1-5
1984: Munster 1-18 Leinster 2-9
1985: Munster 3-6 Connacht 1-11
1986: Connacht 3-11 Munster 0-11
1987: Connacht 2-14 Leinster 1-14
1988: Leinster 2-14 Connacht 1-12
1989: Connacht 4-16 Munster 3-17
1990: No Competition
1991: Connacht 1-13 Munster 0-12
1992: Munster 3-12 Ulster 1-8
1993: Leinster 1-15 Ulster 2-6
1994: Connacht 1-11 Leinster 1-10
1995: Munster 0-13 Ulster 1-9
1996: Munster 2-20 Leinster 0-10
1997: Munster 0-14 Leinster 0-10
1998: Leinster 0-16 Connacht 2-9
1999: Connacht 2-13 Munster 1-15
2000: Munster 3-15 Leinster 2-15

All-Ireland Senior Hurling Titles

28: Cork – 1890, 1892, 1893, 1894, 1902, 1903, 1919, 1926, 1928, 1929, 1931, 1941, 1942, 1943, 1944, 1946, 1952, 1953, 1954, 1966, 1970, 1976, 1977, 1978, 1984, 1986, 1990, 1999.

26: Kilkenny – 1904, 1905, 1907, 1909, 1911, 1912, 1913, 1922, 1932, 1933, 1935, 1939, 1947, 1957, 1963, 1967, 1969, 1972, 1974, 1975, 1979, 1982, 1983, 1992, 1993, 2000.

24: Tipperary – 1887, 1895, 1896, 1898, 1899, 1900, 1906, 1908, 1916, 1925, 1930, 1937, 1945, 1949, 1950, 1951, 1958, 1961, 1962, 1964, 1965, 1971, 1989, 1991.

7: Limerick – 1897, 1918, 1921, 1934, 1936, 1940, 1973.

6: Dublin – 1889, 1917, 1920, 1924, 1927, 1938.

6: Wexford – 1910, 1955, 1956, 1960, 1968, 1996.

4: Galway – 1923, 1980, 1987, 1988.

4: Offaly – 1981, 1985, 1994, 1998.

3: Clare – 1914, 1995, 1997.

2: Waterford – 1948, 1959.

1: Kerry – 1891.

1: Laois – 1915.

1: London – 1901.

All-Ireland Under-21 Hurling Titles

11: Cork – 1966, 1968, 1969, 1970, 1971, 1973, 1976, 1982, 1988, 1997, 1998.

8: Tipperary – 1964, 1967, 1979, 1980, 1981, 1985, 1989, 1995.

7: Galway – 1972, 1987, 1983, 1986, 1991, 1993, 1996.

7: Kilkenny – 1974, 1975, 1977, 1984, 1990, 1994, 1999.

2: Limerick – 1987, 2000.

1: Waterford – 1992.

1: Wexford 1965.

All-Ireland Minor Hurling Titles

17: Cork – 1928, 1937, 1938, 1939, 1941, 1951, 1964, 1967, 1969, 1970, 1971, 1974, 1978, 1979, 1985, 1995, 1998.

16: Kilkenny – 1931, 1935, 1936, 1950, 1960, 1961, 1962, 1972, 1973, 1975, 1977, 1981, 1988, 1990, 1991, 1993.

2000: Joy for Kilkenny captain Willie O'Connor and Charlie Carter

16: Tipperary – 1930, 1932, 1933, 1934, 1947, 1949, 1952, 1953, 1955, 1956, 1957, 1959, 1976, 1980, 1982, 1996.

5: Galway – 1983, 1992, 1994, 1999, 2000.

4: Dublin – 1945, 1946, 1954, 1965.

3: Limerick – 1940, 1958, 1984.

3: Offaly – 1986, 1987, 1989.

3: Wexford – 1963, 1958, 1968.

2: Waterford – 1929, 1948.

1: Clare – 1997.

The minor championships were suspended in 1942-1944 inclusive

National Football League Titles

18: Tipperary – 1928, 1949, 1950, 1952, 1954, 1955, 1957, 1959, 1960, 1961, 1964, 1965, 1968, 1979, 1988, 1994, 1999, 2001.

14: Cork – 1926, 1930, 1940, 1941, 1948, 1953, 1969, 1970, 1972, 1974, 1980, 1981, 1993, 1998.

11: Limerick – 1934, 1935, 1936, 1937, 1938, 1947, 1971, 1984, 1985, 1992, 1997.

9: Kilkenny – 1933, 1962, 1966, 1976, 1982, 1983, 1986, 1990, 1995.

7: Galway – 1932, 1951, 1975, 1987, 1989, 1996, 2000.

4: Wexford – 1956, 1958, 1967, 1973.

3: Clare – 1946, 1977, 1978.

2: Dublin – 1929, 1939.

1: Offaly – 1991.

1: Waterford – 1963.

Railway Cup Interprovincial Hurling Final Titles

42: Munster – 1928, 1929, 1930, 1931, 1934, 1935, 1937, 1938, 1939, 1940, 1942, 1943, 1944, 1945, 1946, 1948, 1949, 1950, 1951, 1952, 1953, 1955, 1957, 1958, 1959, 1960, 1961, 1963, 1966, 1968, 1969, 1970, 1976, 1978, 1981, 1984, 1985, 1992, 1995, 1996, 1997, 2000.

21: Leinster – 1927, 1932, 1933, 1936, 1941, 1954, 1956, 1962, 1964, 1965, 1967, 1971, 1972, 1973, 1974, 1975, 1977, 1979, 1988, 1993, 1999.

10: Connacht – 1947, 1980, 1982, 1983, 1986, 1987, 1989, 1991, 1994, 1999.

CHRONOLOGY

1884: The Gaelic Athletic Association (GAA) is founded by a small group of men at a meeting in the Billiards Room at Hayes' Hotel, Thurles, Co. Tipperary. Its basic aim is 'the strengthening of the National Identity in a 32-county Ireland through the preservation and promotion of Gaelic Games and pastimes.' Maurice Davin (Tipperary) is chosen as first President; Michael Cusack (Clare) is first General Secretary.

1887: The first All-Ireland football and hurling championships are started. However, they are not completed until the following year. Tipperary (Thurles) beat Galway (Meelick) by 1–1 to 0–0 in the first All-Ireland hurling final, played at Birr on 1 April 1888. Limerick, represented by the Commercials club, beat Louth (Dundalk Young Irelands) by 1–4 to 0–3 in the first All-Ireland football final, played at Clonskeagh, Dublin on 29 April 1888.

1891: Kerry win their first – and only – All-Ireland senior hurling championship.

1892: Teams reduced from 21 to 17-a-side. The value of a goal, which up to now outweighed any number of points, is set at five points.

1894: Cork become the first county to win the All-Ireland senior hurling title for the third year in a row.

1896: The goal is re-valued at three points and has remained so ever since.

1896: The All-Ireland finals are held at a ground in Jones' Road, Dublin, which would later become Croke Park. The GAA rented the ground from a company called City & Suburban Racecourse Amusements Ground.

1899: Dublin become the first county to win the All-Ireland senior football title for the third year in a row.

1902: Rule 27, 'The Ban', is introduced. It prevents members of the GAA from playing, attending or promoting soccer, rugby, hockey or cricket.

1908: The Jones' Road ground is bought by Frank B Dineen, former GAA President and Secretary of the GAA, for £3,250.

1913: The GAA becomes the official owners of the Jones' Road ground, having bought it from Frank B.Dineen, former GAA President and Secretary, who acquired the property in 1908 and held it in trust for the GAA. It becomes officially known as Croke Park, in honour of Dr.Croke, Archbishop of Cashel, who was the GAA's first patron.

1915: Laois win their first – and only – All-Ireland senior hurling final.

1918: Wexford become the first county to win the All-Ireland senior championship for a fourth successive year.

1920: Thirteen people are shot dead by the British Army (Black and Tans) in Croke Park during a football game between Dublin and Tipperary. Tipperary player, Michael Hogan, is among those shot and the biggest stand in Croke Park (Hogan Stand) is later named in his honour. The tragic day – Sunday, 21 November – becomes known as bloody Sunday.

1923: Limerick become the first holders of the Liam McCarthy Cup, presented to All-Ireland senior winners. They beat Dublin in the delayed final of 1921. Liam McCarthy was born in London in 1851 to a Limerick mother and Cork father. He served as President and Treasurer of the London County Board.

1924: Mick Gill creates history by winning two All-Ireland senior hurling championship medals in the same year. In September 1924, he played on the Galway team which beat Limerick in the delayed 1923 final and in December 1924, he won a second medal with the Dublin team which beat Galway in that year's final.

1925: The National hurling and football Leagues are introduced as a secondary competition to the All-Ireland championships. Laois win the football title while Cork win the hurling.

1927: The Interprovincial hurling and football championships (Railway Cups) are introduced. Leinster win the hurling title while Munster win the football final.

1928: Kildare become the first side to be presented with the Sam Maguire Cup, which is presented to All-Ireland senior football championship winners. The new trophy was presented by friends of Cork man, Sam Maguire, an active member of the GAA and Irish Republican Brotherhood, who died in 1927.

1928: The All-Ireland minor (U-18) championships are introduced. Cork win the hurling final and Clare win the football title.

1928: Cork's 'Gah' Aherne scores 5–4, a record for a 60-minute All-Ireland hurling final, when they beat Galway by 6–12 to 1–0.

1930: Tipperary win the All-Ireland senior, junior and minor All-Ireland hurling finals.

1932: Kerry win their fourth successive All-Ireland senior football title.

1937: A building strike, which holds up progress on the new stand, prevents the All-Ireland hurling final being played in Croke Park. It is switched to Fitzgerald Stadium, Killarney where Tipperary beat Kilkenny.

1938: The Cusack Stand in Croke Park is officially opened with a 5,000 seated capacity in the upper deck.

1938: Micheál Ó Hehir, who goes on to become a broadcasting legend, makes his first GAA commentary at the Galway – Monaghan All-Ireland football semi-final in Mullingar.

1938: Limerick win their fifth successive National hurling League title, a record which has stood ever since.

1939: Mayo win their 6th consecutive National football League title, a feat which has never since been emulated.

1942: Bobby Beggs wins an All-Ireland senior football championship with Dublin, having been similarly successful when playing with Galway in 1938.

1944: Cork win the All-Ireland hurling title for a fourth successive year, the only county ever to do so.

1946: Cork dual star, Jack Lynch, ensures himself a place in history by winning his 6th consecutive All-Ireland senior championship medal. He won five in hurling (1941, '42, '43, '44, '46) and one in football (1945).

1947: The All-Ireland football final is played in the Polo Grounds, New York. Cavan beat Kerry by 2–11 to 2–7.

1954: Cork legend, Christy Ring, becomes the first player to win eight All-Ireland senior hurling championships medals.

1954: Wexford legend, Nicky Rackard, underlines his scoring prowess by scoring 7–7 against Galway in the All-Ireland semi-final.

1956: A crowd of 83,096, a record for an All-Ireland hurling final, watch Wexford beat Cork by 2–14 to 2–8 at Croke Park.

1956: Galway's Frank Stockwell sets a record for a 60-minute All-Ireland football final, scoring 2–5 from play against Cork.

1959: Kilkenny legend Eddie Keher plays for Kilkenny minor hurlers in the All-Ireland final and comes on as a sub for the senior side in the All-Ireland final replay a few weeks later.

1959: The new Hogan Stand at Croke Park is officially opened with a capacity of 16,000.

1960: Down win the All-Ireland football final for the first time, becoming the first team to take the title across the Border.

1961: A crowd of 90,556, a record for an All-Ireland football final, watch Down beat Offaly by 3–6 to 2–8 at Croke Park.

1961: James McCartan (Down) becomes the first player to win the Footballer of the Year award for a second consecutive year.

1962: Dublin's Des Foley underlines his amazing versatility and stamina by playing for Leinster footballers and hurlers in the Railway Cup finals at Croke Park. He plays at midfield on both teams and crowns a great day by winning two Railway Cup medals.

1962: Sean Óg Sheehy captains Kerry to victory in the All-Ireland senior football final, following in the footsteps of his father, John Joe, who led Kerry to All-Ireland success in 1926 and 1930.

1964: The All-Ireland U-21 hurling and football championships are introduced. Tipperary win in hurling and Kerry triumph in football.

1965: Tipperary's John Doyle joins Christy Ring (Cork) as the only players to have won eight All-Ireland senior hurling medals as first choice players. Kilkenny's Noel Skehan subsequently won nine medals, three as a substitute.

1966: Galway become the first Connacht team to win three All-Ireland senior football finals in a row. Their centre half-forward, Mattie McDonagh, establishes his own record by becoming the first Connacht player to win four All-Ireland senior medals.

1967: Kilkenny beat Tipperary in the All-Ireland senior hurling final for the first time since 1922.

1970: The duration of senior hurling and football championship matches is extended from 60 to 80 minutes.

1971: Rule 27 ('The Ban'), which prevented members of the GAA from playing, attending or promoting soccer, rugby, cricket or hockey, is abolished.

1971: Offaly win the All-Ireland senior football championship for the first time, beating Galway in the final.

1971: The All-Ireland club championships, comprised of county senior champions, are introduced.

1973: Cork beat Galway (3–17 to 2–13) in the highest scoring All-Ireland football final in history.

1975: The duration of senior hurling and football championship matches is reduced from 80 to 70 minutes.

1975: Sligo win the Connacht senior football championship for the first time since 1928.

1978: Cork win a third consecutive All-Ireland senior hurling title for the fourth time in their history.

1980: Galway win the All-Ireland senior hurling championship for the first time since 1923, beating Limerick in the final.

1981: Offaly win the All-Ireland senior hurling championship for the first time, beating Galway in the final.

1982: Seamus Darby scores a late goal for Offaly to win the All-Ireland senior football title, and in doing so prevents Kerry from setting a record by becoming the first county to win five successive championships.

1983: Kilkenny hurling goalkeeper, Noel Skehan, sets a record by winning his 9th All-Ireland senior championship medal. He won three as a sub and six as first choice goalkeeper.

1984: The GAA celebrates its Centenary Year. Special open draw competitions are held to mark the occasion. The winners are Cork in hurling and Meath in football. Cork also win the All-Ireland senior championship final, which is played in Thurles, while Kerry win the football equivalent.

1984: The first International Rules (a combination of Gaelic football and Australian Rules football) test series between Ireland and Australia takes place. Australia win the series 2–1.

1986: Kerry's Páidí Ó Sé, Denis 'Ogie' Moran, Pat Spillane, Ger Power, Mike Sheehy all win their eighth All-Ireland senior football championship medals, creating a new record.

1989: Nicky English (Tipperary) establishes a scoring record for an All-Ireland hurling final, recording 2–12 against Antrim.

1990: Cork's Teddy McCarthy becomes the first player to win All-Ireland senior hurling and football medals in the same year.

1991: It takes four games, two of which have extra-time, to separate Dublin and Meath in the first round of the Leinster football championship. The epic saga is watched by 237,377 spectators and yields gate receipts of £1,111,898.

1992: Donegal win the All-Ireland senior football title for the first time.

1992: Clare win the Munster senior football championship for the first time since 1917.

1993: Derry win the All-Ireland senior football title for the first time.

1993: Work on the re-development of Croke Park begins with the demolition of the Cusack Stand.

1995: Clare win the All-Ireland senior hurling championship for the first time in 81 years, beating Offaly in the final.

1995: Leitrim win the Connacht senior football championship for the first time since 1927.

1997: The format of the hurling championship is changed to allow the beaten Leinster and Munster provincial finalists back into the All-Ireland series. Tipperary and Kilkenny become the first two counties to benefit from the new system.

1997: John O'Leary (Dublin) retires, having created a record by playing in 70 consecutive senior championship games between July 1980 and June 1997.

1998: Offaly become the first county to win the All-Ireland hurling final, having lost the provincial final. They lost the Leinster final to Kilkenny (3–10 to 1–11) but gained revenge in the All-Ireland final, beating Kilkenny by 2–16 to 1–13.

1998: Galway's Michael Donnellan wins an All-Ireland senior football medal to become the third generation of his family to achieve the ultimate honour. His father, John, won All-Ireland medals in 1964, '65, '66 while his grandfather, Mick, won an All-Ireland medal in 1925.

1999: Cork beat Kilkenny (0–13 to 0–12) in the first All-Ireland senior hurling final which fails to produce a goal.

2000: Kilkenny's Philip Larkin follows in the footsteps of his father, 'Fan' and grandfather, Paddy, by winning an All-Ireland senior hurling championship medal.

2000: The GAA decides to change the format of the All-Ireland football championship to guarantee all counties a second game in the competition on a two-year experimental basis, starting in 2001.

INDEX

Picture Credits

The publishers would like to thank the following sources for their kind permission to reproduce the pictures in this book:

Courtesy of Colman Doyle 4l, 18, 24, 26, 32-3, 77, 92br

Courtesy of G.A.Duncan 5l, 21, 22, 23, 129br

GAA Museum 10, 11, 12, 13, 14, 15, 49, 121, 151, 159, 160, 164-5, 168, 176-7, Connolly Collection 50, 147

Inpho Photography / Billy Stickland 5r, 29, 34-5,38, 55, 57, 64, 75, 81, 84, 92tl, 93, 93-4, 99, 102, 103tl, 107, 104tl, 105, 106b, 108, 111br, 116-7, 117br, 118, 122, 131, 133br, 133tc, 134, 136, 142, 143, 144, 154-5, 185, Patrick Bolger 2br, 9, 44, 110, 124, 135, 141, Tom Honan 2tr, 2l, 4r, 16, 100, 130tl, 137, 138, 172, James Meehan 36, 45, 78, 96, 106t, 112, 114, 139, Lorraine O'Sullivan 82, 87, 120, 170

Irish Examiner 19br, 19tl, 27, 28, 30-1, 39, 40, 42-3, 48, 61, 74

Lensmen & Associates 32tl, 51, 103, 146, 148-9, 150, 158

Sportsfile 6/ Gerry Barton 59, Matt Browne 3l, 76 , 89bl, Connolly Collection 25, 46, 54, 58, 60br, 62, 63, 66, 72, 115, 183, Damien Eagers 98, Lay Lohan 97br, David Maher 3r, 180, Ray McManus 47, 52-3, 56, 60tl, 67, 68-9, 70, 71, 73tl, 79, 80, 83bl, 83tr, 85, 86br, 86tl, 88, 89tr, 90br, 95br, 97tl, 103tr, 104br, 109, 111tl, 113, 119, 125, 127br, 127tl, 127tr, 128-9, 130tr, 130b, 132, 140, 152-3, 156, 163, 166-7, 169, 173, 174-5, 179, 184, 187, Brendan Moran 8, 73br, 90tl, 145, 161, Aoife Rice 91, 126

Every effort has been made to acknowledge correctly and contact the source and/or copyright holder of each picture, and Carlton Books Limited apologises for any unintentional errors or omissions which will be corrected in future editions of this book.